Lessons on Love

Sacred Stories on Relationships, Balance, and Becoming Your Authentic Self

By Adam Guzman-Poole

First Edition

Published by Adam Guzman-Poole

Print ISBN 978-0-9958373-0-0

LESSONS ON LOVE

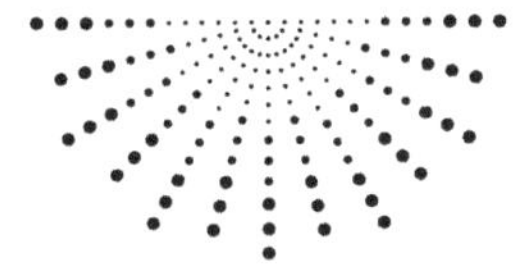

ADAM GUZMAN-POOLE

Mitakuye Oyasin

For All My Relations

CONTENTS

Part V

TRANSFORMING OBSTACLES INTO GIFTS

Part VI

THE POWER OF VISION

Part VII

THE SACRED

PREFACE

If you're reading this book, we need you more than ever. As I write this, the world is in disarray. Small and large-scale wars erupt like volcanoes around the globe. And our political conditions worldwide are just as explosive, with entire nations becoming more polarized by the day. Moreover, our climate is changing, and it's changing fast! Freak floods, droughts, and monsoons have become the norm, with environmental scientists predicting that major weather events will only worsen in the years to come. To add to this already existing chaos, the lingering aftermath of the pandemic has left many of us physically, mentally, and emotionally scarred.

Globally, the inequalities between the rich and poor increase daily, with many scholars warning of total economic collapse. While advances in technology have supposedly made us more connected than ever in history, the rates of loneliness, depression, anxiety, and suicide ideation increase every year, and the youth are facing the brunt of these problems.

While many are hopeful about the rapid advancement of artificial intelligence, many others are concerned about what living in an AI world will look like. Will our very livelihoods be outsourced to computers? Will many of us choose to just escape to virtual worlds rather than live in reality? Is AI even safe? Or will our world and all of us in it end up being blown up by machines? Thoughts like these have haunted many of us in these uncertain times.

Looking at the global arena and the momentous problems we collectively face, it can feel overwhelming, even disheartening. How will we even make a dent in a problem so big? Besides, many of us are just barely hanging on and struggling ourselves. We have bills to pay, children to care for, relationships to tend to, and dreams to fulfill. And quite frankly, we are simply doing our best to keep up with the grind, let alone think about taking on any of the world's problems.

Besides, can we even do anything about it?

But before we answer that important question, even more importantly, we must focus on 'why' and 'how' we are going to do it. Because if we do not first ask *Why?* we fail to find the motivation needed to face the seemingly insurmountable obstacles ahead. If we do not focus on *How?* we will go about effecting change with ill-equipped systems that will only create more problems in the end. The Soviet Union is a perfect example of this—while they wanted peace and equality (the *what*), they went about it through force and violence (the *how*), which only created more chaos.

Great leaders around the world have followed this idea of addressing the 'why' and 'how' as a transformative process for change for centuries, and it was formally brought to light by the thought leader Simon Sinek in his excellent book *Start with Why*. There, he followed inspiring individuals who did the seemingly impossible, like the Wright Brothers, two simple bike mechanics with minimal resources who, despite competing against hundreds of engineers with bigger budgets, degrees, and manpower, were able to fly the first plane.

How did they do it? Well, they didn't just focus on the *what* (flying airplanes). They focused on *why*. The idea of flying inspired them. What would it mean for the world if humans were to soar like a bird? And how would flight make it better? This was their *why*, and it inspired them to keep going even when others around them wanted to quit. It's what allowed them to do the impossible and carried them into the sky.

With this wisdom of the power of knowing the "why" in our minds, we can ask ourselves these pivotal questions: Why is it important to do something about the challenges we see in the world? What will it mean for our kids? What will it mean for our families? Why is it essential that we stand up and face these challenges?

I encourage you to pause for just a moment to contemplate these questions. In them, you will find the energy, motivation, and purpose you need to overcome the obstacles ahead. Because let's face it, we are experiencing more than just trying times. The world is in dire need. It needs help, and it needs someone to do something about it. That someone is you. It's me. It's all of us in this together.

That's our why, and this is our call to action.

If you're with me this far, my prayer is that, like me, you're motivated to create the change our world desperately needs. But now the question is: "How?"

How do we go about changing our lives for the better? How do we go about tackling the collective chaos before us? How?

That's what this book is really about—how we will create change. Keep in mind, to do that, I'm not going to present a simple four-step process for transformation. Because how you go about building a better world will be different from mine.

Because each of us, depending on our respective backgrounds, professions, geography, special gifts, and so on, has our own unique purpose for how we can positively make a difference on this planet. But the "how" I am talking about here is the underlying energy we need to tap into to create that change, meaning the mindset, the attitude, and the intention with which we go about making that better and more beautiful world.

So that begs the question, what is that attitude? What is that mindset? What is the intention we need to adopt as we work to create this change? As you've probably guessed based on the title of this book, as cliché as it sounds, it's LOVE.

It was Love that allowed Martin Luther King Jr. to be so effective in the civil rights movement. It was Love that gave Mother Teresa the energy to work tirelessly in some of the world's most impoverished areas. It was Love that inspired Malala, the education activist, to stand against a tyrannical government. And it is Love that we need to draw from now more than ever in these turbulent times. Because in a world where divisions, selfishness, and egotism run wild, we need access to a force stronger than the troubles of this world.

That force is Love. Because Love, in its purest essence, is our greatest strength. When we connect to it, we connect to a universal force with the power to make anything possible.

While this little book by no means claims to understand every nuance of the vast mystery of Love, it contains stories of my own humble experience of some of Love's lessons.

As you will see, I am just an ordinary guy with a wife, a child, a business, and problems, just like you, simply struggling to be a better person each day and make my little dent in the challenges we collectively face. However, I have had some extraordinary experiences and teachers who have taught me how to meet these trials with a bit more grace. The greatest of those teachers has been Life itself.

In the pages ahead, you will be taken across the globe, to Amazon jungles, to Balinese rice fields, to the feet of Indigenous Elders, and into the hearts of Buddhist teachers. The stories will bring you into the minds of yogis, scientists, leading researchers in psychology, and modern changemakers.

With their help, my first hope is that by the end of this book, all of us will have a little more understanding about this great universal force we call "Love" and how we can use it as a tool to live better, richer, and more meaningful lives. In turn, with that deeper understanding, my greatest hope is that through one loving act at a time, we can truly live the words of Mahatma Gandhi, who invited us to "be the change we want to see in the world."

With Love,

Adam

HOW TO USE THIS BOOK

Before we get started, it may be helpful to understand the best way to use this book. If you skimmed through the chapters, you may have noticed this text is organized into eight parts.

Cover to Cover or Chapter by Chapter

While this book was designed to be read sequentially, which I do recommend for your first time through, you can just as easily pick it up and open it to any random page. Each chapter contains a short story with a life lesson that stands on its own. Each poem contains its own wisdom.

For Busy Lives

If you're pressed for time, don't worry. Every micro-chapter can be easily read with your morning tea or coffee—perfect for those quiet moments of reflection on a hectic day.

For Different Moods and Moments

Based on how you're feeling, you can actively seek out specific stories to support you in your day, for example:

- When you need inspiration for facing challenges, turn to the section about transforming obstacles into gifts.

- When your heart feels heavy, seek out the stories on forgiveness and healing.
- When you're looking to spread more love in your daily life, dive into the stories about sharing and service.

Lastly, after many of the stories, you'll find reflection questions. If you can, I encourage you to take a few moments—even just mentally—to contemplate those prompts. Such thoughtful reflection will help these ideas sink deeper and, in turn, help you to more fully integrate them into your life.

Ultimately, this is your own adventure. Do what works best for you, and let your intuition lead you on the journey ahead.

INTRODUCTION

LEAN ON ME

My wife, Andréanne, and I settled into our seats for the first of two flights back to our home in Bali, thirty hours from Heathrow. This leg of the journey would be seven hours, just enough time to close our eyes and rest for the longer trip ahead. So, even though you're not supposed to, while the flight safety instructions were shared, I sank into my seat and started my evening meditation routine. I guess I figured that with all the years of travel under my belt, I'd seen that video enough times to know from memory what to do in case of an emergency. But little did I know that in a short while, I would face a storm requiring a whole different set of safety instructions.

About fifteen minutes into my meditation, my neighbor, a Brit with a baseball cap and shorts sitting by the window beside me, asked if he could pass to use the restroom.

"Better to get it out now before we can't," I said, eyeing the seatbelt sign.

"That's the idea," he replied as he got up, and both Andréanne and I stood in the aisle to let him through.

We waited to the side until he got back. Then, when I sat down again, I returned to my meditation routine. But not for long. Ten minutes into the flight, our neighbor asked once again if he could get by to use the restroom.

We happily agreed, and at that point, I thought he might have some sort of condition, so when he came back, I asked if he wanted to change places with us and have the aisle seat.

"That way, you have easier access to the bathroom," I said.

He thought about it for a moment and initially seemed to like the idea, but he declined for reasons I did not know.

I shrugged, settled back into my seat, and tried to finish my meditation routine. But again, not for long.

"Can I get through?" he asked for the third time.

Now, at this point, I was pretty shocked, because in all my years of flying, I have never had someone move so many times during the first hour. And I started to think this might be a very long night.

Especially because, between jumping in and out of my meditation, I was pretty sure I had discovered the culprit for his insistent activity. I saw that concealed in the pocket behind the seat in front of him were a couple of beer bottles and a pocket bottle of vodka, from which he would take large gulps periodically. As this was happening, part of me seriously wondered if he was doing drugs in the restroom. Because as time went on, I noticed his demeanor became more forceful and aggressive.

When he returned from his fifth trip to the bathroom, he turned to me and said, "Okay, move over. I'll take this seat."

Despite his rudeness, we happily agreed. Part of me actually rejoiced. I thought, *Finally! I can get some sleep!*

I pulled my eye mask on and started to drift into the sweet, soft place just before sleep. But just before the clouds could take me, someone shook my shoulder.

"What?" I groaned.

"He wants to switch places again," Andréanne whispered.

"What?"

"He wants to go back," she repeated.

"You've got to be kidding me! Are you serious?!" I muttered.

"Yes."

In between worlds and frustrated by all this back and forth, I lost my cool.

"Okay, man," I said firmly, looking at him squarely. "But after this, you gotta make up your mind... You can't just keep jumping around all the time."

He then looked at me like I'd come from some foreign planet.

"I did you the favor," he replied with menace. "You wanted to move."

"What?!" I replied loudly and began to counter with an argument.

But after looking into his glazed eyes, I stopped myself mid-sentence because I realized that behind the booze and possible drugs, I was not going to get through to this guy with logic.

I got up, and we switched back to our original seats. As the transfer happened, you could feel the animosity between us cut through the air. He sat down and then turned on the charm to order a double Jack Daniel's from the flight attendant. And as he did, I started to think this might not end well.

When the food came, he scarfed his meal down and asked if he could go to the bathroom again while our trays were still in front of us.

"What do you expect us to do?" I said as I pointed down at the plates before us.

"Well, pick them up and go," he practically demanded.

By this time, both Andréanne and I were losing our patience, and part of me was seriously contemplating hitting the guy.

But I breathed, stood, and let him through.

Knowing I needed to do something to address the situation, I began contemplating how I would deal with this guy without escalating the confrontation.

First, I asked the flight attendant if we could be moved, but the flight was completely booked. So, to avoid further aggravation, I asked her to stop serving his prized double Jack Daniel's.

While I did this, Andréanne grabbed our food trays and took them to the galley in the back to clear some space. When our neighbor from hell came back, he fumbled over his tray of food in front of his chair. My wife sweetly offered to bring it to the back for him.

He either couldn't hear what she said or ignored her entirely because he quickly sat down.

I looked away for a moment before I turned to settle back into my seat, and when I did, I saw he had opened my tray table and placed his tray of half-eaten food there.

Now, if he was actively trying to piss me off, which I am almost positive he was, it worked. So, when I sat down, I picked up his tray and placed it on his knees without saying anything.

"What's your problem, man?" he said, looking at me directly.

"No problem at all," I replied calmly.

"What's your problem, man?" he repeated.

"No problem at all. Just handing you your tray, that's all. It was in my seat, and now it's with you," I said, sharpness in my tone.

We then stared at each other like two bulls ready to charge.

He backed down first, turned away, and put on his headphones, blasting them so loud every lyric was audible.

After sipping on another shot of his rum and Coke, he then started to spread his elbows like a chicken spreading its wings and, in doing so, almost took the whole armrest of the small seat we shared. At this point, I'm positive it was a deliberate act of aggression. Fighting for my ground, I elbowed him back.

The tension was palpable and felt as if an electric current of hostility was buzzing between us.

But as my elbow poked like a knife, I heard the whispers of my conscience speaking to me like a wise sage.

"You don't need to fight for this, Adam…"

At first, I didn't want to listen. I mean, really? He was rude, drunk, and inconsiderate—this was my chair, too! Of course I had to fight!

But again and again, like a wise elder, the voice within reminded me what was right.

So, with these thoughts echoing in the background, I took a few deep breaths, focused my attention within, and prayed for understanding and strength.

Then, the words from so many ancient wisdom traditions flooded my mind, reminding me repeatedly of the importance of being calm. With this reminder as my anchor, I grounded myself with my breath. Then, from a place of inner peace, I looked deeply to see past my fellow traveler's exterior actions.

As I did this, I was able to move away from the picture I painted of this "bad" neighbor and see a bigger picture—one that encapsulated a much different story. In that space, I saw that the alcohol, possible drugs, and his aggression were really just a cover-up for someone who was deeply suffering.

With this paradigm shift, my heart was opened with genuine concern for the hurt he held within, and then, true compassion was born. From there, I took another deep breath and began to apply Tonglen, the Tibetan Buddhist practice of compassion. Visualizing him in my mind's eye, I breathed in his suffering and, on my exhale, offered waves of love and care to him.

Perhaps it was a coincidence or just me, but as my practice deepened, the palpable tension between us seemed to lessen, and I even noticed his chicken arms retract into his own seat. I kept at the practice. Over and over, I'd breathe in his suffering and offer him love and kindness in return. Now, as crazy as it may seem, given our recent history, with each loving round of the practice, I felt closer to him, until it was as if he were my own kin.

But I won't lie and say it was all easy. Even while I willfully practiced compassion, there was still a war going on inside me, between my lower self and my higher nature. The little part of me that felt wronged was just about screaming, justifying the "badness" of this individual beside me.

Yet, my conscience spoke again to me in the words of Yogananda, the great saint, who said: "We are all children of the Divine," reminding me there is the spark of the sacred within everyone.

With that wisdom guiding me, I began to see my neighbor for who he truly was. Beyond the hurt, the pain, the suffering, there was a spark of this Great Cosmic Force. He truly was an emanation of the Eternal.

But my lower nature did everything in its power to tell me otherwise, repeating the story and the previous sequence of events again and again in my mind.

Yet, I stayed firm in my understanding of who he truly was, an emanation of Love itself, and I imagined him surrounded by white light. With my mind anchored in this truth, I held him to this vision. In the middle of this practice, my wife nudged me. Through all the seat shifting, our neighbor had left his packaged blanket on her chair. She handed it to me to give to him.

I lightly tapped his shoulder. "Hey man," I said, looking deeply into his eyes. "Do you want your blanket?"

Perhaps my changed tone or the gesture confused him because from the look in his eyes, I sensed he was both shocked and disarmed.

"Ahh. Um... Do you want it?" he replied.

Still holding him in the vision of his Divinity, I said, "No, no, it's yours. It's cold. You might need it."

"Thanks," he said, still looking confused.

He pulled his headphones back on and continued to blast his music, and I continued to do my inner work of holding him in his light. In the meantime, I noticedI actually liked some of the music he was listening to. Lucky me!

Then came the classic from Bill Withers, *Lean on Me.*

He started to mumble the words to himself. A mutual fan of the tune, I sang along with him. While his headphones were too loud for him to hear me, we still sang together.

Seeing this as an opportunity to make peace, I grabbed my phone, pulled up my playlist from the day before, and highlighted the fourth title down: "Lean on Me." When the song finished, I tapped him on his shoulder again, then held my phone out for him to see.

He squinted for a second to make out what it said, and when he finally recognized our same musical taste, his eyes widened, and he smiled.

"It's a great tune!" he said.

"A classic!" I agreed.

Then he pointed to the screen on the seat back in front of him and said, "This is another good one!"

"I know," I affirmed. "All the music you have been listening to has been good. You have great eclectic taste," I added honestly.

He smiled. Then, he pulled his hand up and offered it to me to shake. I grabbed it firmly.

"Respect," he said as he shook my hand, still smiling.

He then turned, put his headphones back on, and was swallowed by the sounds. Then, a few minutes later, he took the blanket I'd handed him, pulled it over his head, and was soon fast asleep.

As he snored lightly beside me, I continued to send him a few more blessings before I closed my eyes and did the same. My final thoughts before sleep were of gratitude for the Love within all things and the man next to me.

I don't know long I had been out, but when I awoke, I was met with a surprise so sweet it made me beam. At some point in the night, my neighbor, in his sleepy state, had turned his head and leaned it on my shoulder, in the way one would do with a dear friend. Then, with his head gently resting on me, the words of Bill Withers' tune came rushing through my mind.

Lean on me!

When you're not strong

And I'll be your friend,

I'll help you carry on!

With him at my side and that song singing quietly in the background of my mind, I reflected on my exchange with my new friend. Had I hung tightly to the story of him as the "bad" other, the situation would have most likely escalated into a scene I probably wouldn't have been proud of. Moreover, I would have missed that magical moment and the opportunity to make a friend. But through the loving practice of looking past my judgments and seeing the true essence of this individual, a sacred bond was formed, a bond of brotherhood and shared humanity.

Because the truth is, despite our differences, we are all human. All of us long to love and be loved in return. And I am positive that's what my neighbor was seeking as he sucked down the booze. He was looking to feel better. He was seeking connection. That's why any of us turn to unhealthy habits, be it overworking, eating, or using other substances. We want to feel better, so we lean on these things for support. But these crutches are but counterfeits for what we truly seek: Love.

Perhaps that's why we all need a friend to lean on. Because, as Dr. M. Scott Peck famously said in the opening lines of his best-selling book *The Road Less Traveled*, "Life is hard." But the loving support from another human being can keep us strong and help us carry on when the going gets tough. And it's tough out there right now. More than ever, we need to be the kind of people who can find a friend in all.

With this in mind, as we look at this wild world we live in, with its global calamities and the massive energy of division, let us remember that every human being, at their core, holds a spark of beauty, and that underneath those less-than-agreeable people's actions is simply someone hurting, crying out desperately for a friend.

Let us be those friends and find our common humanity, even in the greatest of our foes. It won't be easy. Like me in this tale, our lower selves will most likely fight tooth and nail to defend their story of "rightness." But that only creates more of the mess we are in. Instead, if we want to create positive change, we need to tell a different story. One who embraces love for ALL beings, even those we'd rather not love. Because stories like these will change the world for the better. And this world certainly could use that type of change right now.

So, with that in mind, as we begin our adventure on love, I hope you will join me in writing a new script for society, one loving act at a time. Let's start this journey with ourselves as we read the next section ahead.

PART I
SELF-LOVE

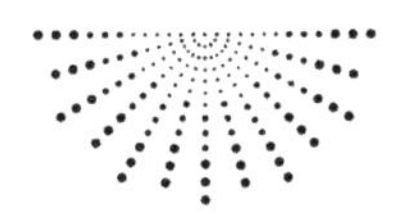

1

YOUR GOLDEN NATURE

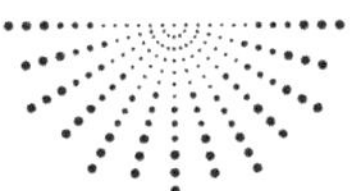

Our first reflection on this exploration of love is about self-love. Just as the well-known airplane principle encourages us to put on our oxygen masks before caring for another, we must first love ourselves if we truly want to love another.

Note, when I say "self-love," I am not talking about a Narcissus-type vanity, staring at our reflections in a pond like the Greek myth. Because that's not love. That's false pride based on external conditions.

Those conditions, in the case of Narcissus, were his handsome looks. But for others, those conditions could be their bank account, their job title, or their social status. Now, the problem is that when we make these external conditions the source of our sense of security, it's as if we are grasping for smoke. Because the minute those conditions change, which, by the nature of this impermanent universe, is inevitable, that so-called "love" will vanish.

So, when I say *self-love,* I am speaking about a love that reaches beyond these superficial and fleeting conditions. A love rooted in the basic goodness within us all. Because "love" is our very nature, our essence, and even if we feel we might be lacking in it, all we need to do is peel back the layers of our past conditioning to reach our golden core. The powerful and true story of the Golden Buddha illustrates this principle perfectly. Here's how it goes:

The Golden Buddha

In a small village in Thailand in 1767, there was a massive Buddha statue made of pure gold. Word came to the villagers that an enemy army was invading, and their swords and force would push the people from their homeland.

Fearing the Golden Buddha would be pillaged in the raid, the villagers decided to cover it with clay to hide it from the fast-approaching troops.

It worked! When the army arrived, they took over the village, but the Buddha's mud-made camouflage disguised his golden center.

The invaders established a settlement and stayed in that village for many years, never noticing the truth behind the mud-covered Buddha. After much time had passed, even the original villagers had forgotten about the richness of his radiant core.

Many years later, when peace was restored, a young monk was meditating by the mud statue. While he sat silently, a large chunk of mud fell from the Buddha right onto his head, shocking him. The monk arose to find out what had happened. To his amazement, he saw the fallen mud left a crack, through which he could see shimmering gold.

He quickly gathered the other monks. They worked together to chip away at the mud and eventually revealed the five-ton Golden Buddha statue, hidden and forgotten for all those years.

Like the Buddha in the story, love is our golden core. It's who we are. But because of life's challenging events, we have covered our radiant nature with mud. That "mud" is our negative thoughts, habits, or destructive ways of protecting ourselves. This could mean beating ourselves up over a mistake or overworking to receive some external validation.

Some of these conditions we have placed upon ourselves. But like the story of the Golden Buddha, much of the mud that covers our lives was put on us by forces in our environment. Our parents, schools, friends, and society have been powerful socializing influences in our lives, telling us what to value, where to focus energy, and how to be safe and loved by the world's standards.

Now, in an ideal world, the socializing forces of the home, school, and community would be forces for good. Unfortunately, Western culture does not always honor the basic goodness of all human beings. Think about it. We celebrate celebrities, influencers, and sports stars, making their lives more important than the grocers in our local supermarkets. Some people are deemed "prettier" based on some illusory metric and thus better. Certain skin tones are considered lesser, while other languages—English, to be precise—are seen as more important than traditional dialects that date back thousands of years.

So, with this underlying cultural narrative where we praise certain conditions like fame, looks, money, status, or whatever, this, in turn, leads many of us to run toward these illusions for security and love. Or as the meditation teacher and psychotherapist Tara Brach pointedly said, we run to "false refuges." They are called false refuges because while we turn to them for security and shelter, like a house built on sand, looking for love in these conditions is unstable and will only lead to never-ending running and grasping.

But the truth is, as cliché as it sounds, the love we are seeking is not out there in the world; it is right here within us. All we have to do is chip away at the mud to discover the gold is who we are.

This inner excavation is paramount. If we don't do the work to uncover the love within us, we won't be able to offer it to others. Because, as the logical adage goes, you can only give what you have. But if so much mud hides our loving core, how can we give the beauty we have within us? How can we love one another, especially the challenging people?! Put simply, we can't. Because the mud clogs our vision from seeing the basic goodness within another. Instead, we see people through a lens of judgment, as not enough, or a "bad other."

That's where the inner work helps. Because let's face it, so often, many of the faults we see in others are the very things we dislike and judge within ourselves. In the words of Jesus, "Why do you look at the speck of sawdust in your brother's eye and pay no attention to the plank in your own eye?" That's why self-love is needed. Because if we do not have compassion for ourselves and our own shortcomings, we will often project our hurts and frustrations onto the world and be less understanding in the face of others' ignorance.

But if we learn to have compassion for those darker parts within us and see the inherent light and basic goodness within ourselves, we are better equipped to see it in others.

This is where the practice of self-love comes in. This quality of self-love has many faces—self-compassion, self-care, kindness, patience, and even fiery and fierce when needed. Because self-love is not just making dates with ourselves for bubble baths or massages, although, as you will see, that's also important. But it's also doing the hard things, like going to therapy, sitting with uncomfortable emotions, discovering your gifts, and pursuing your purpose. It's saying "no" and setting boundaries, to mention but a few actions this type of love requires.

In this section, we will dive into some of these facets of self-love, and hopefully, by the end, we will all have a bit more understanding, love, and compassion for ourselves. In turn, my prayer is that through this inner loving work, we will have much more love to share with the world around us.

BE A FRIEND

~

Be a friend to yourself.
The voice within that barks and bucks
Is not something to kill.
This is violence.
Allow it.
Give up the fight, and do not run.
Instead, let it pass through you
like waves on the ocean.
If we meet our own inner demons
with aggression or fear,
We can only do the same to those around us.
Let us use this body as training grounds
To be kind and friendly
to all who come our way
When we do,
We will be a friend unto the whole world.

~

2

LOVING YOURSELF TO WHOLENESS

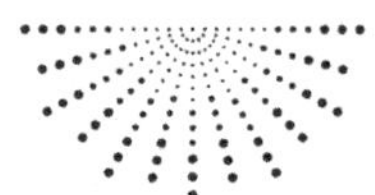

One Saturday afternoon sitting on my deck, my wife, who should have been a comedian, cracked a light-hearted joke that struck a chord in my heart. Standing two and a half inches taller, she sometimes thinks I am vertically challenged—or "short," as most people would say. Now, at nearly 5'9", insecurity about my height has not been much of an issue for me, but that morning, her words hit the roots of an old wound—the feeling of "not enough."

Perhaps you're familiar with some form of this belief. It runs deep through our culture, whether it be not being good enough, not beautiful enough, not strong enough, not smart enough, not rich enough, or not interesting enough.

If I missed any, you can insert whatever version of lack here.

As her words hit me, my throat and chest began to tense. I wanted to run, to lash back at my wife, or to just bury myself in work. I was in what health psychologists call a fight, flight, or freeze response. But as I watched myself reacting, before I spun into a spiral of negative thinking, I did something I had practiced a thousand times before. I took a deep breath and relaxed into the uncomfortable feeling. As I did, my thoughts slowed while I watched the rise and fall of sensations—the knots in my chest, the heat, and the pressure in my throat. At times, it felt like fire. But I did not run or play into my thoughts; I actually discarded them altogether. Because I knew what

I was feeling inside had nothing to do with the story of being "short." I knew what was really going on was an old wound being activated—one that could have been as easily triggered from failing at something new or making a meaningless mistake.

I also knew the moment before me was an opportunity, a road to freedom if I chose to walk toward it. So, there I sat, anchored in mindful awareness, for how long, I am not entirely sure—perhaps it was just five minutes, or maybe even thirty. That's because sitting with discomfort, at times, can feel like forever. But with each passing minute, the tension inside my chest began to loosen its grip, and by the end of it, I experienced a spaciousness surrounding my chest and felt as if I was embraced by a loving, kind, and caring presence.

What was happening?

I was healing.

As a human being, you have no doubt experienced a version of the first part of the story. However, if you're 6'2" and not in the NBA, it's unlikely it was about feeling short. But perhaps something else activated an uncomfortable experience within you. Maybe it was a comment from your boss about the quality of your work, or the lack of response you received from a project you worked hard on, or maybe even a seemingly hostile glance from a stranger you passed on the street.

When these experiences happen, they can activate core wounds long stored in both the psyche and the body. For me, at that moment, the wound was "not good enough." However, other core wounds can also be activated, such as beliefs that we are stupid, not lovable, and so on.

While they can happen later in our lives, more often than not, these core wounds develop in our early childhood. As children, we are so impressionable. So, if we don't receive the love we need from a caregiver at one point in time, the belief of not being worthy of love can develop. Even an offhand remark from an overwhelmed parent can plant a negative belief in a child's subconscious mind that will follow them their whole lives. Without the resources to move through these negative experiences, these hurts often turn into deep-seated traumas that live within the body and will only resurface when something activates them. Thus, the off-the-cuff remark from your boss about your late deliveries can trigger an innate, unprocessed hurt.

This is well-researched in modern psychology. However, it was discovered over 2,500 years ago and written about in Buddhist and Vedic philosophical texts. In these wisdom traditions, these stored pockets of emotions are called *samskaras,* which are energetic imprints of unprocessed feelings. Just like psychologists discovered, the ancient philosophers also found that when conditions are right, samskaras will rise to the surface, carrying with them the same uncomfortable feeling from when they were created.

Most of us have not been trained to move through these uncomfortable feelings. As such, we try to flee through many coping strategies when they arise. Or, as already mentioned in Tara Brach's work, we escape to "false refuges," which are so-called because they present the illusion that they will bring us the security we desperately seek. Some common false refuges are alcohol and other mind-numbing substances, social media, work, food, excessive exercise, or whatever other false refuge we use to escape the feelings we are feeling.

Now, before I go further, there is one important point I would like to make. These coping mechanisms, especially if they are "healthy," might not be the worst thing in the world, particularly if we have not trained ourselves to face uncomfortable emotions. Numbing out on a mindless movie might not be the worst thing in the world every now and then, especially if you are tired and not ready to face your feelings. Diving deep into uncomfortable emotions without the proper resources can actually perpetuate trauma. But it's important to know these coping strategies are like band-aids; they may be helpful—even necessary at the beginning—but if you want to produce deep healing, you have to remove the band-aid and let the wound breathe in a clean and supportive environment. So now the question is, how can we accomplish that?

The Practice

Many different traditions and fields of psychology highlight a similar step-by-step process to heal these old wounds. Tara Brach uses a process where clients witness their negative emotions and, through mindful awareness, accept them. Similarly, Michael Singer, yogi and spiritual teacher, says we must *surrender* to the feelings that arise. Eckhart Tolle calls these stored emotions the "pain body" and teaches that when it occurs, we must be present and watch it. Byron Katie tells us to "love what is."

While their language and approaches may differ slightly, each process has similar essential elements—a witnessing presence (not attached to the story) and a conscious feeling and releasing of the sensations in the body.

Personally, I like how Byron Katie adds "love" to the equation, as I believe it is a supportive ingredient to face those uncomfortable feelings. Just as the loving attention from a friend when you are having a hard time can offer additional support, bringing the energy of love to the witnessing process of old emotions can be an added resource when facing these old hurts.

Be Patient

Healing old wounds is a long, sometimes arduous, but beautiful journey. But if we train our attention skills through mindfulness, meditation, and inquiry, we will be able to pause, feel, and allow those waves of emotion to pass through us and, ultimately, face all of life's storms with grace. But we must be patient with ourselves. Healing is a process, especially when working through these core wounds.

The other day, I spoke with a distraught client. "Not this again!" he said, referring to one of his core wounds that had risen to the surface. "I thought I had dealt with this already!"

Can you relate? Have you ever felt like you'd overcome a challenge, only to find it coming up again a week, a month, or even years later? If that's the case, don't worry. This is normal. While I am not discounting miracle healings—and I have witnessed them—I have found that, more often than not, healing these old hurts takes time. It takes many rounds of conscious awareness as these old emotions rise to the surface. If we are mindful and welcome them with the above-mentioned practices, then some of those old hurts will leave us. And bit by bit, little by little, we chip away at the past pain and, as a result, become freer. As such, we can live in the beautiful present moment and create a more beautiful future. It is possible, but it takes work and time.

Indeed, this heart work is sometimes hard work, but we can do it—one step and one mindful moment at a time.

p.s. If you'd like to explore this topic further, consider reading one of the following books:

Extra Resources:

- *The Untethered Soul,* by Michael Singer
- *True Refuge,* by Tara Brach
- *The Power of Now,* by Eckhart Tolle
- *Loving What Is,* by Byron Katie

p.p.s. If you have not trained your mindfulness muscles, it can be beneficial to have extra support, such as a meditation teacher or therapist, to hold space and be present with you as you process these experiences. Just as a support beam holds the weight of the roof of a house, a person's mindful presence can support you when you are stuck in a story and the ground seems shaky.

MY CAPTAIN

~

Sometimes it feels as though there
is an out-of-tune symphony
screaming in my head.
I hear one voice that is bashful
and another that is mean.
Some are sweet, while others
impatient and rude!
One hundred and one voices all calling to me,
telling me what I must do.
If I am not careful,
I just might mistake one of
these passing guests as the captain of this ship.
But when I slow down,
center my attention in my heart,
and rest in the spaces between my breaths,
that rambunctious crowd that has been
causing so much ruckus in my mind
quiets down,
and their out-of-key sonnets
soften to a still hum.
And even though I can still hear their voices

barking in the background,
I have found a fortress of peace
they cannot penetrate.
And no longer can they dictate
where this ship should sail,
because in the silent chambers of my heart,
I connect with the commander of this ship.

~

3
THE POWER OF THE SACRED PAUSE

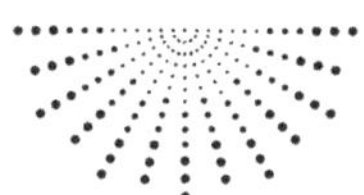

After an epic journey flying across the Pacific Ocean, my wife Andréanne and I landed at Heathrow—one of the world's largest and busiest airports—at 6:45 a.m. After picking up our bags, going through customs, and making our way to our rental car, some 25 miles (40 km) from the airport, by the time we finally pulled onto the highway to make the long drive to Poole, a British coastal town in the south of England, it was already 10:00 a.m. But with the time change from Southeast Asia, our bodies thought it was 3:00 in the morning.

We were both tired. And we'd been in such a daze on arrival, we neglected to grab anything to eat before leaving the terminal. On top of that, even our water supply was quickly draining. To make matters even worse, I was at the tail end of a cold and could feel the stress of my fragile immune system on the verge of breaking.

"There's a rest stop," Andréanne said, pointing to a green sign to the left of the highway. "It's about twenty minutes away."

With all the compounding components putting stress on us, we were both feeling relieved at the prospect of a moment's rest to replenish our water, stretch our legs, and grab a little something to eat.

But Fate had other plans.

"Oh no! That was it!" Andréanne exclaimed as we watched the little rest stop tucked into the trees roll by us.

"It's okay, we'll just find another place," I said, as we both tried to keep a positive outlook.

With Andréanne at the wheel, I picked up the phone to search for a rest stop or restaurant nearby and noticed I had only 13 percent power left on the only phone with access to Wi-Fi. I grabbed my USB cable and placed it in the car port to charge, but, in famous Murphy's Law fashion, the USB port was broken on our rental.

Away from the city and in the sticks in a country neither of us had visited, everything I could find online was forty minutes away, closed until lunch or dinner, or in the opposite direction.

"What about that?" I pointed to what looked like a restaurant sign just off the highway.

Seeing as there weren't too many options, we took a chance. We pulled off the highway and followed a small country road surrounded by trees. While the scenery was stunning, the lack of cars and people did not make it look like a promising choice.

We drove for about five minutes until the little road ended in the parking lot of a National Park. Despite the beauty of the forest, our fatigue, hunger, dehydration, jet lag, exhaustion, and dying phone all amassed into an internal mess, and that's when the bickering began. In our irritation at the situation, we got irritated at each other and tossed little comments of aggression like hot coals back and forth.

We were about to drive away, with the smoke of our quarrel trailing behind us, when something spoke to me. Perhaps it was the trees standing still beside us, or simply the stillness within me, that spoke ever so clearly.

"Pause," it said.

Carrying this wisdom close, I turned to Andréanne and said, "Okay, my love, let's just pause for five minutes. Because whatever we are doing now is not creating anything good."

On edge and eager to get going so we could solve our predicament as soon as possible, we were both a little reluctant to stop, but despite that inner resistance, we pulled over, closed our eyes, and took a moment to breathe in and out. We paused and appreciated the trees around us, the stillness in the air, and the moment itself.

And though it was short, by the time we restarted the car and got back on the road, we were more present, alive, and centered. We slowed down, and as we drove back along the same country road, we were more mindful. We took our time and, in that still space, caught sight of a giant red hawk-like bird, a kite, swirling across the open blue sky. Its majestic flight had a presence so commanding that we slowed down even more to admire it. Then, as our eyes followed it soaring through the sky, I noticed it was circling above a large outdoor garden center, and in the corner of my eye, I could see a tiny hand-painted sign that read, "We serve tea and food."

“There! There!” I pointed. “It's a café!”

“Are you sure?” Andréanne replied, perhaps perplexed that a garden center would feature a café.

“I’m positive. I saw a sign.” And I wasn't talking about the bird soaring through the sky.

We made a U-turn, returned to the center, and crawled down a little bumpy road into nothing short of an oasis. Trees and flowers were in full bloom. Perennials, herbs, annuals, and vines in pots filled the car park with green, red, blue, and violet. People walked joyfully with their dogs and purchased blooms to take home and transplant.

At the end of the road was a quaint little outdoor café with tables that welcomed the sun. A small group of elders sat at one, sipping tea and smiling at us as we gratefully settled into one of the benches. As my nervous system calmed, I began to feel the fatigue that cortisol, the stress hormone, had been masking. Wanting to help with the driving, I was tempted to ingest some caffeine to help me push through it. But, after pausing again and feeling into my body on the tail end of a cold, I knew that pushing it further was not what I needed. So, I settled for ginger tea instead.

We enjoyed a glass of water, quiche, and a salad. I was able to plug in my phone there as well. We laughed and appreciated the British sun (yes, it was sunny!), chatted with the friendly locals, took a little walk around the greenery, and literally stopped to smell the roses. By the time we got back in the car, our water bottles were filled, our bellies satiated, our phone battery had recharged to a respectable level, and so had we.

When we finally arrived at our Airbnb nearly three hours later, we collapsed on the bed for a nap. But before I closed my eyes to drift off to sleep, I turned to the bedside table and plugged the phone in to charge, noting it had only three percent charge left. I laughed, thinking that was literally how I felt. Then, all thoughts ceased, and I fell into a deep and dreamless sleep.

A few hours later, I rose full of energy with the phone fully charged.

As I reflected on the experience, I couldn't help but think about what might have happened had we failed to listen to the wisdom of the voice within that urged us to pause. Had we continued to push, push, push, which is our cultural norm, my phone probably would have died, we'd have been lost in a foreign country with no navigation, the bickering would have increased, and perhaps the cold I had been fighting would have won.

But none of that happened. Thanks to the wisdom of slowing down, we saw the magnificent bird who guided us to the garden oasis to refuel and replenish. This is the gift of rest. Even just five minutes makes all the difference.

This can often feel counterintuitive because in our hustle and bustle culture, we're trained to keep going, to push through whatever is in our way. While there is undoubtedly merit in determination, the idea that we must keep going without stopping is both disconnected from reality and lacking in wisdom.

It's common sense that you would not drive a car empty of gas without pausing to refuel. But in our culture, most of us are so disconnected from our bodies that we don't even know we are running on empty. Masking our fatigue with caffeine and adrenaline, we keep pushing.

But what's the cost? Sure, we may get a little more work done and cross off a few more to-dos, but in the long run, the cost of not pausing will always, always, always catch up with us. Even if we don't see it in the short term.

With this in mind, as you move forward with your week ahead, remember to take those sacred pauses between the busyness of activity. Take a nap, a walk in nature, or just a few deep breaths between tasks. And watch how taking a moment to rest actually gives you time, energy, and wisdom to create a truly remarkable life, one grounded in peace, joy, and balance. That's worth five minutes, don't you think?

4
I CRIED

It was September 1st, my wife's birthday, and on that special occasion, our friend Jaya had invited us to a four-star resort nestled by a rolling river and cradled by the jungle here in Bali. While we are not really resort people, it being her big day, we accepted the invitation and prepared to meet our friend there to celebrate.

"I'd like to get a massage," my wife said while we were preparing to leave. She paused, then said matter-of-factly, "And I want you to get one as well."

"I'm okay," I replied with a smile. "But a massage for you sounds perfect!"

Her look, soft and sweet, turned stern.

"I mean it. I want you to get a massage. You work so hard. You need to take care of yourself, too. We've been in Bali for almost an entire year, and not once have you had a Balinese massage."

She said firmly, just before she put the nail in the coffin of my argument. "Besides, it's my birthday, and I want you to get one."

Now, I am what you'd call a minimalist, with some friends even saying I was a borderline ascetic. I happily slept on bamboo floors or the ground for years before I met my wife. So, in my mind, since my back wasn't broken, I viewed such things as excessive. Besides, the idea of going to a resort was already a stretch for me.

But after seeing the sternness in my wife's eyes and hearing her last point—it being her birthday wish—there was not much to argue with.

"Okay, my love. I will get a massage," I accepted and grabbed her hand as I kissed her cheek. "As a birthday gift to you," I added cheekily with a little smirk.

We rode our motorbike for an hour to the Bambu Indah Resort. To call the place exquisite would be an understatement. It was magical. When we arrived, we were welcomed by a jungle path garnished with stone and wood sculptures, leading to an open-concept reception area on a hillside overlooking a canopy of trees.

At the bamboo reception desk, we were greeted by a young Balinese woman who welcomed us with a golden smile.

"How can I help you?"

"We'd like two day passes, please," I replied.

"We'd also like to book three massages," my wife added. "Two for us, and one for a friend who will be joining us soon."

The woman nodded, still smiling, and looked at her monitor. "I am sorry, ma'am, sir. But we have only two available appointments. We are fully booked."

"Are you sure?" my wife asked.

"Yes, ma'am."

I chimed in, "It's no problem, love. You two can have your massages, and I will happily wait and read by the water."

My wife turned to the receptionist and said, "Okay, we will book those two spots, please."

The young woman looked at her screen, tapped a few keys, and wished us a good day.

We turned and made our way down to the water, which was an adventure in itself! We crossed a rickety wooden bridge suspended fifty feet in the air, marched through jungle paths, and zigzagged up and down stone stairs that eventually brought us to the jungle floor. At the bottom, we found an oasis of stream-fed pools in many shapes and sizes alongside a cozy café that sat comfortably at the river's edge.

We took a seat and ordered tea. Then, very seriously, my wife stared me down from the other side of the table and said forcefully, "I'm not getting a massage. I want you to get one."

"Honey, are you kidding me? It's your birthday. And I don't even want a massage! I am not getting it," I replied defiantly.

"Honey," she said back to me, "I want you to get it. You really need it."

I shook my head in a circle. "Let's see. Let's just take it as it comes and see what happens." I was still convinced I would not take my wife's massage on her birthday.

But she didn't flinch. And as I looked into her beautiful eyes, I saw the look of someone who had decided. A look, as the philosopher Goethe once said, in more or less words, was "the look of a victor."

We dropped the topic for a moment and proceeded to enjoy our day, sipping on our teas and jumping into the spring-fed pools as we reveled in the perfect moment.

About an hour later, our friend arrived, and we welcomed her with open arms. Then, after a small meal, we brought up the topic of the massage again.

"They only have two slots," we told her, sharing the news. Our friend, a single mom with a busy week behind her, was committed to getting a treatment for herself.

"What, really? No, I am sure they can do something about it!" she insisted.

She then summoned one of the staff to make our plea.

"Is there any way we can all get a massage?" she asked.

"Let me check." The worker nodded politely, turned, and consulted with reception on the in-house phone. It turned out there were only two rooms available. But if we were willing to put a third table into one of them, we could all get a massage.

Problem solved. It seemedI wasn't getting out of this one.

"Okay," I said reluctantly. "Let's do it."

When the time came, we made the long climb from the river's edge through the jungle to a row of bamboo huts surrounded by flowering frangipani trees.

Not knowing what to do, I just flopped myself on top of the massage table. I was quickly corrected, handed a pair of disposable shorts, and told to strip. "Sorry, this is my first massage," I said awkwardly. "I don't really know what to do."

"How long have you been in Bali?" the woman asked me.

"Almost one year," I replied.

"What? And you haven't had a massage yet? Not good!" She beamed.

I smiled back with a shrug and then lay on the table, face down, and let the woman, who had probably massaged thousands of bodies before mine, do her work.

That's when I cried...

Not from the pain of her working the knots from my neck, but from love. As her hands made their way through my back, shoulders, and legs, I felt as if the hands of Love itself were cradling me, bringing attention, kindness, and care to parts of me I had long neglected. My body was like a beat-up machineI had kept pushing, without truly tending to it.

With her practiced, caring touch, it was as if years of holding so tight and just soldiering on were being released in a matter of minutes. And with that, my heart opened like a flower on a spring day. Waves of love filled every part of my body. I was grateful for this massage therapist, for this center, for my wife getting a massage beside me, and for the whole world. I was literally beaming with love.

Still on the table, I turned to my wife, and with tears in my eyes, I told her how much I adored and cherished her.

When the massage was finished, I wiped the tears from my eyes, and with the biggest smile, I placed my hands in the customary

Namaste prayer pose to offer my heartfelt thanks to the skilled masseuse and bowed to the woman who had blessed me.

"Thank you so, so much."

She bowed back and gave a gentle smile.

Holding my wife's hand, when we walked down the dirt path to the parking lot, I felt as if I were flying. My cheeks literally hurt the next day from smiling so big. I was so filled with love, I couldn't help but share what I felt inside with all who came my way, whether with a smile, a conversation, or simply mentally blessing everyone I encountered. My heart was so open, it enveloped the entire world.

And to think, I almost did not go. To think I almost withheld such a special and sacred experience from myself.

To think...

Now, the questionI had to seriously reflect on was, "Why?"

Why, in a place where for less than $20 I could receive a life-changing experience, did I withhold such a gift from myself?

Why was I withholding loving myself?

The ascetic in me definitely viewed it as excessive.

My logic for resisting was this: If my body wasn't experiencing debilitating pain, why should I get a massage? I'd rather use my money for something I actually need or in a way that could help others.

But I reflected that even Jesus, the most admirable martyr, allowed Mary to wash his feet with expensive oils and perfumes that could have been sold to feed the hungry. Not that I'm comparing myself with Jesus! Heaven forbid. But, in all respects, this experience of allowing a masseuse to work on me had nothing to do with the massage but with something much bigger.

It had to do with allowing myself to let Love in.

Love, in all her beauty, was standing there with open arms, the door unlocked and inviting me through. Yet, I was shutting her out.

Why do we shut the door to Love?

While this story is highly personal, it also contains universal themes many of us enact in our lives.

Note: I actually felt quite shy about sharing this story about getting a massage. I mean, really, given the state of the world, aren't there more important things to talk about? But here's the thing: It's not about the massage. It really is about inviting Love more into our lives. Because if we aren't already enlightened, regardless of where we live and what we do, we all have the opportunity to let more love in.

Whether we see her or not, Love is there, encouraging us to allow her warm, loving metaphorical hands to touch us. While Love might not always show up as a person, as it did in my case, it can just as easily manifest in sunshine on a dewdrop at dawn.

She can even show up as a challenging situation, inviting you to open your heart even wider. Regardless of how Love wants to show up in our lives, she is there, standing quietly by the door, waiting for us to walk toward her.

Now, the question is, how can we let more love into our lives?

Service is by far one of the greatest pathways, and as you'll see, I write about that a lot.

But, for this reflection, I'd like to talk about filling our own cups.

Even Barack Obama, as he served the United States to the best of his ability, prioritized exercise, family time, and reading. He explained that those gave him the strength to better serve his country, and indeed the world. As such, the answer to the concept of "filling your own cup" will be different for all of us. It could be as simple as finding time to meditate, be in nature, eat healthy food, exercise, or pray. Or filling your cup with love might show up as a bigger demand, like letting go of a long-standing negative habit or forgiving someone you'd rather not.

Regardless of what it is for you, these big and small acts are doorways that can welcome more love into our lives. And guess what? When we take the time to let more love in, like in my massage story, we have a whole lot more love to give. And as we look at the state of the world today, it certainly could use some more love in it.

With this in mind, I invite you to take a moment to contemplate the following questions:

What small acts of care can I do this week to welcome more love into my life?

What little acts of love can I perform daily to fill my cup?

What's one negative habit/mindset/belief/resentment keeping me from letting more love in?

How can I begin to change that?

May you pay attention to your answers and walk through Love's door. And, as a result, may you bring that love to the world at large.

5
ON THE OTHER SIDE OF FEAR

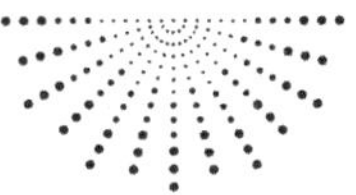

The cave you fear to enter holds the treasure you seek.

— *JOSEPH CAMPBELL*

One afternoon I found myself filled with fear for something so trivial it seems silly to even mention it. But, despite how seemingly small the cause of the fear was, I still found a universal lesson in the experience I'd like to share.

Let me explain.

It started when I went to purchase fruit from my local grocer, which, when living on an island in Southeast Asia, is a much different experience than buying food in a supermarket in the West.

Imagine a little open-air shop tucked into a narrow, busy street with no sidewalks and motorbikes buzzing left and right. The front of the shop is made up of wooden crates laden with watermelons, pineapples, papayas, and coconuts. When you step up two stairs and enter the crowded store, shelves of local crops are piled in every direction, with bunches of bananas, local varieties of apples, avocados, potatoes, carrots, beets, broccoli, and pretty much every food you'd need to make a healthy meal.

After loading my basket with my favorite fruits, I turned to my grocer to offer my thanks.

"Terima kasih," I said as I handed her my cash. Thank you.

"Sama-sama," she said, you're welcome, then handed over my change and sent me on my way.

As I turned to leave, my eyes fell on the stall beside hers, another grocer who, in comparison to the one I had just purchased from, tended to offer a poorer quality selection of produce. She had less variety, often older, and sometimes borderline rotting. But despite the lower quality, she was one of the only vendors in the market who sold *canang sari*—the beautiful traditional Balinese daily offering made with woven palm leaves and flower blossoms.

These exquisite little offerings are placed on altars, stairs, rice fields, or even on the ground in front of businesses as symbols of gratitude to life, nature, and the creative force within the universe. I love this sacred practice of thanksgiving and have made it a habit to place these blessings outside my house every morning.

On a typical trip to the market, I might buy most of my groceries from the primary grocer, go to the next stall, buy some canang sari, and, to make it feel like a more substantial purchase, I'd also pick up some fruit. It had become an unspoken pattern between us.

But on that day, the ATM had run out of money, leaving me with little cash after my primary purchase. While I did have enough to buy my prized canang sari, the only thing I really wanted from that store, I suddenly felt uneasy that I didn't have enough cash to buy the extra fruits I usually got there, which, truth be told, I didn't even want.

So, as I looked at the store and my mind contemplated my possible lack of funds, I began to feel a constriction in my chest. And then suddenly, a small part of me wanted to turn around, hop on my motorbike, and go home.

It was an old, familiar feeling I had felt countless times before—like in moments before sharing an article online, telling someone I loved them, or speaking up about something that mattered to me.

That feeling of constriction was fear.

As strange as it sounds, I was afraid my secondary grocer would be offended if I only bought the offerings.

But thankfully, I've had a lot of practice with that feeling, so I did what I had done thousands of times in circumstances of discomfort. I breathed into the sensations in my chest and relaxed into them. Then, after a couple of conscious breaths like this, I marched over to the second grocer.

"How much is this?" I asked, pointing to a bag filled with the flower offerings.

She gave me the price and told me those specific offerings were an especially good choice. I pulled the bag from the hook, smiled, and handed her the last of my cash. She beamed a radiant glow as she received it. And I beamed back.

I gave her a final farewell before turning to walk away and hop on my bike. Then I looked down at the package of small baskets in my hand, the sacred ceremonial tool used for blessing, and shook my head as a great big grin grew on my face. There I was, holding in my hand a very tangible realization of what exists on the other side of fear—a blessing.

This little experiential story seems so small, really. But I continually find that some of life's most profound truths exist in everyday experiences.

Think of your own life for a moment:

How many times has the feeling of fear held you back from doing what you felt called to do?

Or, how many times has the feeling of "not enough" stopped you from sharing what you had to give?

Isn't it true there's a blessing on the other side of those fears, too?

In the story above, I wrestled with feeling like I didn't have enough money, but that feeling of "not enough" can be felt in so many ways, such as:

Not enough time

Not being knowledgeable enough

Or not feeling good enough

Just to name a few.

If you've experienced one or more of these, you're not alone. It's common for feelings of fear to hold us back.

But just because it's common does not mean we should let those fears run the show.

Because when we listen to fear, we do a disservice to ourselves because we miss out on the gifts that wait on the other side. We also do a disservice to those around us because they don't receive our gifts.

Had I failed to face that little fear, the grocer would have had less money at the end of the day—less to share with her family, her community, and the world at large.

Note: She was HAPPY to receive what I had to give. It was enough.

The same is true with whatever gifts you have to offer. You do not need to be the best in the world to make a difference in it. What you have to give is enough. You are enough.

With this in mind, please, please, please, face your fears, and go out and share your gifts with the world.

You have something truly magical to offer, and in today's crazy world, we need what you have to give now more than ever!

And, hey, sharing your gifts is pretty sweet for you as well.

Because on the other side of those fears is a canang sari—a blessing.

Bringing It Home

To bring this idea into your own life, I invite you to reflect on the following:

Questions for Reflection:

- What fears are stopping you from expressing your truest self?
- Are you withholding from sharing your gifts, yourself, or your time, because of feelings of "not enough?"

- How might what you have to share positively benefit those around you?
- Why is it important for you to face those fears?
- How can you face your fears today?

THE REVOLUTION

~

Go! Go! Go!
Is the story of our culture.
Do! Do! Do!
Again, and again, and again.
It's crazy!
We destroy entire ecosystems
just to keep up with this insidious pace,
and now many forests run bare simply
because we want to build
more and more and more!
It seems we have forgotten that
this precious life of ours
is made up of both an inhale and an exhale.
Forgotten
that there is a time to act
and a time to be still,
That there is a time to sit
and a time to go.
All things have their seasons
and all things must be honored.
But at times, it seems that this world we live in

is in such a rush and so focused on "production"
that it has forgotten the simple act of breathing,
the simple act of being.
And because of that,
consciously choosing to slow down and
be still could almost be seen as an act of
protest.
But this wildly fast-paced way of life
seems to be tearing our world apart,
So, I say "Protest!"
Stand tall with your tree, brothers!
Be as spacious as the open sky!
Be still and strong like the Grandfather Stones!
Be.
Breathe.
And join this peaceful revolution.
For the simple act of being
transforms this entire world.
If you don't think so,
just look at the power of the great white oak.
Just look at him be!
Can't you see that in his perfect act of presence
of resting with who
and what he really is
brings the very breath you breathe?
This is the power of being!
This is the power of breathing!
It brings the beauty of life itself...
Now that's something.
So, I hope you join me in this quiet revolution.
Sit,
Breathe,
and
Be.

6
TAKE A BREAK: YOU'RE TAKING TOO LONG

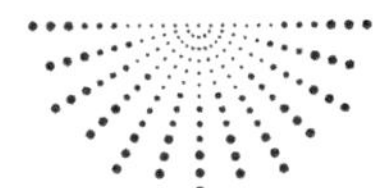

For years, I have prioritized taking a day of rest every week. I was first inspired to follow this practice by a friend who would fast one day a week. Later, my commitment was reinforced when I discovered that Gandhi, who, despite planning a revolution against the British Empire, would still find time every seven days to sit and be silent.

Most weeks, Sunday is the day I slow down, unplug from the world, and dedicate twenty-four hours solely to this soul renewal. After doing so, I am always energized the following day and ready to take on the week. I have found this rest day to be such a powerful practice I have prioritized it as a cornerstone for my overall well-being. In fact, whenever I've made an exception, like the story you are about to hear, I have always paid the price.

It was a Saturday evening in mid-September, that busy month when people are coming back from vacation, kids are back at school, the traffic is chaotic, and, if you're an online entrepreneur and a teacher like me, this is when programs begin and classes start. That fall, I found myself teaching four different programs, and even though I don't like to work weekends, that Saturday afternoon, I was buried in my computer finishing off deadlines.

But just before I closed my laptop to shut off for the day and head to a concert, I noticed my computer had stopped charging. Any computer short-circuit is never ideal. In this case, it was especially worrisome because I had planned to take my regular Sunday off and then prepare on Monday morning for a class that evening.

So on Sunday, I violated my long-standing rule of unplugging completely. The day's original plan was to have a long meditation in the morning, then make my way with a friend to a sacred site, some forty minutes from my house, to connect with nature, be still, and restore ourselves. However, wanting to get my computer problems sorted before Monday morning instead of taking my time, almost immediately after my meditation, I jumped up from my mat and tried to squeeze in the task of fixing my computer within the day's constraints.

I rushed out the door and hopped on my motorbike to head for Bali Repair—the tech maintenance shop twenty-five minutes from my house. My phone rang just as I was leaving. It was the friend solidifying our meetup details for the trip.

"Hey, sorry, I'm going to be an hour late," I told her and stressed the importance of my reasons.

My friend was frustrated with the last-minute change of plans. Defensively, I barked something at her, which I immediately regretted. Unable to soften the blow of my words before the call ended, I was left buzzing down the quiet roads, contemplating my mistake.

As I arrived at the little electronics store, I could almost feel the Universe laughing at me. A big white sign hung from the glass window: CLOSED. Driving back, I couldn't help but think about how much unnecessary stress I had created for myself and those around me. And for what? It was all a complete waste of energy.

Thankfully, when I arrived at the beautiful natural site, with the big body of water practically embracing me, I made peace with my friend, and together, we washed the woes and worries of the week away. But the story really got interesting the following morning. With the repair shop closed until 11:00 a.m., I had ample time to prepare for my class with good old-fashioned pen and paper. By the time I left for Bali Repair with my laptop, I was pretty much finished with all the content for my evening's class.

When I entered the little white store with Apple branding stenciled all over it, a Balinese man in his early twenties greeted me warmly.

We shared a few friendly hellos, and I struggled to utter some words in the foreign language I was still learning.

"Saya computer tidak energi." My computer has no energy. He laughed, probably appreciating my attempt. Calmly, he picked up my laptop, took it to the back to run some diagnostics, and discovered the charger was the culprit. All I needed was a new one.

"We don't have one in stock, but we can have it by tomorrow," the man replied.

Realizing the problem could have been far worse, I counted my blessings I only had to wait one day, thanked him profusely, and we shared a few warm-hearted remarks in Indonesian. Just before I turned to leave, he said something I couldn't quite grasp.

He noticed, smiled, and looked up through the corner of his eyes, as if he were searching the room to find the word.

"Just remember..." he said with a giant grin, "no stress. Because when you stress... it, it, it messes everything up."

Reflecting on the last twenty-four hours, I smiled back knowingly. "You are so right, my friend."

He beamed as I waved and walked away from his sagely smile, his words rolling on repeat in my mind as I drove back home.

When I arrived at my house, I was met with a stack of everyday problems. Some challenges with a colleague pushed a deadline back, family demands required my attention, unexpected interruptions, and a few loose-end tasks were still undone before the class that evening. Yet, the wise words of my young computer repairman, "No stress," carried me through.

Now, don't get me wrong, a healthy dose of stress can be beneficial. Like the string of a bow, the right amount of tension helps direct an arrow to its target. But the problem in our world is we often put too much stress on ourselves, most of which is unnecessary.

Did I really need to rush frantically to get my computer fixed that day? As you can see, the answer was most definitely no. While it would have been nice to have my laptop on Monday morning, it was not necessary. We often think we *must* fulfill an impossible To-Do list every day. But in truth, more often than not, we burden ourselves with unnecessary stress, which doesn't just hurt us; it affects our partners, our friends, and the world at large. All this unnecessary stress, to quote the wise repairman's maxim, "messes everything up."

With this in mind, let's all take that wisdom to heart, take it easy, and relax a bit more.

NOW-HERE

~

Nowhere is where I would like to be,
a place free from
the constant ping of my phone,
free from appointments to rush to
and deadlines to meet,
a place where the only thing in this world
that truly matters
is this perfect moment.
Nothing more.
This belly breathing,
these fingers typing,
just here,
Nowhere.
Wow.
What a beautiful place it is!
I can hear the silent wind
singing a sweet and still song.
I can feel an opening in my chest
vibrating with little currents of electricity.
I can see the dark morning hue drape

across the colors in my room.
Wow, nowhere is a wonderful place to be!
I hope you join me sometime.
It's really quite easy to get to
and only requires a little effort on your part.
But don't you worry
because, as you know,
any great destination is well worth the journey.
I tell you what,
I'll take you right now!
Are you ready?
Don't worry,
no need to pack.
You have everything you need.
Okay!
Ready?
Let's go!
Take a big breath right into your belly
and then hold it for 5-10 seconds.
Release...
Take another one.
Hold,
and release.
Okay, two more times
before you read the next line.
Now listen,
feel the space around you,
pay close attention to the sounds,
let them come over you
like a wave upon a silent shore.
Feel your hands.
Do they vibrate? Do they pulse?
What do you notice?
Keep breathing.
Now look around with new eyes
at this strange and wonderful place
that exists around you!
Welcome to Nowhere.
You are Now-Here.

Isn't it beautiful!?
You're welcome here any time.
It's just a few breaths away.
I hope you come here often 🙂

7
DON'T HATE ME: THIS COULD SAVE YOUR LIFE

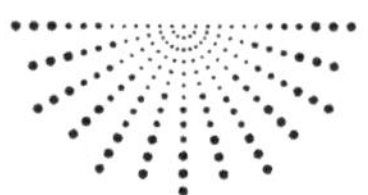

The body is your temple. Keep it pure and clean for the soul to reside in.

— B.K.S. LYNGAR

"If you could have one wish, what would you wish for?" she asked, staring deeply into the Hindu priest's eyes. He looked back at her without flinching and smiled, his timeless face, both young and old, glowing like the sun.

"Sehat," he said. Health.

Sitting beside him, I looked into the sparkle in his eyes and deeply contemplated his answer. We were in the garden of his modest Balinese home, a compound with several small one-room houses, each sleeping whole families. The buildings were arranged side-by-side in a tight circle and shared a central outdoor kitchen. It was a humble home, which he later told me he had built with his bare hands with a handful of friends many years before. And here he was, offered the world in a single wish, and all he wanted was health.

As I contemplated his response, my mind flashed back to the previous week. Images of me sick, lying in bed, came to my awareness. For days, I could barely move, eat, or even think. As I viewed the motion picture play across the screen of my mind, I couldn't help but think of the wisdom of this man's one-word wish.

He understood the adage "health is wealth." Because, at the end of the day, no matter how great your riches, without health, what is left? Not much. An overwhelming body of scientific research agrees, linking health to overall happiness. Spiritual traditions echo this wisdom, often referring to the body as a temple.

But if we look at the current and growing prevalence of physical and mental health challenges, it's safe to say that a large majority of us are not prioritizing health. We are burning the candle at both ends, chasing worldly wishes and hedonic pleasures, only to be burned by them in the long run.

Now, don't get me wrong. I think a large majority of us do want to be healthy. We want to feel good and live rich, meaningful lives. But so many of us are going about it the wrong way.

But here's the thing: Being healthy is actually really, really straightforward. And it just takes a few simple habits which, if practiced regularly, will lead to astonishing results. These are physical actions that also positively affect our emotional, mental, and spiritual well-being. They are backed by scientific literature and are not that hard to implement.

So, what are these magical habits? You won't believe how simple they are: Eating, Moving, and Sleeping.

Tom Rath, the prominent researcher who some have called the greatest non-fiction writer of the twenty-first century, in his excellent book *Eat, Move, Sleep*, tells us that "eating, moving, and sleeping" are the cornerstones for us to live healthier and happier lives. When we engage fully in these three things, we "create an upward spiral and progressively better days."

Think about the importance of what you choose to eat in the morning. In the short term, a healthy meal will make you feel better, give you more energy, and improve your productivity at work. In the long run, you'll likely live longer, spend more time with your family, and contribute more positively to your community. If you exercise, you're not only reducing your risk of a host of physical illnesses such as cardiovascular disease and obesity, but you're also pumping your brain with powerful chemicals that enhance your mood, increase your focus, and help you sleep better. And the better we sleep, the better we think, feel, and act. Consequently, we'll probably be more patient, kind, and caring with people around us, make better decisions, and be drawn to better food choices. It's a powerful cycle that works together like the gears of a vehicle.

On the other end of the spectrum, if you get a bad night's sleep, your blood sugar will drop, making you more likely to reach for unhealthy food in search of some quick energy. You'll have a high, then crash, and will feel more sluggish as a result. Consequently, you'll want to be more sedentary and will be less likely to exercise. You may grab some caffeine to mask your fatigue, and despite being exhausted, when you lie down to rest, your mind will still be buzzing, leading to another bad night of sleep. It's a vicious cycle.

But with a little bit of thoughtfulness, we can transform these things into a virtuous cycle, each healthy habit supporting us to create better and better days. With this in mind, let's take a deep dive into these three practices and see how we can apply them in our own lives, if we don't already.

Food is Medicine

Hippocrates once said, "Let food be thy medicine and medicine be thy food." And while many of the Greek physician's theories are considered outdated, this one by the father of medicine, even after thousands of years, is heavily backed by modern scientific research, which highlights the direct cause-and-effect relationship between what we eat, how healthy we are, and how we feel.

For example, Dr. Mark Hyman, author of *Food Fix*, along with a group of physicians and public health experts, looked at the statistics and noticed a direct correlation between the number of hospital visits by people who were nutritionally vulnerable. They devised a unique study to see if changing their diet could reduce their visits. The research found that simply improving their nutrition decreased hospital visits by nearly 20 percent. Moreover, in *The China Study*, which analyzes data from the most comprehensive twenty-year study on health and nutrition ever done on the planet, researchers found 8,000 statistically significant correlations showing how our nutrition directly impacts our health.

So, now the question is, what makes a meal nutritious?

There is so much debate around this question, some of which even ventures into the philosophical and ethical realms. So I won't go there; instead, let's just look at what makes a meal not nutritious. Because there is an overwhelming amount of research on this, and we know one of the quickest ways to jumpstart our health is simply by removing unhealthy food from our diets.

Eat Real Food

Anything you find in a box, can survive in a bomb shelter, or is highly processed, such as vegetable oils or cheese in plastic slices, will not result in positive returns on your health. This also includes highly refined carbs like white bread, pasta, and white rice.

Sorry, don't hate me. It's just what the research says. Highly refined foods like these often lead to blood sugar spikes, inflammation, and a lack of essential nutrients, contributing to weight gain and chronic health issues over time.

Eating factory-farmed animals is also not going to help your health. These are pumped with toxic chemicals, growth hormones, and antibiotics and force-fed an unhealthy diet, which, if you have them for dinner, will end up with you consuming those additives yourself.

To add to the "no" list is sugar. It truly is a silent killer that leads to more negative health outcomes than many of us would like to admit. Gary Taubes, the award-winning investigative scientist and author of *The Case Against Sugar*, found the common link between ALL chronic diseases, including cancer, obesity, and cardiovascular disease, is metabolic dysfunction. Can you guess the quickest way to cause metabolic dysfunction? If you guessed sugar, you're right. Just drinking a single can of soda increases the likelihood of getting diabetes by 7.7 times. And this is on top of all the negative mental health outcomes linked to sugar.

I hate to be the bad guy here, but seriously, the mere act of cutting sugar from your diet can literally give you a better quality of life than a hundred other little tweaks to improve your health. Don't get me wrong, I like a piece of chocolate every now and then as much as the next guy, but regularly enjoying a soda, a dessert, a cookie, or a scoop of sugar in your coffee is like poison honey. Sure, it may taste sweet at first, but the long-term negative impact on your vitality and mental well-being is a bitter price to pay for something so fleeting.

On the flip side, if you pass on the sweets and highly processed foods today, you'll feel better immediately and, in the long run, live a richer and fuller life with the energy you need to appreciate the journey with your loved ones.

Exercise

While nearly everyone knows the benefits of exercise on our physical health, it also has just as powerful effects on emotional and mental health. In her book *The How of Happiness: A Scientific Approach to Getting the Life You Want,* leading researcher in positive psychology Sonja Lyubomirsky explains how prescribing depressed patients exercise as a treatment method is as effective as the chemical antidepressant Zoloft. Additionally, Tal Ben-Shahar, another leading psychologist in the field of optimal health, tells us, "Failure to exercise is like popping a depressant pill."

With this in mind, move! I don't care how you do it, just get moving. Get your heart rate up for thirty minutes and observe how you feel. If going to the gym is too inconvenient, make it easy. Jog around your house, roam the woods. Do push-ups in your living room, park five blocks from your work. Whatever! Just find opportunities to move.

Sleep

In our hustle and bustle culture that encourages us to endlessly produce, it's not uncommon to cut an hour or two of sleep so we can get more done. Then, we mask our fatigue with stimulants and run our minds and bodies into overdrive. This is a huge mistake. Sleep is essential for optimal health, influencing every aspect of our well-being. Getting a good night's sleep strengthens our immune system, supports tissue repair, and, like food, reduces our risk of chronic diseases. Moreover, on the emotional end, sleep also helps regulate our moods, makes us feel better, and fosters resilience and empathy while at the same time reducing stress. And if you actually do want to produce more, make sure you get quality sleep. It improves your cognitive performance.

However, when we "lose" sleep, our physical, mental, and emotional states can feel as if they are on shaky ground. Personally, when I've had a rough night of sleep, I may feel sluggish, and I may even entertain dark thoughts, and I can be more irritable. Perhaps you can relate. Maybe that's why renowned sleep researcher E. Joseph Cossman once said, "The best bridge between despair and hope is a good night's sleep." This is why prioritizing sleep is such an essential cornerstone for well-being; it can literally be a bridge from despair to hope.

The optimal nightly sleep time for adults is seven to nine hours, a bit longer for teens and children. So if you're struggling to find the time because of stress, anxiety, or increased demands at work, keep up with the other two practices—eat healthy food and exercise—and watch how it improves.

Another great way to optimize your sleep is not eating anything at least two hours before bed, not even a single bite, including honey in your tea. Food heats your body and makes sleep much more elusive. Refraining from eating before bed also includes what the beloved Buddhist monk Thich Nhat Hanh called "sensory food," which is everything we take in with our senses, including conversations, entertainment, media, or games. Just like food, we have to digest every piece of information we take in. This means the work email you opened late at night, the ten shorts you watched on your phone, or mindlessly scrolling through social media bloats your mind with information, making it trickier to sleep.

Moreover, never underestimate the power of a nap. Even twenty minutes of lying down will do you wonders, even if you don't fully fall asleep, and give you a much higher return on your investment than reaching for that midday coffee. I speak from experience. Just as much as the next guy, I have felt the pull to reach for caffeine to keep me going when I've felt sluggish. But I've been burned so many times by that mentality to know it's not worth it in the long run. Sure, short-term, I might be able to go an extra hour or so with intense focus. But it's always at the cost of greater irritability, negatively impacting my interactions with the people around me and my overall productivity for the day. But now, writing this article as the father of a newborn with a series of interrupted nights of rest, I know for a fact that a nap will do greater miracles than caffeine ever would.

So, there you have it, three very practical strategies you can implement today that will give you powerful returns on your health and overall well-being. Just keep in mind, though, that while these are basic principles, it's important not to be fanatical about following them. Our modern world is busy. We may be tired and facing non-negotiable deadlines, and that second or third cup of coffee may just be what we need to get the job done. A few cookies over the holidays won't kill us, and staying sedentary on a cold day won't be our demise. But, as a whole, if we can strive to make a habit of eating healthy food, sleeping well, and exercising regularly, we will see amazing returns on our physical, psychological, emotional, and spiritual well-being.

These three practices are like golden levers which, when pulled, won't just make you feel better in the long run; they make you feel better today! Each practice impacts the others, and as such, should all be practiced together.

With this in mind, it's worth pondering: How can I eat, move, and sleep better?

Pay attention to what you hear and start practicing today.

May health, one of life's greatest wealths, follow you wherever you go.

8
WHAT TO DO WHEN A TREE FALLS ON YOU

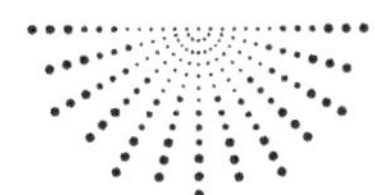

I pushed and I pushed, and I pushed, but no matter how hard I tried, I couldn't hold it up.

The 75-foot-tall tree started falling toward me. But just before the mammoth birch could crush me completely, my friend Janine dove like a soldier pushing me, her platoon mate, from enemy fire. We both tumbled and rolled as we hit the ground, the enormous tree crashing close behind us. Miraculously, it only caught my ankle.

Everything moved in slow motion. I could hear the terrified screams of people around us, while others huddled by my side to check if I was okay. Their eyes were furrowed with worry as anxious sweat dripped from their faces. Yet despite all this chaos, I myself was completely calm.

I just sat there looking at my foot, knowing this was a message from life itself, telling me to *WAKE UP*.

How I Got There

Before I continue, I should tell you how I reached that point. It had been an intense year. I was heavily involved in environmental activism, campaigning, and community organizing while simultaneously running a small business and finishing my third year of university. On top of that, I was always on the go, helping wherever

I could. Meanwhile, having a sick family member in need, created the perfect storm for over-commitment.

While all this seemed good and noble, the truth was that many of my actions weren't connected to wisdom. In all honesty, I was addicted to being needed and looking for my self-worth in what I did. But living on overdrive was taking its toll.

In the months preceding the tree incident, I had gotten sick periodically—no doubt my body's way of trying to tell me to rest. But my need to make my mark on the world kept me pushing forward until... Well, there I was.

Sitting on the ground, clutching my cracked ankle, trying to untangle the message the Universe was sending me.

The Sacred Context

You should know I was particularly observant of the deeper meaning of this incident because the tree that fell on me wasn't just any tree. It was a Sundance tree. And for those of you unfamiliar with this term—and I'm not talking about the film festival—the Sundance is an ancient Indigenous ceremony used for healing, which takes place around a sacred tree. And that sacred tree had fallen on me.

So if I hadn't gotten the message before, given the context of the situation, my ears were wide open and ready to listen. And that's why I was calm. Because despite being unable to see the entire picture, I intuitively knew this was all part of my healing. In the months of stillness that followed, confined to my bed to heal, I was able to unpack the lessons from this journey.

What I Learned

Throughout this book, I speak extensively about the importance of service. I share scientific research and spiritual wisdom from traditions around the globe about this beautiful practice and how it can help us thrive. I even prescribe it as an antidote to depression for some of my clients.

Serve from the Heart, Not from Lack

Yet, before we turn our attention away from ourselves to focus loving energy on others, it's crucial to ensure we're truly serving from love rather than serving from a need for validation. Because, just as we can derive self-worth from our professions, achievements, looks, or bank accounts, we can also wrap our identity around being a *good person*.

When I was honest with myself, this is exactly what I was doing. Feelings of inadequacy were involved in much of my overdoing. While many of my actions seemed selfless externally, some selfishness was still wrapped within them. I wanted to be loved, and my acts of care, and all my achievements got me that. Now of course, that was not always the case.

There were still many times I genuinely felt called to give, and did so from my heart. But learning when I was coming from lack, rather than fullness, was not always clear. Thankfully, that period of quiet reflection, sitting in my bed, provided me with the wisdom to know the difference.

Take Care of Yourself

This brings us back to the airplane metaphor mentioned before, reminding us to take care of ourselves so we can better serve others. For us givers out there, this can be an easy one to forget, which is why we should tattoo it to our memory. We need to take care of ourselves with the same love and attention we offer others. This manifests in both small and significant ways.

A small way this showed up for me after my accident was doing physiotherapy every morning for 10-15 minutes. While it seems so insignificant, we often neglect these small acts of self-care, filling our time with "more important" things. We don't exercise, sleep, or rest sufficiently, and in the long run, we suffer for it. Had I failed to offer myself that little bit of love each morning, I probably would have mobility issues today. That's the power of small, consistent caring actions. They have the power to heal.

Self-love can also show up in bigger ways. After the accident, I pursued therapy to honestly examine the underlying negative patterns driving my tendency to work myself so hard. It wasn't easy, heck, at times it was downright painful. But if we really want to be better instruments of change in this world, we have to do this deep work.

It can't be ignored.

Set Boundaries

An extension of self-care is learning to set clear boundaries. If you have adopted the helper mindset, which I hope you do by the end of this book, it's also important to learn to say no. Prior to the tree incident, when anyone needed anything, regardless of how I was feeling, I'd drop everything to help. While supporting others is admirable, doing so at the expense of your own wellbeing isn't noble—it's simply unsustainable. Just as you can't solve a calculus equation by removing a key variable, you can't sustain a life of service by removing yourself from the equation. Because let's face it —we all have finite time, energy, and resources. Learning to set boundaries helps us manage those constraints and give in a way that is long-lasting.

While many of us struggle with boundaries, women often face an extra layer of pressure to forget about their own needs. Gender socialization research shows that even from childhood, women are praised for prioritizing others, while equally important qualities like assertiveness are often neglected. Moreover, research from places like Harvard Business School and Stanford has illustrated that women often face backlash for assertive behavior like saying no—a challenge most men are not criticized for. That being said, women may have to be extra vigilant in the practice of setting boundaries, ensuring that societal pressures don't prevent them from finding a sustainable balance between service and self-care. But regardless of your gender, this is a balance we all must strike.

Asking for Help and Receiving Support

Continuing our conversation on self-love and self care, I would like to mention the willingness to receive. As a natural giver, it was extremely difficult for me to accept support, and even harder to ask for help.

This lesson began the day after the accident when my mom, who was visiting, insisted on staying an extra week to help me rehabilitate. Knowing she'd lose money changing her plane ticket, I resisted. I felt uncomfortable letting her carry that extra burden. Like many of us, I had been conditioned to equate strength with independence and weakness with needing others. Moreover, on top of this, as mentioned before, I also harbored unconscious beliefs about my self-worth that made me feel like I didn't fully deserve care. As such, when others offered it to me, my natural default was to push it away.

Thankfully, after being bedridden to the point where I had to literally pee in a jug, I was practically forced to open to receive life's loving hands. Because I knew if I truly wanted to heal, I would have to be humble enough to accept another's help.

A practice that supported me—and you might try if receiving from others feels difficult—is to imagine yourself as someone you deeply care about. Ask: "If that person was going through the same struggle, how would I want to show up for them?"

Often, the compassion we offer others is the same compassion we need to learn to accept for ourselves.

Learning to ask for help was equally challenging. In Western society, we often place tremendous value on self-reliance, making seeking support seem like a weakness. This is especially true for men, who are frequently taught to "be strong" and often suffer in silence rather than reach out. Research actually shows that men are much less likely to seek support from others, which may explain why they report higher levels of loneliness and increased risk of depression.

I had unconsciously absorbed these cultural messages, and my resistance to reaching out created unnecessary suffering. However,I discovered that in times of great need, the willingness to ask for help is not weakness at all—it's actually a sign of great spirit. Or as Brené Brown, one of the world's leading researchers in courage and empathy, puts it: "Asking for help is a power move. It's a sign of strength."

After the Storm

While immensely difficult, that wake-up call changed me for the better. Honestly, it shifted my entire life's trajectory. I slowed down, did less, and even took a year off school to get clear on my direction. Filled with more self-love, I realized that much of my activist work wasn't actually my soul's calling—I was doing it because I felt I "should." So instead, I started focusing on what lit me up and my unique contribution to make this world a better place. I said "no," set boundaries, and engaged in service from an authentic, heartfelt place.

While I would never wish such an experience on anyone, I'm grateful it happened to me. For I'm better because of it. Now my prayer and reason for writing this is that you can learn from my mistakes and won't need a sacred tree to fall on you to receive these lessons.

Because in a world that praises what we do, it's easy to get lost in the whirlwind of endless tasks, hanging our worth on our achievements or ideals of being a 'good person.' This often leads us to neglect self-care, push others away, and fail to ask for help when we need it most. But if we slow down long enough to pay attention to life's messages and take small, loving actions day by day, we grow stronger and become capable of taking on bigger and bigger challenges. In turn, we become the kind of people who have the capacity to truly change the world for the better. And it all starts with lovingly caring for yourself.

Questions for Reflection:

- Are there any areas of your life that might be driven by a need to prove your worth?
- If so, how can you approach those situations from a place of authentic self-worth?
- Where do you need to ask for help or allow others to support you?
- Are there any places in your life where you need to set stronger boundaries? What will you do about this?
- What big and small acts of self-care can you offer yourself over the next week, month, and year to help you truly thrive?

PART II
EXTENDING OUR LOVE

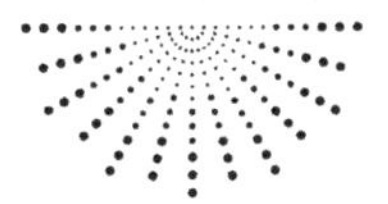

9
LOVING OTHERS

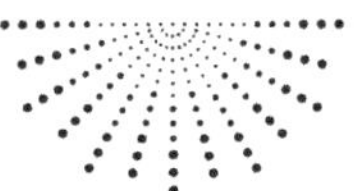

Humankind did not weave the web of life. We are but one thread within it. Whatever we do to the web, we do to ourselves.

— CHIEF SEATTLE

After we've done the initial work of cultivating the gold within, we are better equipped to extend that love outward—to our family, friends, community, and the world as a whole.

Nearly every religion and wisdom tradition worldwide encourages us to reach out and offer love and service to those around us; perhaps that's because it's not just good for others but because it's also good for the soul.

Confucius said true virtue is achieved by serving others and that living a virtuous life will lead one to peace. This same principle is echoed in the Stoic writings, which say a happy life is found through virtuous activity. The Sikhs tell us to help others without seeking reward, and that acts of selfless service purify us. Again, the Hindu and Christian philosophies preach the same doctrine, and the Bodhisattva ideal found in Buddhism encourages us to engage in selfless acts of service, which result in the byproducts of good merit, inner peace, and joy.

Moreover, many findings in modern science have shown that altruistic behavior increases happiness and life satisfaction, lowers depression, raises self-esteem, reduces stress, improves physical health, and results in a greater sense of purpose in life.

Put simply, do good + be good = feel good.

Hang on a second. Can it really be that simple? Yes. The research and wisdom traditions from time immemorial suggest it absolutely can be that simple.

Now the next question is, "Why?"

Why does serving, caring, and loving others support our overall well-being so much?

Perhaps that's because we are not as separate as we may think. Ubuntu, the Zulu African philosophy, is a perfect example of this principle. Directly translated, Ubuntu means "I am because we are." Put simply, we are interconnected. So if you thrive, so do I! Many Indigenous traditions in North America call this interconnectivity "The Great Web of Life." The Ancient Romans called it the *Cosmopolis* (World City). Understanding our interconnectedness, the Stoic philosopher Epictetus put it this way: "What is bad for the hive cannot be good for the bee."

Thus, the more we recognize our interconnectedness, the more we see that every act of service touches the whole community and, consequently, ourselves. This is because when you really break life down to its essence, there really is no "other."

All the great religions preach this same interdependence. Jesus said, "Whatever you do for the least of my brothers and sisters, you do it for me." In Taoism, all things are part of the Tao, which is the ultimate source of everything that unites all beings into a single cosmic flow. Interestingly, this idea of a unified whole is not just a religious belief. It is a verified scientific truth. Look at the study of ecology and observe how a change to one part of an ecosystem affects the whole. Or study quantum physics, and you will find that everything in the universe, when broken down, is energy, and despite our seeming separateness, we are really just part of the same stuff.

When you truly look at the mechanics of our universe, the concept that we are all connected is not just a warm and fuzzy idea. It's a fact. Like cells in the body, we are in this together. But the question is, are we working together to help this universal body thrive?

Interestingly, cancer cells only think about themselves. They take and take and take, and in turn, destroy their host and eventually themselves in the process. This is the cost of the illusion of separateness. It makes us only think and fend for ourselves, an attitude which, unchecked, will eventually break us and destroy our world in the process.

But if we realize we're all in this together and start reaching out to help others, in the very same way we would help ourselves, then we as a community can and will create a more beautiful world. As we explore this idea of love for others, let's remember the far-reaching effects of our actions. Because since we are all connected, that means every good deed and every act of kindness, however small, forms a ripple that expands and extends to the whole. This means that by loving one person, we are really loving the whole world. How powerful is that? Thus, perhaps one of the greatest acts of self-love we can offer ourselves is reaching out and loving another.

10
SAVING YOURSELF THROUGH SERVICE

"What stood out for you most about the video?" I asked my client in our second session. Her eyes were aglow as she reflected on the inspirational story of Dick and Rick Hoyt.

If you're unfamiliar with it, here is the short version.

Rick wanted to run. The only problem? He was born with cerebral palsy. But rather than shutting his dream down, his parents made a decision to find a way. That's when Team Hoyt was born, the dynamic father-son duo where Rick's father would push him in his wheelchair as he ran.

After their first race together in 1977, Rick turned to his father and said, "Dad, when I'm running, it feels like I'm not handicapped." These words struck a chord in Dick's heart and inspired Team Hoyt's thirty-seven-year journey of marathons, triathlons, and Ironman races spanning thousands of miles.

Interestingly enough, after a mild heart attack in 2003, Dick went to his cardiologist only to discover that one of his arteries was 95 percent blocked. It was at that point his doctor told him if he had not been in such great physical condition, he would have likely died from heart disease fifteen years earlier.

Which really makes you question, in the end, who was helping whom?

How Helping Heals Us

After my client recalled how inspiring this story of self-transcendence was for her, I reflected back that this was exactly what she was doing herself. Because when this woman came to me, her intention was to foster a better relationship with her son, which had grown rocky as he approached his teens. Yet, the great mother she was did not want to leave their relationship to chance, and instead, just like Rick's parents, made a decision to take fate into her own hands and see what she could do to remedy the situation.

This decision led to much internal reflection, highlighting that she was parroting many patterns her parents had passed on to her in her relationship with her son. Patterns of perfectionism and unnecessary pressure which, as a child and now as an adult, created self-critical tendencies that brought her nothing but strife.

But the beautiful part was that as she worked to untangle the knots that kept her from connecting to her son, she created a deeper, more loving connection with herself. Standing face to face with those overly critical parts, she was inspired to meet them with compassion and love rather than trying to change or fix them. This freed up massive energetic space and brought more peace into her day-to-day life, which in turn brought greater peace into her relationship with her son. Thus, just like Dick was healed through serving his son, her spirit was renewed through her intention to connect with hers.

A Universal Truth

What my client experienced isn't unique to her—it's a fundamental truth about life. Like Dick Hoyt discovered his own health transformed through serving Rick, she found that by focusing on her son's well-being, it was the very path to her own healing. This pattern repeats again and again and can be found everywhere we look. If you examine your own life and every time you have selflessly reached out to serve another, you will know this to be true. And in the end, you'll see it's actually you who's getting the most help.

The Science of Service

Now, even modern science is confirming this. Researchers at Harvard and UC Berkeley found that acts of service light up the brain's reward centers, releasing dopamine and oxytocin—the very chemicals that help us feel joy, calm, and connection.

This is what psychologists call the "helper's high," and can explain why we often walk away from serving others feeling more energized than depleted. Remarkably, we are actually wired to help. Even our biology reflects this great truth.

Studies on caregivers and volunteers have found their blood pressure was lower, they had stronger immune systems, and were less prone to stress. Additionally, long-term studies have found that people regularly engaged in service are happier, healthier, and ultimately, tend to live longer.

Perhaps it's why Viktor Frankl, the great psychiatrist and Holocaust survivor, said, "Self-transcendence is the essence of existence." He understood it was in helping others that we bring out the best in ourselves.

Ancient Wisdom Across Traditions

Spiritual traditions across the world echo this same truth. In Christianity, Jesus told us it "is more blessed to give than to receive." In the Buddhist tradition, generosity, or Dana, is considered the first perfection and a portal to deep awakening. Hinduism also echoes this wisdom in the Bhagavad Gita, with the path of Karma Yoga—suggesting that through selfless action, we liberate our souls.

Again, many Indigenous traditions highlight this universal principle, too, and they actually see the whole dance of life as one big act of service. See how the tree gives its fruit, its shade, and its nutrients to the earth. In turn, the soil, the sun, the rain, and the animals all give back to the tree. In the end, it's all one beautiful offering of giving and receiving.

Dick and Rick Hoyt's story reminds us that the line between giving and receiving is not as clear as we often imagine. A father runs to help his son feel whole, only to discover that the act of service quite literally saves his own life.

Modern science tells us this is no accident—our brains and bodies are wired to flourish when we step beyond ourselves and support another. And the great spiritual traditions around the world remind us that service is the gateway to awakening our soul's great nature.

Self-Care and Service

Note, this does not in any way mean that we negate self-care. As mentioned before, we are all well aware of the airplane metaphor of putting on your mask first in times of crisis. The same is true as we serve. We need to eat well, sleep, rest, and recharge. And if necessary, do deep inner work like therapy so we are better equipped to serve another. While self-care is critical, it's best not to stop there.

So the next time you find yourself struggling with your own challenges—whether it's anxiety, loneliness, or feeling stuck—consider this: perhaps the path forward isn't found in endless self-analysis or trying to fix yourself.

Perhaps it's found in asking a simple question: "How can I serve someone else today?"

It might be listening deeply to a friend, helping a neighbor, or, like my client, showing up more lovingly for your child.

Ask that question, and follow through on whatever response you receive from your conscience. For at the end of the day, you'll find one of the greatest ways to help yourself is to help another.

11
RELATIONSHIPS: A PATHWAY TO A MEANINGFUL LIFE

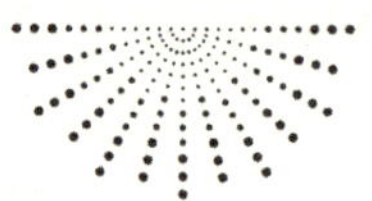

If you want to change the world, go home and love your family.

— *MOTHER TERESA*

I swallowed heavily.

"He didn't make it," cried my friend, fighting through grief over the phone.

I hung up and sat in silence, choking through my own tears. He was gone. My dear friend, mentor, and elder had passed to the other side. Never again would we sit in his little apartment on Somerset Street, sipping tea, reciting poetry, or discussing philosophy. Never again would he offer me his gentle prods of encouragement, as all good mentors do. Never again. All would be but memories in our friendship story.

Filled with sorrow, I couldn't help but think how crazy it was that I was supposed to visit him in two days. He had called me earlier that week.

"How are you, Barclay?" I said enthusiastically as I picked up the phone.

"Nice to hear your voice, my boy," he replied. "Honestly, Adam, I'm tired." His tone was weak, but despite that, it still had that spark of life he always had. "I'd like to see you soon," he added.

It was Tuesday, and he invited me over for Friday. But I was working on an "important" project, and it seemed tight to squeeze in a visit that week. So, I replied, "Well, how does next Tuesday sound?"

We agreed, shared a joke, a chuckle, and I went on with my week. But Tuesday never came. And it never would.

The Event

What happened next was a strange series of events that appeared to be orchestrated by some divine intelligence, or perhaps by the spirit of my mentor, as one last farewell and teaching for me. It was Sunday evening when I heard the news. I was on a break during the final hours of a weekend training program in a downtown convention center. While it was difficult to carry on, I managed to gather myself and make it through. When it was over, I hopped into an Uber and made my way home through the cold fall evening.

That's when it happened.

Scre-e-e-e-ch! Crash! The car shook like a bone-rattling earthquake. Screams sliced through the November night sky. "Oh my God! Oh my God! Is everyone okay?!" Calls came from outside. In a daze, I looked around. A fury of flashing lights and sirens sailed through the darkness. I touched my head gingerly. It throbbed and burned from slamming against the back seat. But I wasn't bleeding, and I felt okay.

Turning around, I looked through the back window and saw what had caused the accident. A speeding BMW had slammed into the rear of our car. I climbed out the door and ran to the vehicle to see if the driver was okay. The smell of oil punched me in the face as I raced toward it. The two cars were crushed, and it looked as if giant fists from the sky had come down and pounded them. I was grateful to be alive.

"Are you okay?" I shouted at the young driver, a man in his early 20s.

He didn't look at me or answer. He just shook his head and shouted through the airbag.

"Oh, f--k man! F--k! F--k! F--k! F--k! F--k!!!"

Physically, he appeared fine, but he was clearly emotionally and mentally distraught, likely considering the consequences of his actions. I yanked the battered door open, and he pulled himself out.

Police had already arrived, and I shuffled to the sidewalk to give them room. Observing the severity of the crash before me, I shook my head in disbelief. Glass, plastic, and debris were spread across the entire road. Cars piled up on both sides. Horns honked wildly, sirens screamed, and red lights streamed through the night sky. Two fire trucks poured into the scene, and a dozen uniformed emergency workers spilled out and assessed the situation.

“Are you okay?” one of them asked, eyeing me head to toe.

Despite the wreckage outside, miraculously, my driver and I were both fine and would walk away with only minor bumps and bruises. Satisfied that I wasn't badly injured, he nodded. He said he would ask the paramedics to do a more thorough check when they arrived, then he was off.

Standing in the cutting cold, surrounded by the wreckage, I knew that Life was trying to tell me something. That somehow, this strange event, mere hours after my friend's passing, was somehow connected. *But what does it mean?* I thought.

Then, looking at the BMW driver still shaking his head and swearing at himself about the damage he had caused, the larger metaphor Life was trying to teach me dawned on me.

The driver who smashed into us was a lot like me at the time. So focused on speeding to where he wanted to go, he failed to notice his surroundings. By not paying attention, he hurt both himself and the people around him. I recognized how I could be like that, operating with tunnel vision, hyper-focused on reaching my goals, so much so that I failed to pay attention to my environment. Getting to the destination and fast is what mattered most. And I'm ashamed to admit this, but sometimes, I even saw people as obstacles that kept me from my long list of to-dos. There were even times when I'd be interacting with someone, and if I was feeling scarce on time, rather than being present with them, I would unconsciously project myself into the future and what I "needed" to do next.

I was constantly in a race. And by living with this mentality, just like that young guy in the BMW, I was speeding by and cutting people off. But really, the person I was cutting off most was myself. I was cutting myself off from one of Life's greatest gifts.

What wisdom did Barclay want to share with me that Friday he invited me to visit him? Would he have graced me with one last insight for how to live a good life? Maybe he would have shared a story he wanted me to pass on to others. Or perhaps, we would have simply sat in silence, laughed, and shared one last smile together. Perhaps. But, of course, this is all speculation, and I will never know Barclay's final wish or kernel of wisdom for me. This was the cost of how I was living my life.

As they say, hindsight is 20/20, and looking back at the last days my friend spent on the planet, given another chance, I would have responded differently. Sure, I was "busy" with work obligations and responsibilities. But I most certainly could have found time to put my projects and plans aside for a few hours to spend a caring visit with a dear friend.

It's true that life gets busy. But it's never too busy to take the time to say hello and to show your love. Because there is always time for that. And if we think we really don't have the time, we should probably reorganize our priorities. At least, that's what I discovered that evening. I believe the accident was my friend's final farewell, the last great piece of wisdom he wanted to share with me as he left this world. Relationships matter. Make time for them. Prioritize them. Work on them. Celebrate them.

Because at the end of the day, a good life comes down to right relationships. But you don't have to take my word for it. Just look at the longest scientific research study done in history by Harvard University. For eighty-five years, researchers followed men and women from all over the world, some wealthy, some poor, some had a positive upbringing, and others had more challenging childhoods. But despite the diverse demographics and socioeconomic backgrounds, the most consistent finding in the study for what made for a happy life was not wealth, achievement, or even physical health. In fact, the most consistent finding among the study's subjects of that decades-long research project was that positive relationships were the definitive foundation of a happy life. Healthy relationships did more than just make them happier; they helped the subjects become healthier and even live longer. So, yes, relationships matter.

Perhaps that's why the Lakota Nation lives by a philosophy known as *Mitakuye Oyasin* (pronounced Mee-TA-kway-A-sin), which translates to "we are all related." This Native American philosophy highlights the awareness that life is all about relationships. It acknowledges that you and I, in spite of any geographic, racial, or cultural differences, are intrinsically connected. We stand on the same earth, breathe the same air, and are nourished by the same sun. Thus, we are all connected in this great tapestry of life.

Once a human being comes to realize this truth of brotherhood / sisterhood, the BIG question becomes, how are we as individuals relating to life? Are we cut off? Lost in our heads, busy with the next thing we have to do? Or are we connected, present, and relating to this moment and the people and things around us with kindness, care, and love? If we want to live a good life, it starts right here, right now, with every relationship.

So with that, let me pose a couple of questions to you:

Are there any areas of your life where you are placing your goals or projects above your relationships?

Is your focus on your destination taking away the beauty of this moment?

If you answered *yes* to those, I encourage you to pause, breathe, and notice the people and other living beings around you, and find a way to let them know you care.

Note, this does not simply need to be for the "close" people in your life, but can include all creation—your dogs, your cats, your neighbors, your grocer, the stranger on the street, and even the trees you walk by on your way to work. Remember, Mitakuye Oyasin. We are all related. And if we feel disconnected, it's simply because we are not consciously connecting to life around us.

If you are finding it challenging to connect to those around you, you can start by relating to yourself with the love you'd like to receive. If that's too hard, the loving embrace of nature is another great place to start. Walk in the woods, gaze at the night sky, or even connect to a plant in your home. Such practice, while simple, can work wonders for the soul.

Since Barclay, my friend and mentor, passed, I have been working on shifting my mindset from my habitual non-stop hustle mentality so often found in our Western culture. I've had many testing times when I failed to be present for the people around me. But I've also experienced many beautiful moments when I succeeded.

Even while writing this story years ago, I nearly ignored spending time with a dear friend because I was so focused on finishing it. Five years later, I had picked up this story to revise it when my wife "barged" into my office and "interrupted" me. At that moment, with my social conditioning pressuring me to push through and "get it done," I almost ignored her. Thankfully, since I'd been working on this challenge for a while, I instead closed my computer, smiled, got up, embraced my wife, and held her pregnant belly. And to thinkI could have missed that beautiful moment because I was so task-oriented seems simply crazy to me now.

Sure, it's taken me much longer than planned to write this tribute to Barclay and acknowledge his final lesson to me—one week, in fact! But I've been able to catch up with my mother, chat with an old friend in Florida, visit my grandmother via WhatsApp video, and volunteer at the community garden twenty minutes from my house. While these apparent "interruptions" may have slashed my writing time, they didn't cut me off. On the contrary, they connected me to all of life and, in turn, made this story all the more beautiful. Because that's what relationships do. They make our lives more beautiful.

So, as you move through the hours, days, and weeks ahead, I encourage you to consciously carve out time for the people you love. Reach out to those around you, and prioritize your relationships above everything else that pretends to be "important." And if you ever feel you are too "busy" to spend time with anyone, whether a friend or a stranger, I hope you can remember the mistake I made the week my friend Barclay passed, and I missed saying my final farewell to him, because I was "too busy." Please remember what really matters. Relationships.

Mitakuye Oyasin.

12
VISIONS FOR A BETTER WORLD START AT HOME

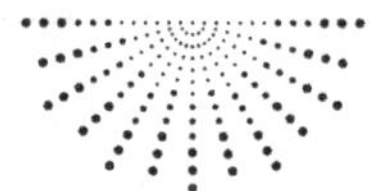

When you are in doubt, be still, and wait.

— CHIEF WHITE EAGLE

The cold wind blew through the trees as black clouds crawled toward me. Thunder rolled in the background as I sat cross-legged on the earth, tucked deep into the heart of the forest, watching the oncoming storm. I took a deep breath and prayed.

You may be wondering why I was there in the middle of nowhere. I was not lost or trapped but willingly entered the wilderness on a four-day solo quest in search of direction. While it may seem counterintuitive to enter the woods to find out where you should be heading, let me explain. I was not searching for a physical destination. I was seeking a spiritual one.

What I was participating in was a "vision quest," a timeless Indigenous ceremony that has been practiced since time immemorial. Traditionally, these quests were used as sacred containers where individuals would unplug from their ordinary world and go off into the wilderness. Through a four-day process of fasting, prayer, and mindful connection to the land, questers would plug back into the

Universal Source of all life and confidently gain the direction they needed to take on their life assignments.

You see, while life is always speaking to us, in the busyness of our world, it's sometimes hard to hear what she has to say. That's why one of the best ways to hear her message is to get really quiet. Spending days out on the land in silence is one powerful way to do that. And that's what I was doing in the forest in the middle of nowhere. I was listening.

What I Heard

I don't know about you, but during the first few years of the pandemic, I found myself confronted with some big questions about our society, how we live, and where we humans are heading as a species. I've been concerned with the divisive energy around the world, which seems increasingly to be pitting people against each other. That, along with wondering what AI will mean for our future, our disconnection from the environment, and the ongoing struggles for peace in many parts of the world, left my heart striving to know my place and responsibility in this cosmic story.

These concerns inspired many ideas about where I could channel my energy to do my part. I was inspired to work with young people, the future leaders, and also with men, to help heal their wounds so they could, in turn, help heal the world. Other ideas I contemplated included working with the land in a community to grow food to encourage a more holistic world. But still, when I wandered into the woods, I had no idea how to bring all those visions to fruition. That's why I ventured there. I was seeking answers, fully trusting the stillness would guide me.

As I sat on that hill in the forest in the skin-stinging wind, I heard a voice within as clear as a summer morning.

"These visions are beautiful and important for you to follow through with," the voice said. "But if you really want to help the next seven generations, start with your family. Love your wife, fully and unconditionally. Make loving your children your first priority. When you do this right, the future will take care of itself."

The sweet words sang to my heart like a songbird in spring. I knew them to be true; I knew if I could bring the purest love to my wife, she would be able to offer that same love to our children, and in turn, those children would have the love they would need to face the challenges of our world. Because if we take care of the kids, the future will take care of itself.

Even though I am hopeful about the future, I'm also a realist, and I know that if we want to live in a unified, just, and kind world, we have *a lot* of work to do. But to change the world, we've got to start with ourselves and our families and then work to spread that love to our communities. Let's keep that in mind as we work to create a more beautiful future.

It's a big job. And it starts at home.

13
HEALING ANCESTRAL WOUNDS

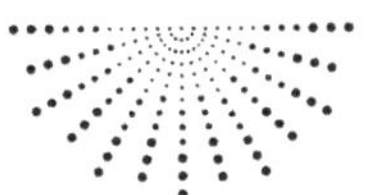

Tears flowed through the stranger's eyes as she sobbed in my arms.

Patrons of the little café ate their food—completely oblivious to the hurt and healing that was transpiring.

After a hearty sob, she pulled herself from my shoulder and wiped the leftover water from her eyes.

"It's really hard," she said through a sniffle.

Why this stranger was crying in my arms is a sad story that all started with a simple smile from my baby boy across the restaurant's dim room.

After a few warm exchanges back and forth between them, she couldn't contain herself and eventually walked over to meet us.

Her name was Francine, and apparently, my boy's joyful and friendly nature reminded her a lot of her son living just outside of Toronto, who, now at thirty-eight, had two young daughters of his own.

The only problem was that the other grandmother, who lived a few doors down from Francine's son in Toronto, wanted nothing to do with his side of the family.

While part of Francine's heritage was French Canadian, the other grandmother, of Asian descent, didn't want the two cultures to mix and forbade the little girls from learning that part of their ancestry. Moreover, Francine felt like her granddaughter's other grandmother —who favored designer clothes and more luxurious things— constantly looked down on her simple, outdoorsy way of life.

So even though she was only a few hours' drive away, Francine felt like a complete outsider to the family.

Having just spoken to the woman for no more than fifteen minutes, I was not entirely sure why the son and his wife would allow this. But my wife and I comforted the woman with our presence and what words of hope we could find. And while those tears on my shoulder were a sign of some release, as she turned and left, I could still feel the burden she carried for the loss of her grandchildren.

For days, Francine's sullen face was etched in my mind, and I couldn't help but think of the sad circumstances that plagued this family. Here were two grandmothers who both deeply loved their grandchildren and, through these kids, in a sense, shared one another's blood.

But despite that, they found themselves in a cold war.

The Wound of the Brothers

As I reflected on Francine's pain, I realized I was witnessing something much larger than a family dispute, and it reminded me of the biblical story of Cain and Abel—two brothers who both wanted their father's love, until jealousy turned that love into violence.

This is what I call The Wound of the Brothers—a deep hurt that happens when people who were once close turn against each other because of fear, envy, pain, or generational trauma.

The Asian grandmother was afraid of her grandkids losing her culture, so she spread her elbows wide and pushed the other family out.

On a larger scale, you can see *The Wound of the Brothers* playing itself out between Ukraine and Russia, two nations that have many shared roots, intertwined histories, overlapping language and culture, and, in many cases, family ties. Yet despite that, they now find themselves at war.

We see this with Israel and Palestine, who, according to tradition, are both direct descendants of Abraham, literally making them brothers. Both these nations have ancient ties to the same land, and both want security for their children.

Yet each one fears the other's existence threatens their own survival.

As we can see when we examine The Wound of the Brothers, family wounds run deep, really deep. They don't just affect the household, but the world at large. Perhaps that's why Mother Teresa so wisely said, "If you want to change the world, go home and love your family." She understood that through healing the conflict within our homes, we end up touching the whole world.

Now, I won't lie and say this is easy. Far from it. Negative family dynamics are often rooted in long-standing ancestral wounds that have been passed down for generations. As such, effecting family change can be a lengthy, arduous process. And it can be especially disheartening if it feels like we are the only ones making the effort to heal.

Your Circle of Influence

So how do we break these cycles that seem so much bigger than ourselves?

In cases like these, it's helpful to take to heart the words of renowned leadership expert Dr. Stephen Covey, who reminds us that if we really want to create change, we need to focus on our circle of influence, not on our circle of concern.

To illustrate this concept further, let's imagine you draw one large circle called your circle of concern. Then, inside that circle, you draw a smaller one, called your circle of influence.

Your circle of concern includes all those things in the world that are concerning you:

- Wars across the globe
- Unjust politicians
- Inflation and gas prices
- And your crazy mother-in-law!

While these things are in your circle of concern, they are outside of your control. Thus, if you truly want to create change, all your energy and efforts should be focused on your circle of influence—these are the things you have the power to change, such as your behavior, your attitudes, and your response to those around you. Note: The more you focus on your circle of influence, the more your circle of influence grows.

This concept is illustrated perfectly through the little story told by an unknown monk written centuries ago, who said:

"When I was a young man, I wanted to change the world. But I found it was difficult to change the world, so I tried to change my nation... Today, I realize the only thing I can change is myself, and with that awareness, I realized that if long ago, I had changed myself, I could have made an impact on my family. Then my family and I could have made an impact on our town... and thus I could have changed the world."

Bringing it Home

Similarly, with family conflicts, whether it's two grandmothers in Toronto or two nations at war, we must work on our circle of influence and embrace Gandhi's wisdom to "be the change we wish to see in the world."

But like I said, this won't be easy. It means we give up all thoughts of victimization or feelings of being wronged, even if the situation seems unjust, and instead accept total responsibility for our part in creating change. Note: This does not mean we should be doormats and actively accept abuse. At times, boundaries do need to be drawn. But it does mean we never stop trying to work on creating peace.

Without knowing all the details of the situation, I am not entirely sure what this would look like in Francine's case. What it looks like for you with your family dynamics, I haven't a clue, but what I do know is that each of us is responsible for bringing about that healing, even if it feels one-sided. We need to do the work and continuously endeavor to create peace, even if it is just finding peace within ourselves.

Because at the end of the day, all this work is not just about us. It's about something so much bigger. It's about humanity as a whole.

For how can we expect to create peace in the world if we can't find it within our family?

With that in mind, as we move forward in the week ahead, let us love our families. Let us put our differences aside and see the best in our relatives. Let us offer understanding in spite of others' flaws. Let us forgive freely, be patient, and find peace within ourselves, so we can bring that peace about. Let us first change ourselves, and in turn, let us change the world at large.

A Practice:

This week, instead of waiting for your difficult family member to change, ask yourself:

What's one small thing I can do to bring more peace and healing into this relationship?

Take action. Then watch how those loving ripples spread out into the whole world.

14
FAMILY LESSONS FROM THE GARDEN

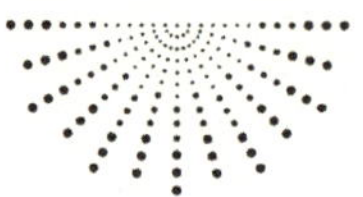

"Almost there!" I said giddily, looking down the twenty feet of track we still had to cover. On my hands and knees, I was covered in dirt as I pushed a stick into the earth to build a living fence—a permaculture wall created from small twigs that would eventually grow into trees.

"So close!" Ayesha, the Australian volunteer, said as we inched our way forward, post by post.

But then, suddenly, from a distance, we heard a great booming voice flying across the field.

"Kopi!" Coffee! It was Kadek, the Balinese founder of the permaculture farm where we were volunteering. Ayesha and I eyed each other, then looked back at the twenty feet of ground we still had to cover. If we pushed, we could finish in twenty minutes. Without saying a thing, we pressed on, completely ignoring Kadek's call.

But again, his booming voice ran across the fields. *"Kopi!"*

Ayesha shook her head and then shouted back, "We're almost done!"

"No! Come now. We'll finish later."

"But we are so close!" I shouted back with a chuckle.

"Come!"

"Okay! Okay!" we finally said and rose, reluctantly.

We took one last look at the patch of earth we were so close to completing, laughed a little, smacked the dirt off our trousers, and then headed for the outdoor kitchen. We approached a small circular stone table, where Kadek was waiting for us, sitting on a concrete stool with three cups of coffee in front of him, along with little sweets wrapped in banana leaves.

"What took you so long?" he asked as he sipped his coffee.

"We were so close. We wanted to finish!" I exclaimed with a smile.

He waved his hand to the left as if swatting a fly. "Don't worry about it. We'll finish later. Now, we eat!" he said with a great big grin.

Ayesha laughed, reached into her bag, and pulled out some banana bread she had baked the evening before and brought to share. Then we sat in a circle and, through sips of coffee and bites of sweets, talked and laughed about the mystic and the mundane—how the crops were growing, the vision for the larger project, a YouTube channel, our families, and life at large.

After twenty minutes, Ayesha picked up her phone to check the time and said, "Well, I had better get going. I promised my kids I'd take them to the library now." She hugged us both and was off.

No more than two minutes later, Kadek's phone rang. He picked it up and chatted for a minute, hung up the phone, and then looked up at me. "That was my son. He wants me to come home to play with him."

"I guess that means it's time to call it a day," I said.

Kadek nodded, and we both slammed back the last of our coffees, bid our farewells, and continued on with the rest of our Saturday. As I left the garden, I passed by the plot of earth we'd been working on that day and smiled, reflecting on how the Balinese people truly know how to live.

Sure, we didn't finish that day, and in Western terms, it might even be considered a failure or a waste of time. But it's because we didn't finish that day that something much greater than a completed task was created—a bond. Relationships were deepened, and life's sweetness was shared.

I have so much more I want to say about this. But my wife just got up as I write this, so I guess it's probably best I go live instead. Besides, I can always edit more tomorrow…

15
WHERE TO FIND FRIENDS

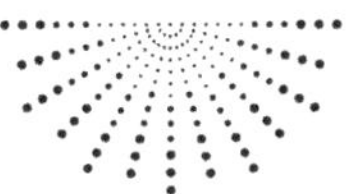

The spring sun rose to greet the day. My mind was like a laser as I focused on my morning's racing deadline, a slide show for a class I was teaching that evening. I was sitting at the outdoor dining table surrounded by rice fields. I squinted as I stared down the challenge on my screen, when, in the corner of my eye, I saw Wayan, a small Balinese man with a smile that reflected the sun. He was my neighbor and the caretaker of the property my wife and I rented in the small Indonesian village of Pejeng. He was responsible for cleaning the yard, managing the plumbing, and doing any other odd household jobs.

So every morning, before leaving for his day job, Wayan would stroll over to my house to do a quick clean of the fallen leaves in the backyard or any other maintenance required on the property. Having just moved in, I had only met him briefly on a couple of occasions, and we were still not fully acquainted.

And on that morning, he shared his radiant smile and waved to me; I mimicked his movements, and after a few casual hellos, I quickly got lost back in the world of my work. This daily exchange went on for about a week. And, I am ashamed to admit, as a productivity nerd who does his best to make all work sessions uninterrupted, that a few times that first week, I actually hid in my office so I could avoid seeing him and feeling obligated to have a conversation.

But something changed in me for the better. What it was exactly, I don't fully know. But on one of those early mornings, I heard a subtle whisper within, telling meI needed to step outside my world of self-absorption and reach out.

The next day, as Wayan strolled into my yard as he usually did, I paused what I was doing and deliberately closed my laptop. We did our usual "hellos" and "good days," but that morning, I made an extra effort to truly engage with him. I asked him about his weekend, his family, the music he liked, and some of those little questions you ask when you're just getting to know someone. Within five minutes, we both shared a good laugh before we got back to work.

That evening, during a walk with my wife, we played the game of highs and lows, where we shared the magic moments of our day.

"So, what were your magic moments today?" she asked as we strolled through the rice fields.

I thought deeply about the day. I had a great call with a client, progressed with a work project, and wrote a full chapter for my book. All meaningful accomplishments. Yet out of all of those, those five minutes in the early morning sharing that sacred connection with Wayan were the most memorable and meaningful moments of the day. I marveled at how something that seemed so small and insignificant could end up touching me so profoundly.

In the weeks that passed, I continued to look for those micro-moments of connection with Wayan. When he came by, I would pause and make a special effort to create a few minutes of genuine caring conversation. Once, even when I was "busy," I got up from my desk to help him clean the yard, which, after a heavy rainfall, was filled with debris; even if I was locked away in my office zeroing in on a deadline, I would still make an effort to run out and just smile and say "hello."

Like this, my relationship with Wayan grew, and so did our mutual caring efforts. Regularly, he would bring my wife and me fresh fruits he had harvested from his trees. We would bring his family sweets. He happily watched our cat while we were away, and we would invite his family over for dinner to share stories, food, and laughter.

Then, one sunny day in June, it became apparent to me how much our relationship had grown. It was late afternoon when I followed Wayan to the garage, where he showed me the brakes he had put on my bike, something he had offered to do the week before. My hand pressed the right brake and felt it clench the tire, and then I shared my gratitude for his help. He smiled at me, but then his normally calm and patient face changed to one of deep concern.

"How is Andréanne?" he asked pensively.

Earlier that week, my wife had come down with the flu and had been feeling like a dark day in winter.

"Oh, much better," I replied.

Two days back, when he had first found out she was sick, he brought three fresh coconuts to help hydrate her. I had thanked him instantly when he did, but there he was, days later, continuing to care.

His face softened. "Oh, that makes me feel better. When my wife or daughters are not feeling well, I get worried, and with Andréanne sick, I was getting worried for her."

Hearing his words, my heart opened. There he was, thinking of the well-being of my family, with the same consideration as he would his own.

"Thank you so much, Wayan!" I said. "Not just for the coconuts, the bike, but everything. You are so good to our family, and I just want you to know I so appreciate you and your whole family," I said warmly.

He softened his gaze. "Adam, of course. You and I, we are... We are friends," he said, then paused as he looked within. "But also, we are more than that—we are like, like family," he added with glowing eyes.

My eyes matched his, and I grinned widely as I wrapped my arms around him like a bear and then leaned back to give him a few gentle slaps on the shoulder.

"Yes, we are, my brother!" I agreed. "Yes, we are…"

This experience with Wayan truly touched me and got me thinking. How did something as small as a five-minute conversation create such a big transformation? Upon reflection, an image of a seed comes to mind. Those little micro-moments of care and consideration were like the water and light it needed to grow into the fruit of friendship. Like the miracle of gardening, I am still in awe of how those tiny acts of care could grow into something so profound.

On the contrary, it also makes me think of the huge loss I might have incurred had I been too self-absorbed to see the potential blessing of friendship before me. With a culture prioritizing productivity over relationships, it's obvious why we, in the West, are facing such a crisis of loneliness.

Are we so self-focused on our projects, our stories, and our own problems that we fail to see there is a whole world out there just waiting for us to reach out and connect with it? But if we have the wisdom and courage to look beyond ourselves, we see the seeds of potential simply waiting to be watered.

Note: Just like watering a garden, cultivating healthy relationships does not mean we need to abandon our whole day. My interactions with Wayan were *tiny* —five to ten minutes at first. Yet, in the end, often, they were some of the most rewarding parts of my day.

Perhaps that's because even though they may have been short, what we were sharing at the deepest level was love. I know, this may seem like a loaded word to use for a little heartfelt conversation. But one of the world's leading positive psychologists, Barbara Fredrickson, would agree with me. She tells us that "love blossoms virtually anytime two or more people—even strangers—connect over a shared positive emotion, be it mild or strong."

In her book *Love 2.0,* she challenges us to upgrade our current cultural views of love, which reserves this word for a select few, such as our spouse, children, or close friends, and suggests that "love" is simply the "micro-moment of warmth and connection you share with another living being."

How helpful is this paradigm to adopt in a world struggling with such record highs of loneliness and depression? This view means we need not search the stars to find genuine connection; we simply need to step away from our self-absorption, perhaps by putting our phones away for a moment, so we can be present and reach out to the world around us. That can mean the stranger walking down the street, the cashier at your local supermarket, your bank teller, or your accountant. Heck, even as I wrote this, my neighbor's dog came wandering onto my patio and lay his head on my lap. His tongue hung from his mouth as I opened my heart, paused, and patted him with care. Fifteen minutes later, I can still feel the burst of warmth running through my chest from this small, simple act. The opportunities are there; we simply have to open ourselves to them.

Lastly, for my fellow productivity nerds out there, I understand the desire for zero distractions. I am well-researched in the stages of flow and even teach the topic in some of my courses.

Thus, there are still many times when I lock myself in my office so I can be distraction-free. But these days, I am looking at these experiences of connection as less like "distractions" and more like opportunities. Opportunities to create one of our most fundamental human needs: Love.

So, while I'm still mindful of the power and processes of productivity, I've long realized our culture has an unbalanced relationship with it. Because in the end, what's wrong with doing less and "being" more? Truth be told, in my honest reflection, it was those moments when I stopped "doing" and started "being" that were some of the most meaningful moments of my day.

So, the next time you're walking down the street, interacting with your local grocery store clerk, or stuck at the DMV, I hope you can remember my experience with Wayan. I hope you can remember that if you treat people like gardeners, sure, you might grow a garden, but if you treat people like friends, you just might gain a new family member—one who truly cares for you.

So, what are you waiting for? There are seeds of potential all around you, just waiting for you to water them with your attention and care.

p.s. If this inspired you, here is a practice from Barbara Fredrickson herself, instructing us how we might create more love in our lives today.

CREATE THREE LOVING MOMENTS TODAY

- Recall how energizing and rewarding it can be to really connect with somebody, sharing a flow of thoughts and feelings with ease.
- As your day unfolds, seek out at least three opportunities to connect with others like this, with warmth, respect, and goodwill.
- Opportunities may spring up at home, at work, in your neighborhood, or out in your community. Wherever you are, open toward others, freely offering your attention, creating a sense of safety, through eye contact, conversation, or, when appropriate, touch.
- Share your own light-hearted thoughts and feelings, and stay present as the other person shares theirs.
- Afterward, lightly reflect on whether that interchange led you to feel the oneness of positivity resonance, even to a small degree.
- Creating the intention to seek out and create more micro-moments of loving connection can be another tool for elevating your health and well-being.

16
THE FOUNDATION FOR THRIVING RELATIONSHIPS

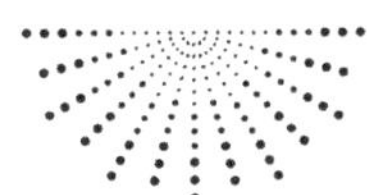

Want to know the secret to truly happy, healthy relationships? Let me tell you a story...

We had been assigned to put up a few screen doors on the outdoor camp kitchen, where I had been volunteering. I was working with an old friend, who, over the years, had grown to be not so friendly.

What I mean is that despite genuinely caring for each other, we fell into the unhealthy habit of belittling each other. And while I am all for cracking a light-hearted joke every now and then, the ongoing stream of negative put-downs got to the point where it just wasn't much fun hanging out with him.

To accomplish our task of hanging up the screens, we needed a few tools from a little green outdoor shed crammed with boxes and crates.

"We should pull out all these boxes so we can find what we're looking for more easily," my friend said as he lifted one of the little red crates.

I surveyed the ground and thought having all those boxes outside would get really messy, so I figured it would be just as easy to side-step some of the storage bins to get the tools we needed. For that reason, rather than listening to him, I simply squeezed through a few of the containers and started digging through one of the crates to find what we needed.

Afterward, a few negative remarks were volleyed back and forth between us, until my friend made a comment so cruel that even after saying it, I could tell by the look on his face that he immediately regretted what he'd said.

While part of me wanted to retaliate, thankfully, that morning, I had just read the wise words from a little book called *Bringing Out the Best in Our Relationships with Others* by Brother Premamoy, which reminded me that the foundation of all healthy relationships was something my friend and I had long forgotten in our interactions with one another—respect.

So with respect in my mind, despite his comment, I put my hands in the air as if to disarm myself and said, "Look, I am really sorry about what I said earlier. I was way out of line. Can we start over?"

My friend bowed his head, still slightly ashamed at his low jab. "I am really sorry, too. I shouldn't have said that."

Then, like good Canadians, we had a "sorry war," shooting our apologies back and forth.

And while this little interaction alone was a testament to the power of respect, what happened next was nothing short of miraculous.

Armed with respect, as my friend and I went about putting up these screen doors in the outside kitchen, I consciously considered everything he was sharing regarding his thoughts on the best way to accomplish the task.

Note: Since these screens were far too big for the size of the small cook shack's little doors, it was not an easy IKEA setup, and some MacGyver-like ingenuity was required to make the screens fully functional.

That being said, even if at times I thought there might be a better way to do it, before shooting my friend's ideas down instantly or suggesting we do it my way, I'd listen to his point of view, his reasoning, and where he was coming from.

Interestingly enough, when I approached my friend with this level of respect, he offered it right back to me. With the utmost esteem, he'd say,

"Well, how do you think we should do it?"

And like this, the usual crass commentary, which had been the norm in our relationship for so long, was transformed into an angelic song of please, thank you, and what do you think?

With respect as the foundation, we became more collaborative, we became smarter, we became better. This is the beauty of respect. It brings out the best in us.

But the problem is, as you saw with my friend and me, often with those closest to us, this key ingredient for healthy relationships is missing.

Why is this?

St. Augustine once famously said, "Familiarity breeds contempt."

Perhaps that's because often when we are too familiar with people, respect gets forgotten.

Think about it.

Culturally, we are trained to meet strangers with respect and appreciation.

Yet all too often, when we get too familiar with people, we get too casual with them. We neglect their value. And forget to offer them the level of respect required to sustain healthy and happy relationships.

Now, this does not mean we have to treat our friends, spouses, or children like strangers. It just means we need to be extra aware not to take those people for granted and to ensure that respect is always at the foundation of those relationships. Because as you just witnessed with my friend and my story, when our relationships are rooted in respect, it creates balance and harmony.

Bringing It Home

So, if you want to thrive in your relationships with others, here is a simple reminder:

Don't take them for granted.

Listen to their points of view.

Take into consideration their needs.

And most importantly, push that big egotistical "I" that always wants its way, out of the way.

When we do this, it doesn't just positively impact us but has far-reaching effects that touch the world at large. Because if we can learn to bring love and respect to those closest to us, we are better equipped to bring that same level of respect and understanding to those who are different from us.

Just imagine what might happen to this world if instead of pointing fingers, blaming, and putting each other down, we started listening, loving, and respecting one another?

Imagine what a world that would be...

That's a world I want to live in. What about you?

The best part? We can start creating that world today, with you and me, and our friends and family.

17
WHERE TO FIND HAPPINESS

When will we realize that true happiness does not come from getting what we want? Instead, it flows from helping those in need. It is only when we forget the little "me" and instead, focus on "we" that we begin to taste the essence of true joy.

The Chinese philosopher Lao Tzu said it much sweeter than I in the ancient text *The Tao Te Ching*:

"A man can achieve his own happiness only by pursuing the happiness of others because it is only by forgetting about his own happiness that he can become happy."

With these wise words in mind, body, and soul, may we forge forward on this day, caring for the well-being of those around us as much as our own. May we celebrate their successes and be willing to share their pains. And may we be friends to all, knowing that each being before us is much more than just a stranger but a reflection of the Divine.

18
REAL LOVE

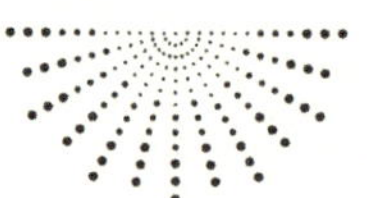

"What's up with that guy?!" Shawn said, shaking his head as he looked into the field of banana trees in the distance. "He doesn't say anything. He eats alone, doesn't talk to anybody, and just stays in his room most of the time. He reminds me of a dog that's been kicked too many times."

We were on the floor of the front porch of his bamboo hut under the overhanging thatched palm from the roof, the traditional design for the Shipibo people in these parts of the Peruvian jungle.

The guy Shawn was referring to was Gunnar, a Latvian whose long, shaggy black ponytail matched a scruffy goatee. His dark eyes made me think of a forest that travelers fear to enter. I'd first seen him on the boat on my way to the Amazonian village of Pao Yhan. I didn't know it at the time, but we shared the same destination, and he was heading to the village to work with the very shaman I was there to see.

"He needs our prayers," I said to Shawn. "I think he has met some bad people along the way."

I had already made several attempts to connect with Gunnar with friendly smiles and head nods here and there, but so far, nothing had landed. He had built a strong fortress that blocked my meager gestures from entering. So, I left him alone and focused on why I had come to the village and to do my own healing work.

Thankfully, by the grace of the Great Spirit, something happened that changed my perspective. But before I tell you what, you should know why the heck I had traveled twenty-two hours by boat into an Amazonian village to meet some shaman in the middle of nowhere. Well, without going into too many details, I took my father there a few days prior to get some healing. In the process, I was hoping to get a soul treatment myself from this long-unbroken line of medicine men whose families had helped people for thousands of years.

The evening after that conversation with Shawn—a fellow traveler there to do the same inner work—I was guided through our first ceremony. Now, the specifics of what happened that evening can't quite be written into words, but the transformation that occurred is what I want to talk about.

The morning after the ancient ritual, my father was changed. I sat on the hardwood floor of the circular ceremonial hut and looked deeply into his luminescent eyes, which beamed with the light of stars as he spoke.

"All I want to do is to serve," he said as he shared his insights from the evening prior. "Last night, I saw how in so many moments in my life, I was only concerned with myself. And that's not right. The most important thing we can do as humans is to serve." At that moment, the light of my father's revelation cracked my self-centered shell. At that moment, I realized just how selfish I had been these last few days. Here I was, on retreat, only concerned with my peace, my growth, my healing. Me! Me! Me! That was all I was thinking about, and this self-focused approach had cut me off from my father, pushing us into unnecessary disagreements. It also cut me off from connecting with the other participants who had also traveled far and wide for similar healing. And at the end of the day, this attitude cut me off from myself.

Later that morning, as I was walking to the kitchen, I saw Gunnar sitting on the wooden floor, smoking a rolled cigarette while solemnly staring off into the distance. Holding the wisdom I'd just received close to my heart, I approached and asked if I could sit beside him. His face scrunched at first, but he hesitantly accepted me.

We began to talk, just a couple of words at first. Not really about anything, just small talk about the weather and such. But the more we spoke, the more he opened up. He told me about his home. He shared stories of his travels and even revealed his deep desire to become a healer one day. Like that, we spent the whole morning together. We walked through the village, met with the locals, joked, and laughed. And by the time I left him that morning, his previously serious face had transformed into a giant smile. For the next couple of days, I took it upon myself to find him before mealtimes to be sure we could sit together. I invited him into conversations with the others, and most of all, I just loved him for who he was. After that, I noticed him smiling more, cracking jokes every now and then, and even opening himself up to others.

Two days later, Gunnar was scheduled to continue his journey down the Ucayali River. After breakfast, my hand squeezed his shoulder. "I'm on my way to my *tambo* (hut), but I will see you off at the boat later." He smiled, and I turned to the jungle to make my way home.

As I hiked back, an unexpected mass of dark clouds sailed through the sky, turning the sunny day into a black sea. Thunder roared, and a torrential Amazonian downpour bore down on us. Raindrops the size of golf balls assaulted the ground while trees waved frantically in the wind. My stride turned into a run, and I bolted for the tambo's shelter. I made it safely, wearing a blanket of rain that slithered to the floor. It was 9:30 a.m. by then. I could only hope the storm would die down before 11:00, when I was supposed to see Gunnar off at the dock. But hoping had no effect, because the rain continued to pour even more ferociously than before.

Sitting on my bed at 10:45, I mentally prepared myself to make the treacherous trek through the storm. But suddenly, out of nowhere, a loud pounding beat upon my door. I crept toward it and yanked the wooden frame open. To my surprise, there were the glowing eyes of my new friend Gunnar with a river of water running down him.

"I came to wish you a good journey, my friend," he said with a golden grin. My smile matched his. And at the same time, we stretched our arms out and leaned in for a wet yet warm embrace. "I am so grateful to have met you, my friend," I said. "It's been an honor." His smile grew even wider.

"For me too," he said. I gave him a hearty slap on the shoulder. "I hope to see you again soon, my friend." With a sparkle in his eyes, he nodded, then turned and ran through the rain. As I watched him go, I sent silent prayers of love and gratitude to his soul, thinking how blessed I was to have gotten to know him.

Back in my room, I thought about just how much had changed within this man in such a short time. From winter to summer, his cold edges melted with the warm fire of love. And at the same time, I realized how much had actually changed in me. While it would have been so easy for me to write him off as cold, strange, or a lost cause, had I done so, I would have missed making that beautiful connection. The irony is that had I continued to focus so much on myself, my work, and my healing, I would have actually missed my healing.

You see, one person's healing is actually all our healing. Ancient spiritual traditions and now modern science tell us we are all connected. This means that one person's pain is actually all our pain. Similarly, one person's well-being is all of our well-being. The illusion of separation is actually the source of our greatest pain. And when we are so focused on ourselves, we sever our connection with the world and, by doing so, we lose our connection to our Source. When we look through the focused lenses of "me" and "mine," we fail to see there are others out there who are hurting and could use our help.

Don't get me wrong. I believe a healthy dose of self-care is essential if we are to truly serve effectively. It's impossible to give if we are running on empty. But it's a very fine line we must observe to ensure our self-care does not turn into "selfish care."

As mentioned before, when we really recognize our interconnectedness with all things, we see that one of the greatest acts of self-love is to lose ourselves in the service of others. We see that by helping one person, we are really helping ourselves. So, if you truly want to practice self-love, go and serve another with the awareness that the other person is you!

Given today's global crisis, we could all use a little more TLC. It doesn't take much effort to help another human. A smile, a chat, or a moment of true presence is sometimes all that's needed. These acts, as small as they may seem, are powerful gestures that can change the course of someone's day. And, under the right conditions, it only takes one loving moment to change the trajectory of someone's life. Try it today. Be that someone who changes the world, one loving act at a time.

19

BREAKING OPEN: PATHWAYS TO LOVE

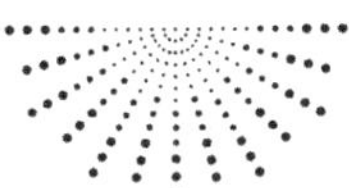

There is a crack in everything, that's how the light gets in.

— LEONARD COHEN

"Are you sure you don't want to come?" Carrie asked me before she hopped into the taxi to the concert in a beach town, a short drive from my place.

"No thanks," I said as I looked around at the quiet rice fields in my quaint village. She shrugged, smiled, and waved before she closed the door and headed north toward the little "tourist gateway." But when Carrie arrived, she was shocked at what she saw.

Despite only being an hour's drive from the rural village where I lived, to Carrie, it felt like she had just flown to another country. In contrast to my peaceful village, the coastal community she had driven to was more like one long resort. The town had traded its ancestral rice fields and traditional culture for high-end hotels, restaurants, and shops catering to tourists. But having just landed in Bali a few days back, Carrie didn't know anything about her destination. In her mind, she was simply following the intuitive call to attend an Erykah Badu concert, a rhythm and blues singer she used to listen to as a teenager. While I had warned her it would be touristy, she wasn't prepared for what she was about to see.

The place stank of partying, greed, and a dying culture. Even the Balinese people she found there starkly contrasted with those she encountered in my village. She noted that they seemed aggressive and on edge and that even if they were smiling (a common trait of most Balinese), it was as if their smiles were plastered on to please the tourists.

When Carrie left her hotel on the first day, the streets were chaotic, with swarms of foreigners marching down the tight pedestrian pathways. Motorbikes buzzed left and right. As she walked through one of the manic roads, she passed by a large building painted pink with a picture of a rosy rooster on a giant sign that read The Pink Cock.

Judging by the characters she saw enter and leave the building, she assumed The Pink Cock was serving a lot more than food, if you catch my drift. Disgusted, she sped past the building. But out of the corner of her eye, she saw a little girl, no more than eight, sitting on the ground to the left of the door, selling leather bracelets.

A cord tugged on her heart, pulling Carrie to the child. The little girl looked up and flashed one of those fake smiles Carrie had been seeing all day. Then, in perfect English, the girl went through her sales routine, holding out a fistful of braided leather bracelets, begging my friend to buy some. It was a routine so flawless he must have practiced it a thousand times before.

Carrie was not hard to convince. She quickly bought a few bracelets and continued chatting with the little girl. As they talked, the child's smile grew authentic, and Carrie noticed she still had a faint spark in her eyes. But it was clouded by an unnatural maturity bred from a life that demanded too much from a girl so young.

They shared one last kind look before Carrie turned to leave, and when she did, she noticed a terrible aching inside her chest, as if there was a rope knotted tightly around her heart. Suddenly, images of the child's possible fate flooded through her mind. She imagined the girl inside The Pink Cock, serving tourists in ways she did not want to think of. Carrie's eyes began to water as the clenching in her chest grew even tighter. As the sun set, she walked back to her hotel, unable to get the girl out of her mind.

For the next few days, Carrie went back again and again to visit the child, offering kind words, money for more bracelets she didn't need, and mostly, her loving attention. But after the concert, as Carrie left the town and rode the bumpy hour back, all she wanted to do was stop the car, turn around, and take the child away from the cruel world before her. She even seriously considered the possibility of adopting the child. By the time she arrived at my house, she was weeping as she recalled the experience.

Yet, in the face of her despair, something awoke within her. Perhaps it was all the time she had spent engaged in social work; perhaps it was all those years training as a Buddhist, or perhaps it was the simple knowing within her soul that the hurt within her heart could only be healed by turning toward it. Whatever the source, that wisdom within her moved her to act.

Looking at me squarely, she said, "I really don't care about traveling anywhere else for the rest of my time here. All I want to do is volunteer at an orphanage." Two days later, she was off to the neighborhood of Nyuh Kuning to visit a center for at-risk youth. She stumbled into the old building, where a bunch of teenagers sat on the floor of a makeshift stage. She offered them all a smile and a wave. They returned the friendly gestures, then went back to their chitchat when she walked past them. In the front office, seated behind a desk, a small woman with jet-black hair and an aura like a still pond was sorting through files.

"Are you Carrie?" the woman asked with a welcoming smile.

Carrie nodded, and the woman stood, reached out, and offered her hand.

"I am Mama Ayu," she said with a gentle glow.

After the greeting exchange, Mama Ayu proceeded to give Carrie an inspiring tour of the place. Carrie was so impressed by all the activities and support programs the small center offered the children. There was a full kitchen for cooking and a classroom to help them with their schoolwork and to learn English, Spanish, and even Korean! The second floor housed an art room, a music room, and even a computer lab!

Then Mama Ayu took Carrie to a little office in the back, where a photograph on the wall of a peaceful-looking man with dark, square-framed glasses stared directly at Carrie from the frame.

"This is Kadek Suambara," Mama Ayu said, shining. "He's the founder of the center. He helped me a lot."

Mama Ayu looked fondly at the picture, then explained. "Many years ago, my husband left me and our small son. It was very hard. I was alone, without money, and I actually had to leave my child with my parents so I could work abroad to provide for him. It was difficult for me, but I think it was even more difficult for my son," she said.

"One evening, when I was home visiting my son, we were out walking in our village and we saw a happy family with a mother, father, and son. I could see the sadness in my son's eyes, his longing for the father and family he did not have. After that, I also became very sad. And that's when I started to drink." She said as she shook her head, remembering those trying years. "Thankfully, a friend encouraged me to meet this man and attend Kadek's yoga classes." Mama Ayu said as she pointed to the founder with her eyes.

"It took some convincing, but eventually, I agreed to meet him. He started working with me. He counseled me, prescribed me yoga practices, and all sorts of other healing exercises. And it worked! After a few months, my addiction stopped, and I was feeling so much better." She said as light beamed around her.

She then shared how the founder invited her to work at the center, doing odd jobs here and there, training her in every aspect of the operation, until eventually, he stepped away from the daily responsibilities and handed the executive role to her.

Carrie listened intently as Mama Ayu spoke, deeply touched by how this single mother who had struggled to help her only child had now become a mother to so many. Then, after she offered one more fond smile to the founder's picture, Mama Ayu said, "Well, let's go meet the children."

Carrie returned her smile and then followed her down the stairs to where the children had greeted her on arrival.

"Children, this is Carrie," Mama Ayu said, waving her hand to Carrie.

"Why don't you introduce yourselves to her?"

With big smiles, the children immediately formed an orderly circle. Speaking in tentative English, the kids proceeded to share their names, ages, and what they wanted to do when they graduated from high school. Carrie smiled and listened attentively as each child shared some of their most cherished dreams.

After every kid spoke, the group dispersed to participate in the day's activities. But a few of the older girls stayed behind to chat with Carrie. Then, they took her by the hand and brought her back to the art studio, where they proudly showed off their artwork. Carrie admired and praised them, and to inject more confidence in the girls, offered to buy a few of the paintings from them. The girls lit up in delight.

Afterwards, they all sat together in a circle, scribbled on paper, and shared stories, laughs, and genuine human connection. In what felt like no time, Carrie's volunteer shift was up. She turned to wave goodbye, and a half dozen smiling girls waved their arms in warm farewell.

As she left, Carrie noted that her heart, which was so tender just a few days back, now felt as if it was overflowing with so much love it could be felt emanating in every direction.

A stone's throw from the orphanage, Carrie stumbled upon a quiet restaurant. Having barely eaten that day, she went inside and ordered a meal, and then contemplated the series of events that had led her to that moment. She thought about the beach town, the little girl selling bracelets at The Pink Cock, the transformation of Mama Ayu, and the orphaned girls radiating with such confidence.

As her mind went over these thoughts, the food arrived, along with a blue napkin with cutlery tucked inside. A light brown string threaded through a small white card wrapped around the napkin to keep it all together. She tore it open, not noticing she had ripped the piece of paper in two.

At the end of her meal, she looked down and noticed the white paper was like a slip inside a fortune cookie. She placed the two halves together, revealing her message from the Universe. It was a quote from the philosopher-poet Kahlil Gibran: "Your pain is the breaking of the shell that encloses your understanding."

That evening, when Carrie shared her experience, I was in tears, as I contemplated the wise words of Gibran, pointing out that on the other side of pain, there lies a deeper truth. Yet, in order to touch that truth, we must be willing to be broken open.

But how often in our world do we run from pain, numbing it with social media, drugs, shopping, food, or whatever we can to avoid sinking into the discomfort within ourselves or another? Yet, if we are willing to be vulnerable and divest of our armor, as Carrie did, pain can be the gateway to healing and transformation. It was through Carrie's willingness to feel another's pain that she was moved to reach out and offer care. This is, by definition, the very essence of the word "compassion," which literally means "to feel another's pain and offer care."

A few days later, I visited the youth center with Carrie to watch the children's weekly talent show. To say I was impressed is an understatement. I was mesmerized! The kids were outstanding, joyfully performing everything from traditional dances to complex hip-hop sequences. They spoke Korean, played instruments, and sang classic Western songs with interpretive dance.

Then, as I watched with my mouth wide open in awe, I saw something in the corner of my eye to the left of the building that brought the whole experience together. It was the center's sign that called my attention. An image of a huge green heart and the inscription: *Permata Hati.*

At the time, I was in the process of learning Bahasa, and knew only one of the words, so I grabbed my phone to plug the meaning into my translator. When I read what it said, I was brought to tears once again.

Permata Hati means "The Jewel of the Heart."

With happy tears flowing from my eyes, I looked back at the kids dancing, smiling, and singing with such confidence. Then, in that moment, I saw the gift, the magic, the jewel that comes from living in our hearts.

It was through the orphanage founder's open heart that he was inspired to start the center in the first place. It was his open heart that moved him to support Mama Ayu. It was this love that helped Mama Ayu heal, which, in turn, provided the energy and love she needed to serve all of those children so powerfully. Moreover, it was Carrie's willingness to feel another's pain that allowed her heart to be broken open to love. That love within her touched me, and my deep prayer is that the same love will also touch you. That's the power of living with an open heart. It gives birth to a jewel that can positively touch and heal the whole world.

20
SERVICE AND THE STREETS

The hero of this story is Daniel, an 11-year-old boy who lives on the streets of Pucallpa, Peru. His spirit and caring heart touched me in such a beautiful way that he will never know. I write this to honor him and the wisdom he shared with me.

It was evening in the jungle city of Pucallpa, Peru, when I met him. I was sitting with my friend in an open-concept restaurant without walls, which allowed the city's humid air to waft in. It was packed—not an empty seat in the house. The place buzzed and boomed with voices.

We were nestled beside the outdoor grill that sizzled with chicken and fish. Not a vegetarian at the time, the smells of smoke and meat brought saliva to my mouth. We had placed our order shortly after sitting down, and with stunning service, minutes later, the waitress pulled two large chicken breasts the size of my head from the fire and served them with yucca and salad.

"Holy crap! This is huge. I can't eat this all," I exclaimed wide-eyed.

"Good! You can give it to me when you're done," my friend replied with a chuckle as he chomped away at his own mountain of food. I tucked into mine. That's when I met Daniel.

From the blackness of the streets, barefoot, he approached our table.

Without a word, he held out his dirty hand and looked at us through distant eyesI could see carried deep pain.

I frantically searched my pockets for some money to give the boy. Apart from large bills, I only had 50 centimos, about 15 cents. I handed it to him. With the same hollow stare, the boy took the money mechanically, then turned and moved to the couple at the table beside us.

They handed the child a few more coins. At this point, our waitress gave the boy a sad stare. Shaking her head, she said, "I'm sorry, but could you please leave?" He was unfazed. With the calm of having been told the same thing a thousand times, the boy turned and left.

I watched him go around the corner into the dark night, my heart constricted into a million knots. I looked down at the mammoth plate in front of me and wanted to cry.

"This isn't right!" I said, jerking my head.

"What?" my friend replied between mouthfuls of meat.

"Here I am eating this huge frickin' meal when that boy has nothing. I should have given it to him. But all I did was give him a few cents!"

The pain of the injustice and my guilt made it hard for me to breathe and even think of what I should do. Thankfully, Spirit must have been watching and spoke through my friend. "Well, if you see him again, why don't you invite him to eat?" I nodded and looked eagerly towards the streets, praying he would pass.

Within less than thirty seconds, my prayer was answered.

I saw the young boy across the restaurant. My heart jumped. *"Venga!"* Come! I shouted, waving him over.

The boy slowly approached our table with the same muted glare. "Are you hungry?" I asked. The boy nodded solemnly. "Well, come and sit," I said with a warm-hearted grin. Then I pulled out a chair and invited him in. My friend approached the grill and asked them to prepare another plate for him. The cook suggested we give him a small chicken leg. My friend agreed at first, but then, shaking his head, insisted they prepare him the same plate as ours.

"What's your name?" I asked the boy.

"Daniel," he said, not looking at me.

"Daniel! Wow, that's a great name! I know a hero whose name was Daniel. He fought a lion! You must be a hero too!"

The boy responded with a small smile. I commented on his SpongeBob SquarePants shirt, saying that I really liked the character. He offered another small curl of his lips, then turned to the TV in the corner. We joked with him as we watched the antics on the reality show. I asked questions about what he liked. We found out he was good at soccer and could dance. "Me too!" I said, and started to dance like a fool in my chair. That earned a full-on grin and a little chuckle, too.

As we ate, I noticed Daniel slowly forking away at his food, taking only small bites of his veggies and little nibbles of his yuca. "Come! Eat!" my friend and I said, encouraging him to try the chicken. With his knife and fork, he struggled to cut, and he took a modest taste. After a while, I understood what was happening. I'd noticed another little boy pass the restaurant earlier. He peered in quickly, looked at Daniel and us, then swiftly darted off. I realized Daniel was saving his meal to share with his friend.

"Do you want to take the rest to go?" Daniel nodded in eager agreement. *"Para llevar,"* I told the waitress, asking her to bag the food.

The waitress handed Daniel his meal, and we said our goodbyes. "Well, Daniel, it's been great to meet you!" I said as I raised my hand in the air. "Give me five." With a grin and a modest slap, Daniel hit my hand. He was shining now with eyes glowing so brightly they could have lit up the entire city. He got up, turned, and exited back to the streets.

Only now, after reflecting on this story, do I realize who the real hero was. It would be easy for me to think it was me, having seen my shortcomings and surpassed them by inviting Daniel to join us. But the truth is, Daniel was the one who truly did something remarkable.

Just think—even though he was hungry and had nothing, he saved what little he had to share with others. This act of radical charity and kindness is something we can all learn a great deal from. It's easy to share when we think we have a lot. But it takes a great deal of love and generosity to give when we have little. Daniel beautifully demonstrated this selfless way, thinking of others regardless of his own challenging circumstances.

As we have discussed previously in this book, in our world today, there is so much self-centeredness. Left and right, it seems like everyone is just thinking of what they can do to make themselves feel better. So we buy things and have experiences to cut the edge of the longing we feel inside. While these things may help us feel better for a moment, the truth is, they actually keep us from the joy we are all truly seeking. In the Buddhist tradition, we are taught that happiness comes through compassion and care for others.

The Hindu teacher Sai Baba said, "No joy can equal the joy of serving others." The Christians have the Golden Rule, which instructs us to do unto others as we would have them do unto us. In other words, it is in sharing and giving that we find the peace, happiness, and love we are all seeking. And a love like that is what the world truly needs right now.

With this in mind, I pray that we can humbly bow to the wisdom shown by my friend, Daniel—who reminds us to serve in times of strife. Because just like Daniel's act of generosity changed me, acts of service like these have the power to change the world.

p.s. I humbly ask you to take a minute to pray for the life and well-being of Daniel, his little friend, and all the children whose circumstances force them to rely on charity.

THESE HANDS

~

These hands were made to build
gardens, sculptures, and great works of art.
They were made to work.
But not just for me.
For when I put them to use for my own desires,
I am filled with endless cravings.
Like the ancient Greek monster, the Hydra,
the minute that
I fulfill one of these fleeting wishes,
another one grows
even more fierce than before.
But when I forget about myself,
and instead, lose myself in the service
of my fellow man,
a joy wells up inside that no personal desire
could ever quench.
Knowing this, I know where to put my energy.
Yes, these hands were made to work,
but not for me...

~

21
LOVE, WORK, AND SERVICE

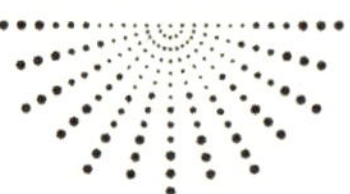

I'm not religious, but my father is, and I can still appreciate any place that honors the sacred, be it a church, mosque, temple, forest, or, on this particular day, a coffee shop.

It was exactly 5:00 p.m. in Cusco, Peru, when my knuckles banged on the bright blue wooden doors of *The Spot,* a coffee shop by day and a church every Sunday afternoon. But the doors were bolted.

"Maybe it's not open?" my father squinted.

"They should be. It's Sunday," I replied and dealt another few heavy blows.

Just then, from the streets, a foreign gentleman and Peruvian fellow marched across the square dressed in the common attire of the cool, high mountain city: jeans, a simple collared shirt, sweater, and windbreaker.

"Buenos tardes! ¿Están aquí por el servicio?" Good afternoon! Are you here for the service? The foreigner's Spanish was distinctly accented but fluid and grammatically perfect. We nodded and smiled in agreement.

"Great, great! The name's Steve, I'm the pastor here, and this is Marco," he said, offering his hand.

After the introductions, Steve unlocked the door and led us through the restaurant's main room. It was simple, with only a few tables painted black and sheltered by chalk-white stone walls. There were a few generic paintings of the city's landscape. And while the place was so plain, there was an air of excellence to it that carried a quiet strength.

Passing through the main floor, we made our way up a set of stairs and through a hallway to a large room decorated with the same simple black tables and chairs. "Can I grab you guys a tea?" Steve offered, now in English, with a British accent and a smile.

"That would be great," we replied, mirroring his grin. With those words, Steve quickly turned and was out the door.

Then my father, the other man—Marco—and I nestled into our seats and waited. My dad turned towards Marco and asked, *"¿Cuándo van a venir las otras personas?"* So, when is everyone else gonna come? The man's face crinkled into a modest smile, and he replied, "Well, there used to be a lot of people, but now, this is everyone else..."

Our eyes widened.

"What happened to the rest of them?"

"Many people moved for work. A few had some family troubles, and others just lived too far away to make the regular commute, so now it's just me."

"Doesn't seem like much of a church," my father murmured to me. Then we sat in silence, staring at the walls.

Steve came sliding through the door with two small teapots steaming with Earl Grey.

"We just have to wait a couple more minutes before we start. My wife and daughter are on their way." He poured us each a cup.

Sure enough, a few minutes later, a Peruvian woman came in with a 14-year-old girl.

"OK, let's get started." Steve rubbed his hands together.

"Now, we don't have a band yet, but we've got a TV." He chuckled then reached for a remote controller and clicked towards a screen in front of us. Suddenly, the once-black box became illuminated with a majestic scene of mountains. Then, the sound of rock and roll guitars filled the room, and in karaoke fashion, white words danced across the tube for us to follow. Then, with big smiles on our faces and hearts full of devotion, we sang. And at that moment, I could feel a presence around me that was so sweet and pure. The closest word I can use to describe it is "love."

Now, what happened next amazed me. After the singing was over, Steve led us in heartfelt prayer and then pulled out a stack of photocopied sheets of paper for us to pass around. About ten or so carefully picked scriptural verses were typed on them, and there were an equal number of thought-provoking questions regarding each verse. We passed them around and began to take turns reading each text; then, using the questions as stepping stones, we reflected on how the wisdom related to our own lives. A deep discussion ensued, filled with revelations, insights, banter, laughter, and new perspectives. And after two hours had passed, my father and I, full of love, waved a heartfelt goodbye to Steve and his humble congregation.

It was dark by the time we walked down the city's cobblestone streets, but there was a light burning so bright in me that was sparked by the commitment, love, and devotion offered by Steve. I was so moved by how much care, attention, and effort this man put into a sermon that, had my dad and I not been there, would have only landed on the ears of his wife, daughter, and one man. And I could tell he did so with joy, without thoughts of grandness, and instead with great humility, doing the task in front of him to the best of his abilities.

When I think about it, Jesus worked like this, too. When he started teaching, he had a mere twelve followers. At the time, he didn't complain and say, "Geez, God, could you give me some more!" Instead, he approached them with all his love and gave his entire self to the job. In turn, these men transformed into beautiful beings who passed that same love on to all they met. And like that, one person at a time, they created a movement of people committed to that same message of love.

While it is true that many people would use this message as a means to profit, control, and appear superior over others. But that is not the message I am talking about here. I'm talking about how one person accepted life's task with a spirit of humility and gratitude and did their absolute best at it. They did small things in great ways and focused all their efforts on serving.

This message of simplicity motivated that pastor to take up his assignment with such reverence and joy. That same love motivated me to write this. And now, my hope is that it inspires you to take up whatever task is in front of you with that same type of thoughtfulness and care. Because at the end of the day, this is how we change the world—doing our jobs with love, one action, and one person at a time.

TODAY'S OFFERING

~

Let your love be an offering today
that spreads freely
like pollen blowing in the wind.
Don't hold anything back!
Give it all!
Plant seeds of kindness with all those you meet.
Sow care, compassion,
and understanding to your foes.
Offer smiles like the sun,
and shine your light on everyone.
Use this precious day.
Share the warmth that rests
in the sanctuary of your heart
and illuminate this whole place.
The world needs your light,
so go out there and shine bright!

~

22
LOVE WHAT YOU DO

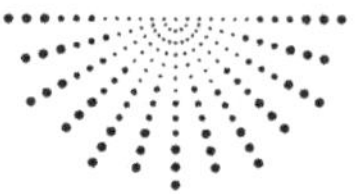

Work is love made visible.

— KHALIL GIBRAN

It was half past 11 a.m. as I was buzzing around Hintonburg, a funky neighborhood in Canada's capital, Ottawa. I was stressed with a long list of to-dos rolling around my head as caffeine pumped through my veins. I hadn't eaten, so I dashed into a little café and beelined it to the counter to grab something to bite before I rushed off to my next task.

The special that day was eggs Benedict served on a sourdough English muffin. It sounded decent enough, and the price was right, so I ordered one, sat down, and then continued to feel the stress of deadlines, decisions, and the pressure of the constant go that comes with city life.

How long I was there ruminating over my problems before my meal came, I don't remember. But I will always remember that first bite. The egg and toasted bread just about melted into my mouth, while an explosion of flavor filled my palate, followed by warm waves of peace that extended into every part of my body. My mind literally stopped. Captivated. Taken. Raptured by the experience. I kid you not. Everything before me was blank. The only thing that existed was me and that sandwich in a beautiful and perfect moment.

About four bites into the eggs from heaven, a skinny young man in his early thirties with a well-kept beard approached my table. "How are you liking your meal?" he asked with a saintly smile.

I looked up from the sandwich I had been celebrating and then into this man's piercing eyes. "It's absolutely amazing," I replied with awe.

With the same beautiful smile, he nodded and then placed his hand on his heart before speaking softly. "I am so happy you like it."

He told me he was the chef, about the source of each ingredient, and detailed how he had prepared the meal. As he spoke, I stared at his angelic glow, looked down at the sandwich, then back at him. I did this a few times before it dawned on me. *OMG!* I thought, *I am eating this guy!* His love and peace had transferred into that very sandwich. And I could taste it!

It's been nearly ten years since that morning, but I will always remember the lesson the chef gave me that day: The love we put into what we do is palpable. It transfers from us into everything we touch.

Many mystic traditions around the world agree, believing the energy we carry creates vibrations that emit into the world. Thus, everything we do, and the level of attention with which we do it, has a direct effect on our environment. While the ancients have known this for thousands of years, science is catching up with this age-old wisdom of how the power of the mind interacts with the world around us.

Take the example of food, as we just witnessed in the story. Several studies have found that food prepared with "love" was perceived to taste better and significantly elevate the enjoyment of the entire dining experience.

But here's the thing. This idea runs much deeper than just food. It extends into literally every aspect of our lives. This is an empowering realization for all of us to contemplate, because it tells us the intention we bring to every action can literally change the world around us.

Think about that peaceful chef for a moment. His love and care for his work transferred into that meal, and simply by eating it, all the stress I had been carrying that day faded away. After that, I moved forward with more clarity and calm. I made better decisions and was kinder to the people around me, thereby affecting their day as well. And now, nearly ten years later, I am still reaping the benefits from that single meal. And as you read this, so are you. Are you beginning to see just how much power there is when we bring love into what we do? The effects are not just positive for a fleeting moment; they are sustained and can last for years. Even though that chef will likely never know the extent to which his act of loving presence touched me, his simple action created positive ripples that have stretched across time and space.

Wow, all that from a sandwich? Really? Yes, really! The little things matter. Things done well, with great love, literally change the world. With that in mind, it's useful for us to contemplate how we can bring more love into what we do. While this list is not exhaustive, I'd like to highlight three key principles to help us bring more love into what we do.

1. Presence

"The most precious gift you can give to the one you love is your true presence," said Thich Nhat Hanh, the revered Buddhist teacher I've mentioned before. He is not alone in thinking this. Many philosophical writers, psychologists, and spiritual traditions echo these same principles.

Perhaps that's because when someone is truly present with another, that other person feels seen, heard, and acknowledged for who they are; they feel safe and, consequently, they feel loved. Perhaps you have even felt what it was like to experience the feeling of being blessed by someone's true presence. If so, you know it's a remarkable experience. On the contrary, I am sure we have all felt the emotional strain of what it feels like when another party is not present in a relationship. It can feel like the other person doesn't care, leaving one feeling unsupported, frustrated, or even lonely.

Relationships rooted in this type of interaction have far-reaching negative implications. Take children with parents who are emotionally checked out. Generally, kids who experience this type of parenting will develop unhealthy attachment styles, which could easily negatively impact their relationships for the rest of their lives. Moreover, the research shows that children from such upbringings are statistically more likely to exhibit behavioral problems, heightened aggression, and even decreased academic performance.

Why? Those children are crying for attention. They're crying for love.

But just being beside someone is not enough. The research on this subject highlights that the quality of the time we spend with someone is more important than the quantity. If you've ever tried to have a deep conversation with someone while they are on their smartphone, you know it's difficult to feel someone's loving presence in that space.

In fact, the smartphone problem is so pervasive in our modern world that it's worth a separate conversation. Notable studies have found that even having a phone on the table diminished a person's feeling of connectedness with another by 30 percent, even if the phone is upside down and set to 'silent.' Why a phone's mere presence would hinder connection is not certain. But speculation suggests it's because the sight of a phone could make someone feel as if the other person's attention is divided, and thus, unable to offer that person the deep presence we as people are all yearning for in our relationships.

As true as presence is the gateway to love with people, it's just as true with what we do. Think about it for a moment. It's hard to bring our love (presence) into our actions if we are not fully engaged in what we are doing. How can you bring love into the moment if you're so busy running around in your head from the past to the future? You can't.

With this in mind, if we want to bring love into our activities, we have to get really good at being present. How we can train ourselves to do that is another discussion altogether, but in short, practices like mindfulness, meditation, and striving to do one thing at a time with our deepest attention can help train our minds to bring our full presence to this moment, and consequently, bring our love to the moment.

2. Make It an Offering

Chapter 9, Verse 27 of the Bhagavad Gita encourages us to work in the spirit of sacrifice. "Whatever you do, whatever you eat, whatever you offer or give away, and whatever austerities you perform, do that as an offering to Me." This verse essentially means to offer up your work to something bigger than yourself. Research on happiness and purpose suggests that contributing to something beyond yourself is a key to fulfillment. You see, when we realize how our activities directly impact the world around us, we feel a sense of meaning, joy, and even bliss that comes from the spirit of service.

Thus, whatever task is in front of you, you can inwardly perform it as an offering, as a service. For example, if I am doing dishes, writing, or coaching a client, as a man of faith, I like to mentally offer up my work to my Creator. But if that doesn't work for you, try to imagine all the people who will be touched by what you do. Even if it's something so small and no one is looking. See how that action helps you build your character to become a kinder, more patient, or more disciplined person who will positively touch others in the future. And for the bigger things, imagine all the people, seen and unseen, who will benefit from your actions. Let your love for that bigger purpose fill your heart, and do everything in the spirit of service. You are part of a greater whole, and everything you do touches that greater whole, even if you do not see it.

This mindset of offering won't only affect the quality of what you do. It will also result in powerful positive impacts that directly touch your life. In fact, research suggests you'll be happier, more productive, and more creative if you simply bring more love into your work.

Perhaps that's because offering up our work to something larger than ourselves helps us connect to that Bigger Force and, thus, draw loving energy from that source.

3. Keep Practicing

Funnily enough, as I was writing this, my wife asked me to make her something to eat. With these ideas fresh in my mind, I was so conscious of the energy I had inside that I found myself singing to the eggs as I made them. Yet, despite my awareness, in a moment of distraction, I over-salted them! And consequently, I turned my wife's dining experience into something far from the one I had with my eggs benny all those years ago!

And guess what? That's okay. There was still love there. We laughed about it, and life went on. With this in mind, it's important to remember that as we strive to bring more love into what we do, we should acknowledge we will not always do this perfectly. We're bound to have moments of forgetfulness. And that's really okay!

The more we practice, the better we'll get, and in time, these small incremental improvements will eventually lead to one never-ending stream of love. How beautiful is that?

So, there you have it, three powerful principles that will help you bring more love into your work. They are worth cultivating and practicing regularly. Because every day, we are tasked with doing thousands of big and little things, and as such, we are provided with thousands of opportunities to bring more love into the world. Every single day.

Wow. What a gift.

So, wherever you are, and whatever you may be doing, like that chef, you have the golden opportunity to bring heaven to earth. One loving act at a time.

23
SEEDS OF CHANGE

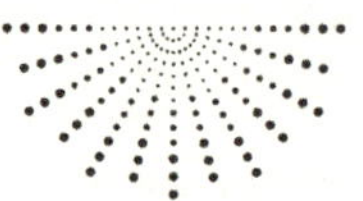

As the land, so the seed; as the seed, so the harvest.

— EKNATH EASWARAN

"I learned that I don't have to be on my phone all the time," said Jessica, the eleven-year-old, during the closing circle of the summer camp I helped run.

My jaw dropped as I witnessed the transformation of this beaming youth who, just five days before, held her head down with a blank face and answered in one or two words when I tried to engage her in conversation. And here she was on the final day of the program, filled with enthusiasm, playing with the other kids, leading games, and standing tall with confidence.

Now, as I looked back with a warmed heart, I was left pondering what conditions create such a radical change. While good programming obviously played some part, I believe the most effective tool by far that we organizers applied was creating a culture of love and kindness.

From the very beginning of that camp, we did our best to affirm every child, to recognize their gifts, respect their likes and dislikes, and to be genuinely curious about every child's unique world. I firmly believe that this environment of love, kindness, and care helped young Jessica feel safe enough to come out of her shell, share her heart with the world, and not look for her sense of security in her phone.

This is because our environments are one of the greatest shaping forces in our lives. Scientific research across fields like social psychology, developmental psychology, neuroscience, behavioral economics, environmental psychology, and habit formation shows that our surroundings are among the biggest drivers of human behavior.

And this principle—the power of environment—extends beyond humans and can be seen operating in the natural world as well. Just as a seed thrives in fertile soil but struggles when the conditions are poor, so too do people flourish in environments of love, care, and support, just like Jessica at camp.

Now, it would have been so easy for me to look at her glum face those first four days of camp and say, "Well, that's just the way she is," and leave it at that. But if I had, both the world and I would have suffered a loss because we would have failed to see the great treasure she held within.

This environmental principle is universal and can be applied to all areas of our lives. Especially now, given the turbulent times we are facing as a species, I believe it is a principle our society greatly needs to embrace and apply to the challenges we are currently facing. You see, if we want a more loving world, we need to create environments to foster that love. We need to create spaces that see, affirm, and acknowledge everyone's basic goodness.

We need to create environments that encourage us to suspend our immediate judgments of those who are different from ourselves. And we need to create spaces that look past people's hardened exteriors and instead look to the beauty and sacredness that lives within them.

So, as we move forward and examine our world, its challenges, and the many difficulties we witness, whether our own or others', may we strive every day to create environments of love, care, and kindness so the conditions are in place for those beautiful seeds to grow.

Questions for Reflection:

- What kind of environment am I creating in my daily interactions with others?
- Who in my life might be hiding their true potential, and how can I create an environment to help them feel safe enough to shine?

COMMUNITY

~

Let us be like little worker bees
and work diligently to extract life's sweetness.
Like bees, let's work in unity
in the service of the community.
The world needs this honey.
Let's get to work!

~

24
THE POWER OF "WE"

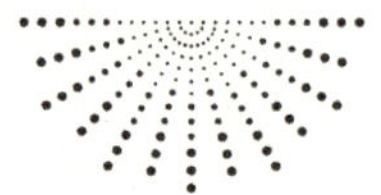

Screams filled the night as an avalanche of water cascaded down the mountain through the narrow, cobblestoned streets of Pisac, Peru. A brown river rushed down the alleyways as high as my waist. Artisans' wares, bags of rice, and families' entire lives floated swiftly down the flooded roads, never to be seen again. Men, women, and children shivered through stinging rains, pleading: *"Ayúdame! Ayúdame!"* Help me! Help me!

The next morning, I shook my head as I heard the owner of the place retell the terrible tale that happened just hours before while I slept. Though we were in the very same village, we had been spared. I counted my blessings but still felt deeply for the people's loss. Then, with a sigh, I turned, waved goodbye, and left to go on with my day. Thankfully, through the actions of a woman named Erica and her husband, San Francisco, I was inspired to do more than just shake my head in sympathy.

Almost immediately after stumbling from the hostel walls, I bumped into my neighbor, San Francisco, a local man built like the mountains around us. His eyes were heavy that morning, but his face was determined. From his mud-encrusted shoes, it was easy to see he'd been close to the action.

He told me he had been up all night pulling people from gutters and rescuing others' belongings the storm had scattered. Then he glanced over his shoulder to his spouse through the doorway of his blue metal gate and told me, *"Ahora, mi esposa está cocinando comida para la gente."* My wife is cooking food for the people.

I followed his eyes into the kitchen of his adobe home, where I saw faint steam rising from a massive pot on an open flame. At that moment, my neighbor's fire to serve the people sparked a fire within me.

Minutes later, I was sitting in his kitchen with his daughter and wife, peeling potatoes at a rickety table resting on a dirt floor. Erica, San Francisco's wife, commanded the room with a bright smile. Standing tall, she stirred the pot with eyes intent on feeding the masses. As time went on, more people came to join our efforts; first a friend, then a sister, then another neighbor.

In ninety minutes, our pedestrian convoy marched through the muck-filled roads, hauling a pot of food that took two people to carry. We arrived at ground zero, where hundreds of city workers and volunteers, most in orange vests armed with shovels, were digging out the submerged homes.

"Venga a comer!" Erica bellowed. Come to eat! It took a few more shouts to pull the workers from their focus. But once a few laborers discovered the service she was sharing, the whole lot came flocking, no doubt tired, worn, and hungry from hours of heavy labor. Plate by plate, we passed the food to eager hands that quickly snatched it up. The men bowed their heads, thanked us, ate quickly, then got back to the task at hand.

When the pot was empty, with her same bright grin, Erica signaled our crew to leave. But after seeing the enormous need still in the village, I bade my kitchen friends farewell and marched to the nearest police officer and asked for a shovel.

He gave me one and directed me to a nearby building almost submerged in sludge. Literally, the entire ground floor was buried. I watched as twenty men and women shoveled mud into wheelbarrows, then began the heavy work of transporting the sludge to giant mud piles on the main road, where a bulldozer would later clear.

I held my shovel and surveyed the enormity of the task at hand. It was daunting. But I went to work. And after seven hours of one shovel load at a time, I clapped, hollered, and whooped in delight with the crew as we removed the last shovel of mud from the house. Together, we had done it!

I looked around at my new friends-in-arms, leaning on our shovels, arms around one another, like brothers and sisters. A warm appreciation filled my chest for all who had made it possible for us to accomplish this towering task. During those long hours of demanding physical work, people from all walks of life, men and women, left their work, their families, or their studies to offer their time and financial resources to help. Like Erica, many women came with giant pots throughout the day to fuel us with food. Others brought water, and still others simply shared words of appreciation and encouragement. This same type of thought and care was not only given to the small group of us clearing that one home but spread to the hundreds of other workers and volunteers who shoveled the streets that day.

Meditating on this experience later, I saw firsthand the immense power of community. With our collective strength, we can accomplish what at first seems impossible. And in fact, if tackled alone, just might be. But when we come together with the same vision and purpose, we truly can accomplish the impossible.

Personally, I find this heartening because right now, there is a whole lot of metaphoric mud in the world. We just need to turn on the news for five minutes to know what I am talking about: another war, a famine, a natural disaster, inexplicable climate chaos, and economic scarcity, just to name a few. And I know that sometimes the mere thought of facing the world's overwhelming challenges seems like an impossible task. Because all too often, it can feel like none of our small actions will make a difference in the grand scheme of things.

Yet, even if we may not see the results of our efforts, they do. Just like Erica and San Francisco's actions fed the volunteers and inspired me to serve physically, all our thoughtful, loving actions dedicated to making this world a better place have a positive effect on the whole. And if we compound those actions, one shovel at a time, together, we can pull ourselves out of this metaphoric mud and create the world we want to live in.

We can, and together, we will.

Questions for Reflection:

- Looking at your daily life, where do you see opportunities to serve others or contribute to your community?
- What specific action will you take this week to be part of the solution to a problem you care about?
- How can you connect with others who share your desire to create positive change?

Action:

Start serving this week!

25
LOVE AND LEADERSHIP

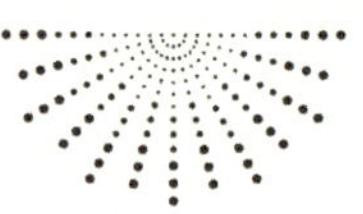

Leadership is not about titles, positions, or flow charts. It is about one life influencing another.

— JOHN C. MAXWELL

What happens when we let love lead our lives?

I first met Robin Lim in Bali, Indonesia, when my wife was pregnant with our son, Arjuna, and I will never forget my firsthand experience of seeing just how vast the power of leading with love can be.

Birth, as you probably know, beautiful as it can be, is also coupled with a host of challenges, be they physical, mental, or emotional.

During the process, for nine whole months, a woman's body goes through a powerful transformation. Surges of hormones make it difficult to sleep, eat, and even just be at times. These chemical changes in the body can give rise to mood swings, anxiety, and, at times, even feelings of depression.

All this and more, plus the heroic effort it actually takes to push a baby out, is the cost of life.

But Robin, the lead midwife and founder of Bumi Sehat Birth Center, changes all that.

I will always remember five months into my wife's pregnancy, when one evening, her urine was slightly pink. This was met with the thoughts, worries, and fears that come with any parent-to-be who wants nothing more than a healthy birth. That evening, I sent Robin a text regarding our concerns. I thought I would have to wait till morning to get a response, and I set my phone aside as my wife and I anxiously awaited the next day. But within the hour, Robin sent a heartfelt message that made us feel at ease while at the same time recommending we come in the following morning for a checkup and some additional tests.

When we arrived, Robin welcomed my wife with a hug and a smile and put her arm around her as she brought her to the center's office for a thorough examination.

Then, after a preliminary checkup, she took my wife by the hand and walked her to the on-site clinic for some blood tests.

As I watched them walk hand in hand, like dear friends, Robin making little jokes as they went, I can distinctly remember the feeling I had inside. It was one of feeling so cared for—that our lives and our baby's life mattered.

The whole experience was so moving that I practically cried right there on the spot. You may be happy to know, as were we, that there were no problems.

This was but one of many experiences of compassionate care we experienced from her during my wife's pregnancy. And this treatment was not just for us; I can vividly remember watching her support each mother who entered her clinic with the same warmth and tenderness.

When you first meet Robin, she will most likely greet you with a warm smile, a caring look, and a gentle hand on your shoulder. You'll probably feel at home, and when you leave the conversation, she'll tell you she loves you.

Now, unlike most people, who hoard this four-letter word for rainy days, special occasions, and anniversaries, as if it were some finite resource, Robin shares those sweet and affirmative words as if she had tapped into the eternal spring of love and thus shares them freely with all who come her way.

Another time during my wife's pregnancy, despite Robin's heavy schedule of evening births, prenatal visits, training, and speeches, she personally took me upstairs to the center's office to give my future baby clothes for his first year of life. We walked through an open office with about seven people working at desks, managing many of the center's day-to-day administrative activities.

All looked up from their desks and beamed brightly at Robin and me. She waved her hand in the air, said something in Indonesian, then smiled even brighter and said, "I love you all!" before she led me through to another room.

And this love she shared spread through every part of Bumi Sehat's culture—the internationally renowned organization she created.

Even when other midwives treated us, they would end our visits by letting us know we were loved. At our prenatal classes, they asked us all our names, because in their words, "When you know someone's name, you can love them more."

When babies were caught at Bumi Sehat, the staff was trained to pray and offer mantras of love and protection for them. Hell, even the automated message on their WhatsApp helpline ended by saying: “We love you.”

And this translated much further than just cheap words; on the contrary, loving action was manifested in every corner of the organization's ethos.

Everyone on staff, from the receptionists to the cleaning ladies and the doctors, beamed with a feeling of warmth when you met them. Even just by being at the center, you felt as if you were being embraced by the Great Mother.

That motherly love reached out and touched the world, literally. The Bumi Sehat Foundation has directly impacted hundreds of thousands of lives, helping women, children, and families with free, compassionate healthcare and education.

More than just a birthing center, it's also a clinic that offers exceptional care free of charge to anyone in need. They even help the babies thrive into responsible adults with a state-of-the-art youth center that offers mentoring, scholarships, and education programs to help the youth become leaders of their communities. There are wellness programs to help the elderly.

They even extend their loving reach to care for the environment around them by consciously using sustainable materials and solar panels on their buildings and supporting recycling programs all over Indonesia.

It's worth noting that Nyuh Kuning, the village where their main center is located, is reported as the cleanest village in all of Indonesia. No doubt a testament to the transformative power of love.

And their love does not end there; with three additional centers, two in Indonesia and one in the Philippines, they continue to do their best to offer safe, loving care to families in need. This includes general medicine for the sick, injured, and homeless.

Moreover, ready to act and spread their love, Bumi Sehat has been known to be one of the first responders in many disaster zones, putting up clinics at ground zero after earthquakes, typhoons, and tsunamis.

They do all this powerful work across the world because they believe that through lovingly caring for the birth process, positive waves will ripple into the future.

In their own words, Bumi Sehat believes that," Each baby's capacity to love and trust is built at birth and in the first two hours of life."

Thus, by making pregnancy, birth, and the postpartum period a loving experience, they will, as their tagline puts it, be "Healing the world one baby at a time."

How's that for a model to change the world?

Research suggests it could be a pretty effective one.

If we look at postpartum depression—one of the many complications that could result from not having supportive systems in place during pregnancy and birth—we begin to see the far-reaching implications of this model for change.

Note that postpartum depression has a global prevalence of about 15 percent.

That's about one in eight mothers. But in developing countries, those numbers can rise to 30-40 percent—about one in three.

Mothers are not islands that suffer in isolation. On the contrary, the negative impacts of mothers experiencing postpartum depression directly affect the child, family, and society as a whole.

For mothers, postpartum depression can lead to sadness, fatigue, and poorer health choices. This often cascades into their inability to meet life's daily demands and effectively bond with their child.

The burden of increased demands often touches the family, as partners and other family members gather their resources to support the mother in her time of need while, at the same time, supporting a new child in their home.

This added responsibility can add additional strain on family members, potentially leading to feelings of distress, anxiety, and overwhelm.

With a less present mother, children exposed to depression during this critical developmental period can experience cognitive, emotional, and social difficulties they may wrestle with for their entire lives.

For example, research suggests that children exposed to mothers experiencing postpartum depression are less emotionally regulated and more prone to anxiety and depression later in life.

Moreover, infants and toddlers with mothers struggling with postpartum depression have been shown to score lower on language and IQ tests. On a social level, children with mothers who suffer from postpartum depression are more likely to have poorer relationships and more likely to withdraw socially.

These challenges have long-lasting consequences that affect the child's future and often reach out and touch society.

Children with behavioral challenges may add additional strain to healthcare systems, struggle with employment, and even run a higher risk of encountering problems with the law.

With this 10,000-foot view, it's much easier to see that through having a healthy, supportive, and loving birth, we can truly create a healthy earth.

This, by the way, is the very meaning of Bumi Sehat—Bumi means "Mother Earth" and Sehat means "healthy."

Thus, with all this in mind, perhaps it's not that far-fetched to think that if we can infuse love into the entire birth process, we truly can transform the world.

As I reflect on Bumi Sehat's model for change, I can't help but think how applicable it is as we strive to lead and create a better world.

Sure, we may not all be birthing babies, but as leaders, we are always birthing something—be it new ideas, policies, or dreams. We are treading new trails and giving birth to visions.

Now, the question is, are we leading with love?

Are we ensuring that our visions are grounded in actions motivated by care and compassion?

Because, just like babies, these cherished visions are just as delicate and require the same attentiveness and care if we hope to see them thrive in the future.

Imagine what might happen if we all pulled a page from Bumi Sehat's model for change and let love lead the way.

Imagine if every farmer were not simply thinking about what he could get from the seeds he planted, but instead, how he could best support the seeds and land to thrive. With love in his heart, he would think holistically and seriously question the long-term impact of using pesticides on the soil.

Imagine if every business owner had a similar leadership style and looked at the products they sold not as simply a means for personal profit but as vehicles to serve the social good. What if every government was not simply trying to hoard its power but instead truly worked to create a vision for the collective good?

Imagine what might happen if we all let love lead the way...

Well, we can get a preview of what our world might look like by observing Bumi Sehat's global reach.

Put simply, it would be beautiful.

And guess what?

Before Bumi Sehat was a global organization that touched hundreds of thousands of people across the world, it started with one woman in a little village on a small island in the Pacific Ocean, simply motivated by love and a desire to make this world a better place.

She let that love lead her life, and that love reached out and touched the world.

And that one person motivated by love could be you, too.

It could be all of us.

One loving act at a time, our leadership can and will heal the world.

Questions for Reflection

- Where can you lead with more love in your life?
- Who and what around you needs you to step up?
- What might happen if you did?
- With this in mind, let's get out there and work together to give birth to a bright and beautiful future.

26
LOVE IS A VERB

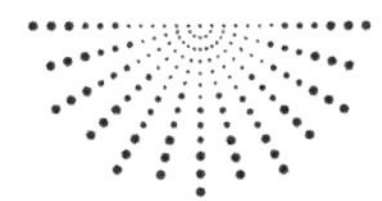

I almost lost my wife in the Pacific Ocean—not through some freak accident, but through my own carelessness. She slipped through my hands as I swam against one-hundred-ton waves. Metaphorically, that is. In actuality, what flew through my fingers was the gold and silver wedding band that confirmed our marriage.

While losing your wedding ring is never a good omen, it's particularly worrisome when it happens on your anniversary just after having a quarrel with your wife.

Dumbfounded at what had just occurred, I sat on the beach staring at the rise and fall of the surf, contemplating what this all meant.

My wife and I had just moved to Bali about three weeks back, and while we were filled with enthusiasm for the new life ahead of us, it came with all the stresses that come with an international move—finding a new home, learning a foreign language, and the initial isolation from lack of community, just to name a few.

With that, during our first stretch in Bali, many of our old unhealthy relationship patterns we thought we'd already dealt with came rising to the surface like a sea monster on a sunny day. Criticism, animosity, and aggression filled almost every interaction, which at times made the simple act of being together feel like a battle.

So, as I sat on the sand and played out the last few weeks, I had this strong intuitive sense that if I didn't shape up, I'd lose something a lot more valuable than my gold wedding ring.

When my wife found out what happened, she was worried as well. Particularly because just the day before, we heard that the statistic of separation for people who move to Bali was a whopping 60 percent. Why that is, I am not entirely sure. But some have attributed it to "the healing spirit of Mama Bali," suggesting that simply the energy of the island has the power to shake things up and help you get rid of what no longer serves you. Whether this is true or not didn't matter. Thoughts that we would be another sad statistic shaken apart scared her.

But hey, maybe this was all just a coincidence?

If I didn't get the message then that our relationship was on the rocks, it all came to the forefront after we drove back from our weekend getaway. But before I tell you what happened next, let me give you a little context.

Two years prior, on our wedding day, we incorporated a traditional Indigenous marriage ritual. In it, like with rings, we exchanged two white tail eagle feathers. While there is a lot more metaphoric meaning attached to that sacred feather ceremony, the simple version is this: The husband takes the wife's feather and agrees to watch over it. His wife does the same with his. Then, they're bonded, committed to holding and caring for one another. After the exchange, like your love, you keep those feathers safely together, usually in a special box. And if you're ever going through a straining period, you take those feathers out, and with each partner holding the other's feather, you have a serious heart-to-heart.

That being said, with everything that happened that weekend, when I came home, I figured it might be a good idea to pull those plumes out to have one of those deep, honest conversations. But to my shock, when I did, I noticed our feather box had a long crack down the middle, practically splitting it apart. While it had probably been that way for weeks, broken in our suitcase on the long international flight, I failed to notice. In retrospect, it was the perfect symbol for my lack of awareness of what was going on within our marriage. Because just as I hadn't even realized the box was breaking apart, I had failed to see our marriage was too.

Love in Action

With this insight, I brought my vulnerability, my worries, and deepest concerns to my wife. We shared, we cried. And rather than pointing fingers, I took responsibility for where I was falling short and promised to work to make it better.

Personally, what this looked like in practice started with lots of self-reflection. I journaled extensively about my role in creating the havoc we found in our relationship and honestly looked at where I was the problem. In doing so, I saw how I walked around with many sharp edges, all of which came from internal places that lacked love. And unconsciously, I would project those feelings onto my wife and not always be the nicest person.

With this realization, I started incorporating the practice of loving-kindness into my morning and evening meditation practices. I reread my vows every day and even visited some old teachers for advice on how I could improve. I worked at it. And through the process of working on myself first, we were better able to work as a team. Together, we started reading more books on relationships, had hard conversations, reworked intimate rituals, and even created a family mission statement we would read weekly. And while all the hurts weren't healed overnight, day by day, and bit by bit, through our attentive loving care, we worked at repairing what was broken.

This is real love, because while many people associate love with butterflies in the stomach and a Hollywood kiss at the end of a movie, the truth is, as Bell Hooks and other great thinkers have said, love is not a feeling—it's a verb. Or in other words, it's an active force, it's work, and at times can even feel like a grind.

It's important to realize this and not let some romantic fantasies of what an idealized relationship should be cloud your vision, because if you look at a partnership like that, you'll be deluding yourself, and out the back door the moment things get rough. And it will get rough—many times over, and that's okay, provided that each party is willing to put in the effort to make things right.

Perhaps that's why Brian Johnson, author and modern-day philosopher said that it's so easy to fall in love, but it's a lot more important to stand in love. This idea of standing in love is a powerful image for us to contemplate as we work to create happy and healthy relationships. When we stand in love, we are like a mountain holding its ground as life's emotional storms confront us. Standing in love is about meeting our relationship's challenges rather than retreating. Moreover, it's a firm commitment to bringing even more loving resolve when the going gets tough.

When the Going Gets Tough

This brings up another important point: When things are challenging, you're going to have to make more emotional investments to bring things back into balance. *The 7 Habits of Highly Effective People,* the bestselling book by Stephen Covey that sold over 40 million copies worldwide, speaks about a useful concept called the "emotional bank account."

To explain this idea further, imagine that every relationship you have is like a bank account. You have an emotional bank account with your spouse, your kids, your friends, and even strangers on the street. Every kind word, moment of total presence, and good deed done to someone is like an investment you're making into that account. Similarly, every cruel word, disregard for another's opinion, and broken commitment is like a withdrawal from that fund.

Now, just like with regular banking, if you've made lots of investments into a relationship, a few withdrawals of you not being your best self are not going to put you over. But if you are continuously making these withdrawals without investing lovingly into that relationship, you're going to be in the red. As such, at this point, you'll probably be having a lot more conflict with your partner.

Additional relationship researchers from the Gottman Institute's Love Lab have found this trend to be true, noting that healthy relationships tend to have about five positive interactions over every one negative interaction—calling this the 5:1 ratio. In their research, they suggest that those positive interactions act like a buffer against negative interactions. Now this highlights a very important point: negative exchanges with our partners tend to have more weight.

Said another way, every time you make a withdrawal, say by sharing criticism or a cruel comment, you need to make five investments to bring things back into balance. Why this is, is still up for speculation, but could be because the brain seems to have a negativity bias, or as Dr. Rick Hanson, the prominent neuropsychologist, has said, "the brain is like Velcro for negative experiences, but Teflon for positive ones."

This is probably because in more primitive times, being hyper-focused on negative experiences—say a poisonous red berry that could kill you, or a saber-toothed tiger around the corner—could literally mean life and death. Thus, holding onto negative experiences actually proved to be to our evolutionary advantage. Unfortunately, this adaptive advantage in the past mean sour relationships in the present need a lot more TLC. Which is why it's super important to keep making those deposits—especially when you are in the red. In times like those, you need to really focus on doubling down and seeing what actions you can take to bring your emotional bank account back into balance. And just like you might need to work overtime to pay off some debts, you will probably need to put in extra effort if your relationship finds itself in a deficit.

Bringing This Practice Home

Relationships with others are probably the most rewarding gift of life. They nourish, fulfill, and make everyday moments meaningful. But if we want them to be beautiful, we can't expect them to grow by themselves. Like a garden, we need to tend to them, weed them, and water them. Put simply, we need to work on them. And it's not always easy, and at times can even cause great strain.

Sometimes that emotional strain is the result of environmental experiences like the droughts of major life events such as a sick family member, the loss of a job, or the lack of sleep that comes with newborns. At other times, that stress is caused through our own inattention and lack of effort—we forget to water our partnerships with our affection, we get too busy to weed out our shortcomings. And in the end, we feel the weight. Regardless of how that pressure comes about, if at times your relationship doesn't look like a neatly cultivated garden, and instead resembles a wild jungle, that's okay, provided you're willing to keep chopping away.

Thus, if you ever find yourself in a jungle, pulling through the weeds, take heart. Because, while it might be challenging, it does not mean you should run away. On the contrary, it should be a sign to roll up your sleeves and get to work—both inside and with those around you. Because as Covey reminds us, "Love is not a feeling.

It's a verb. The fruit of love is the feeling." But in order to get the fruit, you've got to do the work.

Questions for Reflection

- Are you practicing love as a verb? If not, how can you start today?
- How can you apply the 5:1 ratio in your relationships today?
- Are there any personal issues you are projecting onto your partner? If so, what can you do to tend to those parts within yourself?

27
LOVE, LOSS, AND WHAT'S KILLING US

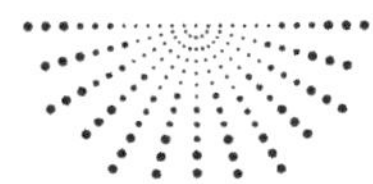

Oh no! I thought to myself, as I watched the three-year-old boy march defiantly with the cardboard bin over half his size down the street.

"We can't leave them!" he said, looking down into the big brown box.

"I will take care of them," he said confidently to the four adults around him—his parents, my wife, and me.

"I will name them Bob and Wendy," he added proudly.

The box moved wildly as it shook with each of his little wobbly steps, until eventually, the two baby kittens, no more than a month old, jumped out and started running down the road, one nearly getting hit by a motorbike, and the other chased by a dog.

My wife quickly snatched them up and placed them back in the box. I stared at her as I thought about what we should do. Because, as much as that little boy wanted to save those cats, his parents' landlords wouldn't allow it. And both Andréanne and I knew if we did not take them in, they would die.

Now, having these two rescues in our home was particularly a big deal, not just because we had a six-month-old baby, but because just two days before, someone had literally dropped a barely alive, starving kitten on our front porch. If we took those two new kittens in, it would mean there would be five cats we had rescued that year roaming around our house, three of them needing hand feeding every few hours.

Looking into my wife's eyes, I shook my head. "It's the right thing to do," we agreed. "And hey, what's a couple more?"

We could not have been more wrong...

The next morning, I woke to piles of wet s*** all over the kitchen where I had laid them to rest. It was understandable, though. It was their first day, and they had yet to learn how to use the litter box. So, we did what we had done with all our other cats to teach them: offered them the litter when they went and gave them ample opportunity to figure it out.

Most cats learn pretty quickly, usually in a couple of days. But there was something off with these new kitties. They were slow, docile, and couldn't seem to figure it out. We even thought they may have been hit on the head and suffered brain damage. One even comfortably slept right in its own huge pile of poop.

So we quickly had them checked out by a vet. He administered a simple parasite medication to deworm them and said it should all resolve itself in a few days. But over the next week, the diarrhea continued. So, we called the vet again, and again he prescribed another dose of the parasite medication and suggested we feed them warm milk every two hours.

But the treatment plan didn't work. Poop pickups became a regular event in our household; every morning, afternoon, and evening, the cats would meow, walk in their s**t, and trail it all around the house. I won't lie and say I did not lose my patience more than once. It was not easy to say the least.

But despite how hard it was to care for the little guys, we did our best to support them with the energy and resources we had. But after the third week of diarrhea and blood in their poop, I called the vet and told him I was pretty sure it was more than just parasites.

He had the kittens come in, and after a couple of tests, discovered they had FPV (Feline Panleukopenia Virus), a terrible disease that attacks rapidly dividing cells. With no known cure, there was only a 5 percent chance the kitties would survive.

He said, "We'll keep them for seven days, and if they survive, there is a very good chance they will make it."

Andréanne and I stepped back and waited, without any expectations.

Day one passed, and they were okay. Two, and their condition was still stable. During this time, I continued to consult the vet about the safety of our other new rescue, the one someone left near death on our doorstep, who had yet to get a vaccine for this disease.

"It's highly contagious with other cats. The best thing you can do is monitor him for the next three to five days. If he gets diarrhea, bring him in immediately, because after that starts, he won't have much time. It starts with diarrhea, then vomiting, then loss of appetite, then, well…" He paused for a long moment before he answered the cold, hard truth: "Death."

After I got off the phone with him, I was concerned our other cat may have contracted the illness from the infected kittens. But then my mind wandered to Bob and Wendy.

The vet said diarrhea was the first noticeable sign of illness, which could appear in only a few days. After that, they'd experience vomiting and loss of appetite, just before death came to take them, a mere one week later. Yet, we had already had these cats for almost three weeks, and they were still alive.

Then I had flashbacks to the first few days of week one with the cats, when Wendy, the noticeably weaker of the two newcomers, had lost her appetite. When that happened, even though we didn't know she had this rare disease, we knew Wendy was fighting to live, or perhaps better put, deciding if she wanted to live. So with that, we prescribed the best medicine we knew for someone who had just lost their mother: Love.

For several days, we made a point to give her extra attention, cuddle her, care for her, and even feed her some prized kitten wet food. While she still had diarrhea, in the following days, she ate more and even played with the other cats a bit.

So, despite there still being five days left to see if the kittens would make it, I was pretty positive they already had. It all happened that first week when we loved them through their struggle and helped them want to live.

Love as Medicine

This is the power of love. It gives us the strength and the will to carry on.

By the morning of day seven, we were pretty sure the cats had made it out. Yet, I was alarmed to findWendy's health had taken a turn for the worse; her breath was shallow, her body was frail, and she would not eat.

I quickly made arrangements to get off work, and that afternoon, I brought her trembling body home, where I held her just before she passed.

It was too late for Wendy.

A couple of days later, her brother Bob, the stronger of the two, came back screaming with life. And we could tell right away, he was crying for his sister. While we did our best to love him, we had to keep him locked in a cage because he was still contagious to our other cats.

This broke our hearts, and unfortunately, it broke Bob's, too. In six short days, this high-energy, plump kitten, which the vets were certain would live, turned into a frail, meek creature without the will to go on, and he passed.

Love and Loss

As I reflect on the brief lives of these two creatures, I am still making sense of it all.

When I first started writing this story, my initial premise was about the power of love and how it gives us the strength and will to carry on.

While I still believe that to be true, after the two souls passed, I am left contemplating how a lack of love can cause us to give up on life.

As I said before, FPV, the disease the cats had, is most active in the first week of contracting the illness. After that, the chances of survival are high. This means that prior to going to the vet, the kittens had already faced the hardest part. So then why did they die?

In retrospect, I don't think they should have been admitted. Sure, the vets were doing their jobs to care for the cats, but there was no attention, no real affection, no true love. With no known cure for the virus, they weren't doing anything particularly special. They simply gave them a little medication to help with nausea, fed them, and that was that. For the rest of the time, they were locked away in a cage with very little human interaction.

I truly believe it was love and attention that helped these cats live for as long as they did, but it was a lack of love that made them give up on life. Being alone and isolated literally killed them.

I'll admit, I still feel pretty raw about Bob's loss, and continue to question if I could have done more. Because on reflection, when he came home, I was much like the vets. I would feed him, clean him, pick up after him, and pet him some, but overall, taking care of him turned into another task on the long list of things for me to do. Yet, he had come home without a sister to turn to, not permitted to interact with the other cats, and locked in a cage with little love to lean on. As a result, that strong-willed kitten simply gave up on life.

It's hard for me to say, but this story has no happy ending. Instead, just a powerful lesson I am still processing, which I believe is helpful for all of us to contemplate.

Love and connection can lift us up, and the lack of them can make us give up.

And right now, with all the chaos and craziness in the world, there are so many hurting souls out there, feeling isolated and alone.

While we're all busy with so much going on, taking some extra time to reach out and connect with those we know are having a hard time can make the difference between someone giving up and carrying on.

A Call to Love

Personally, in my work as a counselor, again and again, I've seen firsthand how someone's caring attention and loving affirmation can make the difference between someone giving up and holding on.

And the research supports this, showing that love and close emotional bonds are linked to lower rates of depression, anxiety, and suicide, while encouraging greater resilience in the face of stress.

This is the power of love, and I truly believe it is the most powerful prescription.

With this in mind, my prayer for us all is that, despite the whirlwind of tasks that need to get done, we still make space to open our hearts and take the time to reach out to those tender souls who could use a little love.

This could be something as simple as a phone call to tell someone you're thinking of them, or a surprise visit to take them to lunch. Whatever it is, big or small, these gestures of love and care have a profound impact. They have the power to give hope when everything within someone wants to give up.

With this in mind, in today's trying times, let us be those beacons of hope and offer one of life's greatest medicines—let us offer love.

With that, I will leave you with three final words, which I hope you take and share with all those you meet:

I love you.

Truly, I do. And if you ever need anything, please do reach out.

Questions for Reflection

- Who do you know who could use a little bit of TLC right now?
- What's one thing you can do to help brighten their day?
- When will you do it?

PART III
LOVE AND THE LAND

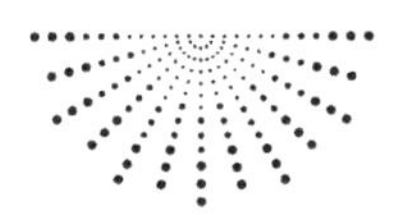

28
LOVE FOR NATURE

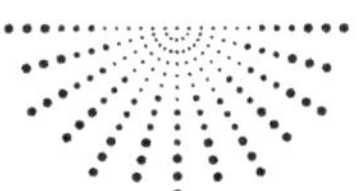

As we deepen our exploration of love, I would like to point to a very important relationship often neglected in our modern world—our relationship with the natural world.

Mother Earth, or Pachamama, as the ancient Incas called her, is one of the greatest examples of selfless service we know. Like a great mother, see how she tirelessly gives. Everything you see, from the paper in this book, the home in which you sleep, the food in your fridge, the roads you travel, and even the very air you breathe right this moment, is a result of Nature giving freely of herself. Is this not one of the greatest examples of love we see?

For thousands of years, our ancestors shared a deep reverence for the land. Mind you, the degrees of separation were not that far off. They grew their own food, fetched their own water, and faced the raw and rugged terrain in the most beautiful of ways, and as a result, they understood the importance of maintaining balance with the natural world by only taking what they needed. They rotated crops, avoided overfishing, and lived harmoniously with the seasons and natural resources. Moreover, being intimately connected with the land, people were more connected to their community. When crops needed harvesting, the entire village would come to share in the labor. If a home needed to be built, the community would band together to make it happen. In turn, this deep connection with the land was not only good for the earth, it was also good for us.

However, since the industrial revolution, globalization, and the many advances in technology, our intimate relationship with the earth has been far removed. Nowadays, children are more likely to think that food grows in grocery stores and milk comes from cartons rather than the earth itself. While we used to harvest crops ourselves or purchase them from our nearby neighbors, now, we get them from farmers thousands of miles away. And rather than sitting around a fire hearing stories under the stars with our community, we sit indoors alone under the dim artificial light of our phones. Moreover, in our increasingly urbanized world, where nearly 50 percent of the population dwells, this relationship with the land and a greater community has almost been severed entirely.

This severed connection has a big cost because when we see the earth as separate, as opposed to sacred, it becomes a resource to be exploited rather than a relative to be protected; the consequence is the overuse of natural resources, deforestation, pollution, the loss of biodiversity, and climate change. Turn on your TV, and look at the latest forest fire, the earthquakes, and the freak floods, and you'll see the overwhelming price we're paying for this disconnection. The earth is suffering. However, since we are intimately connected to it, so are we.

Look at the rising rates of stress, depression, anxiety, and chronic illness due to such sedentary lifestyles. Do you really think these issues are separate? Is the loss of community support and an engaged lifestyle not part of this mental health pandemic we currently find ourselves in? We're not separate. The health and well-being of the earth are intimately related to our health and well-being.

Thus, if we want to be healthy and we want to be happy, we'd be wise to open up our hearts, let our love grow far beyond just humans, and extend it out to include the animals, the elements, and all things on this earth.

29
LEARNING FROM THE LAND

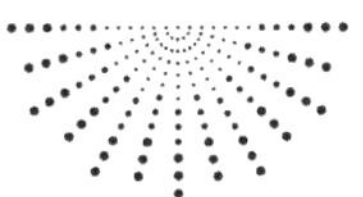

Our driver honked obnoxiously as our charcoal black van drifted around a bend of the one-lane mountain road. Holding my breath as we turned each corner, I silently prayed that no oncoming traffic would come. With one slight shift, we would fall 3,500 feet and say our final farewell to this earth, and frankly, I still felt like I had some good years ahead.

Now you might be asking what brought us through such rugged terrain, and the answer lies in an ancient Quechuan ceremony that only happens once a year, high in the sky on the top of a sacred mountain.

After two hours of swirling like a snake up the peak, our eclectic caravan of locals and world travelers pulled up to a small rushing river that flowed from the base of a great green valley. We still had 1,500 feet to go, and it would have to be made on foot. And that's when the mountain's first test began...

The struggle struck me the minute my foot exited the vehicle. The air was so thin it felt like I was breathing molasses. A little shaky and lightheaded, I followed our group skip across a rocky stream into a trail-less path up a steep valley. With the high altitude, every step felt like there was a fist squeezing my lungs like a sponge. I continued to move forward, but my vision began to blur. Tested by the elements, my mind began to race like the fierce wind around us.

"Breathe!" I commanded my attention, doing my best to center myself.

The act gave me some ground to walk on. But after a few strides, my mind barked back, complaining that I couldn't. Again, I tried, and for a few short moments, I could bear my steps. But again, with every advance I made, my mind came contesting back.

And it appeared that I was not the only one being tested by the terrain. After about an hour's walk, a young Peruvian woman fell to her knees from lack of oxygen at this altitude.

I rushed beside her and placed my hand on her shoulder. "Are you okay?" I called to her.

"I'm fine," she replied through foggy eyes. Then she turned to grab my hand and yanked on it like a rope to pull herself up. But after standing for only a few seconds, she collapsed to the ground and vomited clear liquid.

I patted her back as I looked across the land, wondering how much further we would have to travel.

Rising together, we pushed our way forward while dark clouds gathered in the distance. A coming storm almost mirrored my mind. I so wanted to just "be here" because I knew that's where my peace resided. But try as I might, my thoughts kept searching the future for freedom. And to make matters even worse, I judged my mind for its wild antics.

But as we walked, something beautiful touched my heart and stopped the war with the moment. It was a wise woman, a sage, a reflection of the mountain itself. Her name I did not know, but with reverence, they called her the leader, *la Kamachiq,* the leader. She was one of our guides on that voyage.

An old Quechua woman, she came from a long lineage of healers. She was three people ahead of me when she turned to take the vibrant vista in. Standing about five feet tall, she beamed a smile that resembled the sun and held eyes that sparkled with childlike wonder and awe. Staring upon her face, I could not find a single burden etched there. Not one worry of the past, or tinge of fear for the future, nothing. On that luminous face, I saw the peace that comes from being completely absorbed in the moment, and as I did, my soul longed for the sweet, sweet joy that shone through her eyes.

Quickly after gracing me with her glow, she turned back and bounced up the mountain in her traditional red blouse and black skirt with a colorful rainbow tapestry strapped to her back like a knapsack.

Finally, we approached a small lagoon where Kamachiq and two of her helpers invited us to stop to prepare a *despacho* ceremony, a traditional Quechua ritual of thanksgiving and offering to the land and to the Great Spirit within all things.

Just like it is important to offer gifts of gratitude when entering someone else's home, the wise grandmother and her helpers laid down a colorful blanket to offer presents of food, trinkets, and special items as gifts to all of creation before carrying on to the community.

Gathering in a circle, the ceremony began with one of the helpers beating a drum. Then, as one, we each turned to the seven directions sequentially to call in the energies of that place. From the east, to the south, west, north, to the earth below, the sky above, and the Great Spirit within, we turned.

Then, with the fullness of Spirit in our breath, we sat down on the warm earth and meditated to the sound of the wind. Then, one by one, we placed our gifts of offering on the blanket before us. And by the time we had laid down the last treasure, my heart and mind were filled with a loving presence larger than the land we walked upon.

And I believe the mountain's spirit was respectfully waiting for us to finish. Because the very minute the ceremony was over, the black cloud that loomed over us roared with a triumphant thunder. Then white pellets of hail pounded upon the valley. The majority of our company scattered frantically, searching their knapsacks for their plastic ponchos. But even with the dark clouds pouring upon us, Kamachiq's face still shone with a smile.

Thankfully, the general chaos of the rain only lasted a few minutes and soon transformed into a kind and gentle patter. Following behind Kamachiq, I marveled at the grace with which she carried herself. It appeared as if she was walking on a calm cloud. And again, deep within, I longed for such tranquility because it seemed that my mind, in comparison, was like a wild dog trapped in a cage.

On we marched, and after some time, I looked far off into the distance and saw vibrant colors of blues, reds, and yellows painted on top of a far-off peak. But I realized those lively colors were the ponchos of the people from the community we were here to see, and they were all huddled together, keeping warm from the rain.

We had arrived! Well almost. We still had a far distance to get to them and one last bend to climb. So, as a unit, our company pushed toward our destination against the chilly mountain winds and began climbing the towering hill to them. On the top, a hundred or so faces sat in little circles of five or more. Despite the sting of the rain and cool air, everyone was smiling. And they welcomed us with the same warmth one gives to dear friends and family. With full grins, the men and women gave us hearty handshakes. "Please sit!" a member of the community gestured with an open palm, inviting us to join them on the earth. We accepted, and then, as soon as we sat, someone placed a colorful tapestry in the center of us and laid out a feast of freshly roasted potatoes and corn.

I let the warm meal enter my cold body, and a smile grew on my heart as large as my face. The people were so present, so simple, yet so happy. Connected to the land, many looked to the clouds, puckered their lips, and blew with great force in what seemed to be an attempt to push away the rain, and it seemed to work.

Then I turned and watched a large group of men gathering in lines. They were preparing for the annual ceremony we had come to participate in. They began slapping on hand-embroidered regalia, which consisted of long white cloth draped down their hands. Snow white wings from the traditional bird of this territory were fastened to their backs and sewn atop their red-felted helmets. It was supposed to be symbolic of the metamorphosis that would take place, for on that magical day, the men would deepen their connection with nature, shed their worldly forms, and transform into the flying white bird of this land.

After some time, various community members stood and started to walk down the steep hill towards the next peak across the valley. "OK, it's time to go," one of Kamachiq`s helpers remarked as he stood brushing his pants clean of any scraps of food.

I thought the ceremony would take place here, but I guessed I was wrong, so I followed, but wondered where we were going. It had been about ten minutes of traveling through the terrain when I realized the men preparing for the ceremony had stayed behind.

"Why are we walking ahead of them?" I questioned.

"To get a head start!" The helper chuckled. "They are going to win anyway!" I shook my head, not really sure what he meant. But I understood very soon.

Suddenly, powerful drums began to beat from behind me, and then the warriors' celebrating cries filled the sky. I turned around and marveled as human-sized white birds ran like shooting stars up and down the valley's troubling terrain. After every eight beats, they roared more robustly, raised their wings to the sky, and spun in unison. And within a few moments, they surpassed us and continued to fly to the next far-off hill. They were so fast; it took us 15 minutes to just catch up. And when we did, the giant birds gifted us with their great smiles and nods as we passed them.

From the top of the cliff, I could see so much more, and what I saw amazed me even more. It appeared to be one of the world's first stadiums. Like fans at a ball game across the valley, hundreds more people sat on the neighboring hill, and the grassy knoll was their bleachers.

It turned out this mass of people was made up of three of the nearby communities, and they were all here to commune and celebrate this ancient ceremony together. And with the energy of the masses, you could feel the excitement rising in the air, for in a few moments, the birds would come flying down the mountain and into the clearing where they would offer a sacred dance to the land and to its people.

But before that, we crossed the valley to join the herd. The sharp wind continued to sting, and my body resisted our steps. But as we climbed the final bend, a mighty warmth came over me as I looked at the people's peaceful faces. Wearing nearly half my clothing, they sat untroubled, smiling, with eager yet patient eyes for what was to come. Settling on a seat of rocks, I joined them.

In a few minutes, the drums roared once more, and the beautiful birds came flying down the mountain to the clearing for all the communities to see. Dancing the sacred dance, they moved with grace, making it feel as if each step was one of honor for the land and sky.

After eight beats of dancing to the drum in unison, they turned 360 degrees, chanted in celebration, and repeated the process.

Eight beats turn, chant, repeat.

Eight beats turn, chant, repeat.

Eight beats turn, chant, repeat.

Again and again, they went, and with each round, a building power could be felt. It was almost as if there was an equal exchange being made between the dancers and the mountains and the Great Creative Force within all things. Like the valley in which we stood was giving them the very stamina they needed to offer that sacred dance to bless the land and all of life.

We cheered, and the men who transformed into birds beamed with looks of gratitude. They would keep dancing with this growing force until the sun returned home. But unfortunately, with the day's waning light, our small group would have to make the lengthy journey back before the ceremony was over.

Rising with our guides, I followed them as they made their way through the crowds. Silently, I whispered: "Thank you..." to the Spirit within all things and the mountain I stood on.

But my blissful state flew fast like the wind we were up against. Because after only a few moments of walking, my thinking mind took hold. But not in the form of frustrations, but fantasies. Imaginings of what I would eat for dinner, how I would write this story, where my next adventure would be in the next few days, and so many miscellaneous thoughts that robbed me of that precious moment.

"Breathe!" I told myself again.

And for a few short moments, it worked. I was "here." But it would not be long before my frantic mind came running back like a wild child. And while I kept trying to bring myself to the moment, I failed over and over again.

I couldn't believe it, I had spent the whole day climbing a mountain, and here I was scrambling around in my mind! Then the voices of judgment came barking in like a terrible taskmaster, wishing I were better. And while I was at war with the moment and myself, I completely missed much of the magic presenting itself with every step I took.

And again, my peace was restored the moment I saw Kamachiq`s radiant smile. She was so completely present, so in love with life, it was impossible for it not to be contagious. My mind's grip fell with one look of that radiating smile. With that, I consciously stayed right behind her, letting her presence be my anchor. Slowly and steadily, she walked. Bending down every now and then to pick up various plants to make medicinal teas. And at that moment, I knew if I really longed to carry the same peace as this beautiful woman, I would have to be patient.

Like the very mountains we walked on, Kamachiq's beauty did not come overnight. It was crafted through deep devotion, patience, and time. Every day she worked at deepening her relationship with life, the land, and the plants, and in turn, through her practice, she had become a plant herself, a bright flower with an angelic fragrance for this world. I knew that if I wanted to radiate such beauty, I would need to become slower, take my time.

The land carries this wisdom, this presence, and this peace. And if we slow down for long enough to pay attention, it can be one of our greatest teachers. The seasons have many stories to share, each element a tale to tell, every animal a secret to share, but we have to take the time to deepen and develop that relationship. When we do so, that peace is readily available to us. That's what the ceremony was about. It was a reminder to the people of their connection to the Great Spirit, their deep roots to the land, and their very dependence on it.

While the Western world may not like the word "dependence," like it or not, unless we are highly advanced beings that can live on universal energy alone, we are dependent on the earth. And no matter how many technological advancements we make, we still need the earth. She, like a great mother, gives us the food, the fuel, and the very stuff we need to engineer all the toys we as a species are so proud of. Think about it. Where would we be without this beautiful planet?

But perhaps I am wrong; some say we will find a way to live on Mars. Maybe that's true. But really, is that the world we want to live in?

Not me, and I find it a shame so many of us have yet to develop that intimate relationship with this beautiful blue planet. And that's probably because our cultural story has turned the earth into a resource, as opposed to a living being, with a consciousness, a soul, and part of the Great Spirit, to which we are all connected.

I believe one of the greatest gifts Indigenous traditions around the globe can offer this world is the reminder of our close connection with all of life, that everything is our kin, that the rocks, plants, trees, and animals are part of us, and as such, are entitled to just as much respect as our neighbors.

It's worth noting that this view of an interconnected universe is not limited to Indigenous traditions and is found in spiritual and philosophical traditions around the globe. This view is even widely accepted in our sciences, where the principles of quantum mechanics express that particles are all interconnected on a subatomic level. Put simply, while we may feel separate, we are like cells in this universal body.

I know this may be a radical shift for some and may not even make sense to others. But it is worth entertaining the thought and imagining how living with this worldview would transform our culture.

Think about it for a moment with me.

When we acknowledge our interconnectedness with all of life and that everything is sacred, our thoughts and actions toward the world dramatically change. It is hard to clear-cut a whole forest when we see that the trees we want to log are actually part of us. It is difficult to take more than we need when we see that our greed is causing great suffering to our family. When we can truly see how connected we are, taking care of this earth and one another becomes a no-brainer.

Moreover, perhaps if we lived with this worldview, we too would gain that same peace and happiness I saw on the faces of that community in the highlands of Peru. But it will take time.

Because, as a culture, we have been disconnected from the land. So perhaps we need more reminders, rituals, and ceremonies that help us to remember our deep relationship with all of life. Or perhaps, like any healthy relationship, we just need to take some quality time:

To walk alone in the forest, sit silently on the land, listen to the trees' songs, hear the wind's stories, and simply pass the time and be together.

We can let Kamachiq's radiating smile serve as a reminder of the great treasures that come from deepening that connection. It won't happen overnight; just like these ceremonies and the mountains in which they take place, they have grown in strength over the years. And as such, so can that deepening relationship with this beautiful life. It will take time, practice, and patience, but any worthwhile relationship is well worth that love and effort.

I pray that through offering such love, we, as people, culture, and society, begin to glow just as bright and beautiful as Kamachiq.

WISDOM FROM THE WINTER WALKS

~

The cool air kisses my face as I walk
through the evening's embrace.
Tap. Tap. Tap.
My feet go as I move.
The background chatter of my mind is
fighting hard to be front and center.
I do my best to drown them out.
I say my mantra,
"Thank you" "Thank you" "Thank you"
with each moving step.
It works for some time,
but there I go again, right back in my mind,
planning my long list of to-dos and looking
for solutions to all my problems.
"How many moments have I missed?" I wonder
from not being here.
How many sunsets lost,
laughs with loved ones,
moments of awe
were never fully touched
because of this addiction to thinking?

I come back to my breath and
clench the beads I'm carrying in my hands.
Why would I want to be
anywhere else but here?
I breathe in and out,
in and out,
in and out...
I rest in this moment,
and when I do, I see just how miraculous
this life really is.
The snow takes on a new texture, like satin,
and sparkles in the evening light.
I hear my feet click on the ground with
the rhythmic crunching sound.
And oh, this warm feeling
I feel within my chest—"Man!"
This is amazing!
One word.
Peace.
No goal was achieved,
no problem solved,
but I found all I ever wanted.
It was right here.
It always was.
And it always will be...
I simply have to stop,
breathe,
and pay attention.

~

30
WHERE TO FIND PEACE

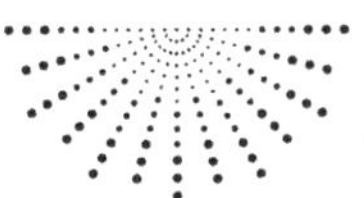

My body tensed as we pushed our way through Cusco's busy streets. Darting left and right, I used all my attention to keep from bumping into the oncoming crowds. The piercing sounds of cars honking and pedestrians yelling pecked at my ears while the stench of exhaust and industry burned my nose. This city's chaotic buzz had gotten me buzzing! And now, within all the clamor, chaos, and noise, my friend and I began to bark and bicker at each other over the smallest of things. The tension between us grew into a mild argument as we walked.

As we pushed forward, I couldn't help but think about how crazy Saturday shopping could be!

Finally, after five hours of running through the constant ringing of the downtown core, we settled onto our bus to make the forty-five-minute journey home to Tarry in the lush Peruvian valley. From my window, I overlooked the urban crawl, so grateful to be heading away from it. Then, looking toward the green landscape where I lived, I breathed deeply, trying my best to calm myself from the busyness of the day. While this helped some, I still felt subtle waves of tension stored in the corners of my body. From what, I wasn't quite entirely sure. It could have been due to the chaos of the city, or maybe the argument, or a mix of both. But whatever it was, the feeling followed me all the way home.

When I arrived at my house, it gnawed at me beyond my conscious awareness. Unknowingly, I was drawn to one of my favorite avoidance strategies: burying myself in work. While it worked for a while, the edge was still there, and the minute my mind was left alone, the feelings of unease came right back to me. Again, I turned to all sorts of strategies to soothe myself. I grabbed a tea and a spoonful of honey; I even wanted a cookie! Something! Anything to get rid of what I felt inside.

When I finally realized what I was doing, I began to breathe in and out and then willed myself up and out the door.

At first, I must have marched somewhat frantically, but after a short while, my steps slowed as the cobblestone road transformed into mud, and a canopy of trees cradled me. I saw a little blue hummingbird resting on a branch. Then it was as if the rushing river, a few feet from me, was inviting me in. I knelt by its side and sank to the earth. My breath began to slow, and my body opened to the calm. Dogs started to bark, no doubt feeling my unruly energy.

"Dear Mother, take what I do not need," I called with an exhale.

Then, it was as if the earth herself was cradling me and relieving me of all my burdens. My breath then became deeper, and suddenly, I started to smell the sweet scent of citronella flowers caressing my nose. The dogs hushed their barking as gentle cool air pressed upon me. And at that moment, it was as if the breath of the earth was breathing me, and I was breathing her. Then I remembered who I was as tears of joy flooded from my eyes.

"Thank you, Great Mother! Thank you for bringing me home."

Coming Home

As I reflected on this experience, I began to understand something deeper about our modern predicament. With the loud buzz of our modern world, it can be easy to forget who we are and where we came from. This can be especially true in the thick of the city. Now, don't get me wrong—cities certainly have their place. I have lived, worked, and played in them for years. Yet cities tend to be melting pots for a materialistic culture, which is not a culture that encourages us to remember our true nature.

But wherever you are, be that a city, village, or forest, there is hunger in the human condition. This hunger is rooted in our disconnection from our Source and manifests as a never-ending quest for "more." Whether it be stuff, success, wealth, or whatever it is, the underlying energy is a sense of not-enoughness.

When we are surrounded by a field that vibrates with the frequency of lack and separateness, like the busy marketplace I rushed through in Cusco, it can consume us. Once filled with that sense of lack, we search the material world, looking for some sort of fulfillment to fill that void. This happens in small and big ways.

The small ways are like in my story when I looked to work and common comforts to restore the sense of peace within. But it also expresses itself in big ways, like striving to reach a goal, thinking our peace and fulfillment can be found on the other end of its achievement. While in our culture this is a normal practice, the truth is, none of these strategies work in the long run and only leave us feeling empty in the end.

However, we don't need to get down on ourselves for engaging in these behaviors, because, truthfully, more often than not, we are just doing the best we can to help ourselves feel better; we are simply looking in the wrong places. Thus, we can have compassion for ourselves if we find ourselves acting out these less-than-ideal behaviors, knowing these actions are simply our soul's way of saying:

"Please, help me reconnect."

Practices like deep breathing and meditation are great ways to bring us back to our center. However, just like in times of great emotional conflict, it's helpful to connect with a friend to support you as you move through a difficult challenge; it's just as helpful to turn to the natural world for that support.

There's even a growing body of scientific research validating what many Indigenous and spiritual traditions have always known: spending quality time in nature significantly reduces stress, lowers anxiety, and improves mood and cognitive function, with studies finding that even a brief walk among trees or sitting quietly in a park can create measurable shifts in our well-being.

Perhaps that's because Nature knows who she is and has not forgotten her sacred connection with all of life. This is why spending quality time with her is a perfect gateway to remembering our inherent connection with all of creation. Mind you, I know many of us don't have the luxury of just getting up and finding our way to a stream like I did at that moment. With our increasingly industrialized world, easy access to nature is not always accessible. But just like we would make time to visit a friend across the city, taking the time to cultivate a relationship with the natural world is well worth the effort. Because, like a good friend, she will silently care for us, comfort us, and most of all, remind us who we are when we have forgotten. And while it certainly would be nice to sit under a great sycamore tree in all our times of stress, you can also create that connection with a houseplant.

Because the truth is, none of us has really left home—we just forgot how to recognize it. The earth has been breathing with us all along, waiting patiently in the wind, the sun, the stars—just waiting for us to remember we belong to something infinitely larger than our busy minds can comprehend. Her hands are open. The invitation is there. Now the only question is: Will you accept it?

Questions for Reflection:

- When do you feel most disconnected from yourself? What triggers that "buzzing" feeling in your body?
- What's your version of tea, honey, and cookies—the small comforts you reach for when seeking peace?
- What are other more positive ways you can bring yourself back into balance?
- How can you deepen your relationship with the natural world?

THE MIRACLE OF THIS MOMENT

~

If you stop for just a moment,
you begin to see just how miraculous
this world really is.
Just think,
it took 13.6 billion years of
atoms spinning and stars exploding
to bring this moment into being.
Countless forces,
both known and unknown, brought it before us.
There will be no other moment
like the one we have in front of us.
With this in mind,
I take a breath
and smile,
because I see that the gift
of this air that I breathe comes from trees
that manifested from stardust made eons ago.
Isn't that beautiful?
With every breath, we touch galaxies.
With every breath, we connect to our ancestors.
With every breath, we tune in with the

Great and Mighty Force
that created all things.
Wow, oh wow,
how special this moment really is!
And with this in mind,
I am inspired to make the most of this miracle
that stands before me.
I hope you do too.

~

CONVERSATIONS WITH A CEDAR TREE

~

Are you willing to stand for me,
like I stand for you?
Will you offer yourself like me,
giving my body so you can
make your medicines,
sacrificing my life
so you can build your homes?
Will you do the same for me?
Will you be a dear friend and
speak on my behalf?
Are you willing to sacrifice those comforts
of foreign foods flown over
from some distant land,
all of which waste so much oil
that eventually ends up in my sands?
Will you cut out as much plastic as you can
and protect this earth with your hands?
Will you avoid the instant gratification
of ordering another book from Amazon?
Do you really need that much stuff?
Another cup of coffee, another bite of food?

Will you stop taking what you want
and only take what you need?
Will you do your part to help
and overcome your own greed?
Will you be my ally and help ensure
that our Mother does not die?
I know it will not be easy
to change these old ways of yours.
Time it will take.
But I need your help.
And I need it now.
Please...
Please help me.

~

31
LETTING WISDOM GUIDE THE WAY

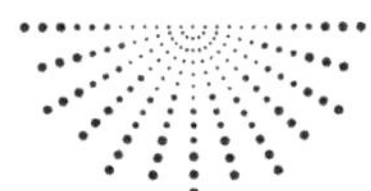

We do not inherit the earth from our ancestors; we borrow it from our children.

— *NATIVE AMERICAN PROVERB*

We were lost. We had been traveling for hours down the Urubamba River in the Sacred Valley of Peru. We were pushing through thick cornfields that seemed to go on forever. Our path, if there was one, was the side of a muddy irrigation ditch that rushed with water. It would seem our simple stroll through the valley had turned into an unexpected adventure.

Trekking down a vibrant grassy trail, we hit a fork in our path. Going straight, we would follow the river and hopefully get to town. But in order to do so, we had to bypass a broken barbed wire fence and walk across an unsteady mound of dirt that dropped into turbulent waters. To the left was a path that led to more cornfields, but with power lines in the distance.

Uneasy about dropping into the water and assuming that power lines meant "civilization," we turned to our left.

The path was large at first and comfortable enough for us both to walk. But after trotting for just a few minutes, it narrowed into a thick forest of corn that pressed upon us as we walked, so much so we needed to wave our hands left and right to swat the stalks and clear the way.

"Are you sure this is where we are supposed to go?" my friend said with a sarcastic chuckle while he batted a stalk of corn from his face.

"Ahhh... No..." I laughed back, still pretty light-hearted about the whole event.

But suddenly, I screamed. "Ahhhh!"

My hands cupped my face, attempting to shield myself from the pain. When I brought my fists down, my right palm was covered in blood. I looked up to find the culprit; it was a prehistoric cactus the size of a car, hiding just behind the stalk of cornI had just slapped from my face.

"Are you OK!?!" my friend exclaimed.

"I'm fine, I'm fine," I quickly replied as I eyed the blood on my hands. We pressed on, but now, there was no more laughter. With the light going down every minute, we finally began to see the seriousness of the situation. And with that, the tension was as thick as the field we struggled through.

The power lines were still a couple of kilometers away. With each step and each bit of light escaping the day, we prayed the road out of there was on the other side of those lines.

Our prayers were not answered. Once we finally exited the thick of the field and were closer to the lines, we entered a small clearing with nothing but more cornfields stretching in every direction.

We were in trouble. We were really lost now, and the day's light kept fading away.

But grace was with us.

Miraculously, out of the cornfields emerged an old mountain woman wearing the traditional attire of the Indigenous Quechua people, a rainbow cloth draped over her shoulders, and a felted fedora hat.

"Mamicha! Dónde está la calle?" We asked. Ma'am, where is the road?

She tilted her head and squinted her eyes. "There's no road here."

Our jaws dropped; we had really gone off track now.

"Then how do we get back to the road?" we exclaimed.

"It's difficult to get to from here," she replied, not letting her gaze leave ours. Then, perhaps after seeing the desperation in our faces, she waved her hand, instructing us to follow.

She then led us down an irrigation ditch rushing with water; cornfields cradled us on both sides. Slowly and steadily, she moved down the narrow grassy path, instructing us when the ground was uneven or slippery. Then, after a few minutes of walking, we came across a small, unnoticeable trail that opened through the fields—something only an expert in the terrain would be able to see.

"Go down there and up a hill, and you will get to the road."

"Muchísimas gracias!" we said, looking into her eyes. Thank you so much! We waved and left.

We traveled down the tight trail and trudged forward until, eventually, we emerged in an open clearing with a dirt and rock hill as vertical as a wall. Using our hands to pull ourselves up, we climbed up the rock crevice. Once we surfaced to the top, we stood on a well-worn dirt road that would eventually lead us home.

We had made it and would be safe for the night.

As I walked calmly down that brown, well-worn path, I couldn't help but see how we might still have been wandering had it not been for the care and guidance of that wise grandmother.

When we first started our walk, my friend had said, "You lead, I will follow."

At one point during our walk, the little voice of my ego emerged and said, "Yes, you are the leader; this is what you were called to do." It was a slight voice, almost unnoticeable at first, but I still remember the arrogance all too clearly.

But after seeing what happened, I was shown how misguided our direction can be when we let our ego lead. It can bring us off course, get us lost, and, in turn, put us and those around us in danger.

The real truth is, we must let the wisdom of our elders and the ancient teachings lead the way, for they are tried, tested, and built on solid principles that will always take us home, just like the wise grandmother.

The ego longs to feel special, and through that, it separates itself from the whole and leads without much foresight for the larger picture. This type of leadership has disconnected us from the earth and is the cause of many of the issues our planet is currently facing.

But ancient wisdom leads with an awareness of our interconnectedness with all of creation, an awareness that each part, no matter how small, is just as important as the others. It takes a humble heart to go home, to see that all parts are important to the whole, to see everything is equal.

But so often in our modern world, we tend to think we know. We think our way is the best way. The West is the leader in scientific advancements and technological triumphs; while we look to these supposed "advancements" to save us, the truth is, just like those power lines in the story, if we chase them in hopes of salvation, they will lead us off our true path.

But the truth will not be found by following power lines; it can be known by following the wisdom of the old ones, the wisdom that teaches us how to walk gently on this earth and in harmony with all things.

Our elders have paved a path to peace and happiness for us to follow. I can only pray we are humble enough to let their guidance lead the way.

PART IV
LOVE IN THE DARKNESS

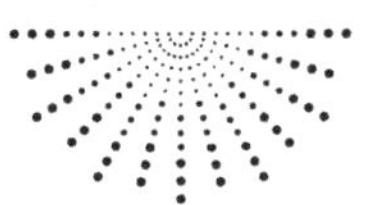

32

DEALING WITH DARKNESS

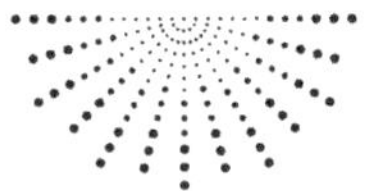

Hatred does not cease by hatred, but only by love. This is the eternal rule.

— THE DHAMMAPADA

As our circle of love grows, from ourselves to our families, to our neighbors, and even to the earth below us, we must stretch ourselves even further and extend this love to the place it may seem the hardest: to our enemies—or at least the people we find less agreeable.

Because, for the most part, it's easy to love when everyone is somewhat decent. But what about when they're not?

What about when you offer a smile and, in return, receive a scowl?

What about when you do your best to be kind but are criticized?

What about when you go out of your way to help but get spit on—literally or metaphorically—in return? What then?

Or worse, what about when people are so swallowed by ignorance that they harm and hurt others? What about racists, sexists, nationalists, and those enacting genocide? What about corrupt politicians and greedy corporations whose selfish desires for power and profit make others suffer? What then? Are we really supposed to love in the face of this? Can we even love such beastly behavior?

If we look at the ancient wisdom traditions, we find that, yes, yes, we can!

Look to Jesus, who, even as he was crucified, opened his heart to the very people who tortured him—fully embodying the teaching he gave in his famous Sermon on the Mount, which said to "Love your enemies and pray for those who persecute you."

Again, in the Dhammapada, the central text of Buddhism, we hear the same wisdom: "Hatred does not cease by hatred, but only by love. This is the eternal rule." Once more, Islam encourages the same sentiment of loving and forgiving those who have hurt you. I could go on, but you get the point. From the wisdom traditions around the globe, loving in the face of unloving behavior is a central practice for living a good life; it has transcendent qualities and transforms not only those who practice it but also anyone who comes in contact with it.

Perhaps that's why Brandt Jean brought the world to tears when he was called to testify against the unjust shooting that brought his brother's death at the hands of a Dallas police officer. While he could have easily reacted with hate and anger, Jean chose the higher road, forgave the officer, and even asked the judge during the trial if he could get up and give the officer a hug. The two embraced and touched the world and reminded each of us of the transformative power of love.

Moreover, this wisdom extends far beyond the books of scripture. Science has also heavily researched it, finding that when we love in the face of difficult people and differences, it improves our health, reduces stress, fosters healthy relationships, changes our brains for the better, and improves pro-social behavior.

In short, this idea of loving in the face of hate and ill will is not just good for others; it's good for us, and the world at large!

However, if we are honest with ourselves, most of the time, this is not always easy. On the contrary, reaching for love when others offer us ill will is probably one of love's hardest teachings.

But it's the place where love is most needed, for a place without love is like a desert, dry of some of life's most beautiful qualities like kindness, care, and compassion. Without these as an oasis, people become hardened, closed, and defensive.

Thus, while it can be easy to turn away from people so far from love, they need it more than anyone. This is why, as hard as it may be, we must turn toward them with open hearts even more earnestly.

Because when we love in the face of hate, we literally feed the dry deserts of their souls with healing waters. In the process, we transform ourselves, them, and the world around us for the better.

Love is what's needed for real lasting change. Because love is like a light, and light and dark cannot exist simultaneously. The darkness of this world knows this; it can only feed on its own energy. That's why it tries to pull us down with its negativity. It wants to bring us to its level. However, if we stand firm on the high ground of love in the face of such darkness, darkness can only rise to our heights. And as it does, it shall transform into light.

Like gravity, this is a universal law.

As such, while loving in the face of darkness is not always easy, it can be one of the greatest healing balms for ourselves and the world at large.

Now, let's explore some ways we can shine the light of love on the darkness we see in this world.

33
HOW TO CHANGE THE WORLD?

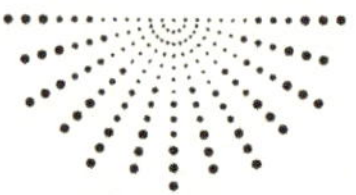

We cannot create the world we want to see by focusing on what we do not want. The great civil rights activist, Martin Luther King Jr., once said:

"Darkness cannot drive out darkness. Only light can do that. Hate cannot drive out hate. Only love can do that."

This is a universal truth.

Just as a seed grows when we water it,

The same is true with all of life.

Whatever we focus our attention on grows.

Now the question is: What are we focusing on?

Are our thoughts and actions in alignment with the world we want to see?

Or are we spending our time complaining, blaming, and pointing fingers?

If the law of cause and effect is true, what do you think might be the effect of using our precious energy to speak and act with the same level of anger, animosity, and hate we want to get rid of? What do you think might be the cost?

Mr. King was able to do some amazing things. His work helped to transform a whole nation. But this was only possible because he let love lead the way. If we want to create such a change, I think we'd be wise to do the same.

How about you?

What seeds are you watering in your life?

Are your thoughts and actions in alignment with the world you want to create?

If not, what's one thing you could start/stop doing today that would help create that world?

Start today.

34

A WOLF AT THE GREYHOUND STATION

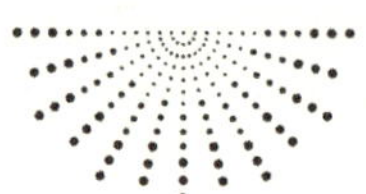

The dim light of the Calgary Greyhound cafeteria welcomed me as I nestled into a four-person booth at the far corner of the room. I swung my rucksack off my shoulders and pushed it to the far end of the booth. It was hard to believe that just a few hours ago I'd been surrounded by the rolling prairie pastures, tipis, and old medicine men guiding me with their wisdom. And now here I was, in a whole new world, surrounded by concrete walls, box shops, and horns honking in the distance.

Yet, even though I was sitting, my mind was still on the move. Vancouver was a twenty-one-hour drive away, and my bus would arrive to fetch me in three. I felt a weight upon my shoulders as I thought about the dozens of details that needed tending to for the new life I was creating in British Columbia.

Would my boxes arrive in time? Should I pick them up before I get to Nick's place? How do I get there anyway? Jumbled questions raced through my mind.

Fixed on my phone, I searched for directions to my first destination. And at that moment, in that tiny cafeteria, something magical happened.

A six-foot-plus Aboriginal man entered the room, wearing scruffy jeans, a white hoodie, and a single long black braid draped over his left shoulder. His cheeks were chiseled, with obsidian eyes as sharp as knives.

Among all the empty seats available to him, he beelined directly to my booth and sat opposite me. Positioning himself sideways, legs in the aisle, he stared off at the distant wall.

My head was still down, staring at my phone, but I could feel tiny waves of uncertainty roll in my stomach at this character's unexpected presence.

The man shook his head and grunted, the smell of bitterness and alcohol on his breath. "I'm waiting for someone."

At this point, I placed my phone to the side and looked up at his profile.

"Oh yeah?"

"Yeah."

"Who are you waiting for?" I asked, genuinely interested.

Again, he shook his head and replied even more bitterly than before, "F*cking someone! They're supposed to be here!"

"Oh," I responded cautiously, wondering whether this guy was a threat.

"You smoke weed, man?" he prodded, still not looking at me.

"No, man... not anymore," I replied.

He chuckled and shook his head. "Me neither." He paused, then asked, "You drink, man?"

"No, not anymore," I said, still trying to figure him out.

He shook his head once more and now replied with a hostility as fierce as war. "What good are you then?"

My heart raced for a moment, but I did not react. Instead, I took a deep breath, allowed the silence from those sacred prairies to fill me, and drew strength from the wisdom of the wise medicine man I'd been sitting with mere hours before. And in that silent space, Spirit spoke.

Looking directly at him, I said, "I pray."

His shoulders kicked back, and from the look on his face, I could tell my words had gotten his attention. He pivoted, now finally turning to face me, and looked into my eyes.

"Where are you comin' from, man?" His tone was still belligerent, but his curiosity seemed to temper it.

"Stand-Off," I replied, naming the Blackfoot reserve two hours west of the bus station, where I'd just spent weeks sleeping under the stars with my Elder and adopted father, who went by the spirit name, Owl Talks.

His eyes widened. "I'm Blackfoot. *Piikáni.*"

"Íkssoka'piwa," I said, the Blackfoot phrase for "good."

"Íkssoka'piwa," he echoed.

He reached out his hand in greeting, but I could tell from his eyes he was still reluctant to trust me. I grabbed his hand and held it firmly. He looked me up and down, sizing me up and still trying to read me. I did the same. His stare was penetrating. And, at moments, even terrifying. But I held my ground, not letting my eyes leave his.

Our hands were held firmly in a shake, and at that moment, I felt called to do something to gain his trust. Still a tobacco smoker at the time, I said, "Would you like a smoke, brother?"

"Yeah…" he replied, his head tilted suspiciously.

I released his hand and then retrieved my red leather pouch filled with loose-leaf tobacco. Then, I began to pray silently for his spirit as I rolled him a stick.

"Can you roll me two?" he barked, more demand than request.

"Of course, brother, of course," I said. "And I can give you something else as well," I added with a smile. I pulled out a palm-sized piece of red cotton cloth from my pack, opened it up, placed a pinch of tobacco in the middle, folded it, and placed it in his hand.

You see, just like how certain cultures offer flowers and fruits as offerings in spiritual rituals, in many Indigenous tribes in North America, tobacco is seen as a sacred blessing and is often used in times of prayer, worship, and ceremony.

"Here is a prayer for you, my friend," I said.

Then, I held my hand on top of his, and with both of us clenching the red cloth, I said, "I give thanks to your spirit, dear brother. I give thanks for your journey and send blessings to you and your ancestors. I send prayers of peace and happiness for your life. I give you this gift of tobacco, so that you may pray just the same."

He said nothing but inhaled deeply, as if he was a child taking their first breath; the offering had touched him. His hands squeezed tightly around the sacred gift, and then he looked at me with sudden respect and cupped my hand with force. A bond was formed.

"Thank you. Thank you. Thank you," he said, with new warmth in his voice as he nodded his head gently.

His eyes locked with mine once more. But this time, they did not try to pin me against a wall, but instead, sought to embrace me. Gazing deeply at one another, we sat in a sweet silence, where no words were exchanged, yet there was a deep, implicit understanding between us that seemed to say: 'I see you.'

"Who are you?" he asked, finally breaking the stillness.

I didn't answer from my head; instead, I looked to my heart. "I am a human being, with many flaws, just trying to be better every day."

"Emmm, a human being. It's nice to meet another," he replied.

I could see flickers of light shine through his eyes, but not for long. Like a flash of lightning, it disappeared, as he defaulted back to the fierce tone he first addressed me with.

"I am Makoyi!" he hissed. "I am Makoyi! (mah/KOH/yee) The Wolf. That's me! Makoyi!"

His stare beat fiercely upon me.

"Who am I?!" he demanded.

My heart raced for a moment, but the land grounded me, and I did not mimic his tone. Instead, I echoed his words back to him with the calm of a still pond: "You are Makoyi, the Wolf. It's a pleasure to meet you, brother."

"Not a pleasure, an honor," he corrected.

"An honor," I agreed.

Our hands were still cupped, holding the red cloth, embracing the prayer.

Then, suddenly, with his other hand, he used his index and middle fingers and began stroking my right cheek in a ritual motion, then my shoulder, then moved his fingers to my left side, and finished his sacred action on my forehead. As he did this, I closed my eyes and felt a powerful healing energy pulse through my body.

The Wolf then placed both hands on the table and spoke like a commanding officer. "You have been marked. The Spirit of the Wolf now protects you."

"Thank you, brother," I responded, my gaze fixed on the wise wolf before me.

Hostility still in his words, Makoyi drilled me.

"What do you see when you look at me?! What do you see?!!" he hissed, fire burning in his voice.

Again, I allowed silence to take us and looked deep within the being before me. As I did, I remembered the words my adopted father and wise Elder, Owl Talks, used to say to me: "Open yourself to people. Do not judge them."

And, as I reached for my Elder's wisdom, I looked past the man's fiery eyes, past the alcohol that escaped his breath, past the hurt, past the pain, past it all… and from that place, I spoke:

"I see a beautiful spirit, a man with so much medicine, a healer. I see Makoyi. I see the Wolf."

As I said those words, I saw the barriers of aggression drop that had kept this man's heart safe from the bitter and brutal world he inhabited. And at that moment, he allowed me in.

"You know why I drink?" he asked, shaking his head in defeat. I didn't reply, but left the space for him to tell his story. "To hide the pain," he admitted.

He then told me of his journey, the toils and suffering he bore. He spoke of his father and mother hating him. How he worked so hard to provide and support them.

"Even then, they hated me. Then they died. Then my brother died. Death follows me wherever I go."

He trembled as he revealed the series of tragic events that had punctuated the hard and cruel life he had lived. I listened fully with an open heart.

Then he explained how he had been a healer back home, and described the things he had done, how his hands were blessed, how he'd helped so many people, but how the burdens from his past became too much for him to bear, and how he had lost his way.

Now, with new sight, I began to understand how his cruel world, with its constant violent blows, had shaped his story. His aggression was but a byproduct of his painful past, which in turn caused him to wear a suit of armor and keep his fist raised in an ever-ready stance to protect his heart from yet another blow. And as I stared deeply into his dark eyes, I saw that even though most of the world may have judged him cruelly, deep down, he judged himself even more.

"Be gentle on yourself, brother. Be gentle," I said. "We all get lost sometimes. But you can always come back. You will be stronger for it, and you will have so much more medicine to give from the lessons you've learned. You are so strong, dear brother, I can see it, I can feel it. You have so much medicine to share. I see you."

An unexpected smile filled his face, and the light began to shine again through his penetrating eyes.

It's difficult to describe what I saw at that magical moment, but the word that comes to mind is: *Forgiveness*.

It seemed at the moment when I cast away my judgments and saw him for who he really was, he was able to do the same for himself, forgive himself, have compassion for himself, and allow the spirit of Love to tend to his scars.

And in that space, we both were transformed. We then shared a meal filled with prayers, laughter, and insight. We told stories filled with teachings, spoke of journeys, and asked questions about how we could make a difference.

Three hours passed quickly, and my bus had arrived. I had to go.

"My ride's here, brother," I said.

"Call me Miína'pi," he replied.

"Mee... nah... pee," I said slowly, trying my best to pronounce it right.

"It means brother," he said.

I smiled warmly. "It was an honor, Miína'pi."

"An honor," he agreed as he opened his arms to embrace me.

"I will pray for you, my brother," I whispered. "Every day, I will pray for you."

He looked at me with gentleness and said, "I love you, Miína'pi."

"I love you too," I replied and grabbed his hand firmly one more time before I looked into his wolfish eyes, and then we exchanged one final stare that seemed to say, *Thank you. I see you.*

And with that, he turned, made his way through the cafeteria, and exited the doors without turning back.

I watched him go and said a silent prayer for this beautiful soul who blessed me with his presence. I gave thanks to my Elders and to the Great Spirit within all things for the powerful teaching I had just witnessed.

As I reflect on this experience years later, I am still overwhelmed with gratitude for the wisdom bestowed upon me by my adopted father, Owl Talks, who taught me never to judge people and to always strive to see the best in them. He did that with me when I was an unsure kid filled with anxiety, aggression, and self-doubt, and in doing so, he brought out the best in me. It was this wisdom that gave me the power I needed to sit patiently with my brother, the Wolf, in the Greyhound station when parts of me wanted to let my judgments take control and dismiss him. And it was this same loving force that dismantled the Wolf's shields and allowed for life's healing energy to come through.

To be honest, there were many moments throughout my conversation with Miína'pi, the Wolf, when tinges of fear, annoyance, and aggression arose within me, so much so that I just wanted to turn away, get up, and leave. After all, I was busy. I had a trip to plan. Hell, at times, he was yelling at me. Why should I stay? Despite all that, I had to consciously lean into my discomfort, feel it fully, and choose love instead. It was this loving choice that helped me look past the Wolf's pain and aggression, and see him for who he really was, a beautiful spark of the Divine, with so much medicine to share with the world. Seeing him in this way became a healing balm for his soul. It helped him step into his medicine, and in turn, he shared his medicine with me. This is the power of choosing love. It is the power that transforms darkness into light, and foe into friend, and it is the power we need to draw from in our ever-changing and challenging world. Let's choose it today.

Questions for Reflection

- Do you have judgments keeping you from truly seeing the people around you?
- What might happen if you dropped your combative stance towards a supposed "foe" and saw them for who they really were?
- How can you apply this teaching in your own life today?

35

HOW TO FIGHT FIRE

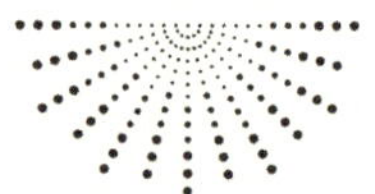

A ball of rage welled up inside my chest.

Just after meditation, I sat at my altar and began to pray for the many souls I knew were hurting in these difficult times. Then, as I began thinking of their pain, their challenges, and the injustices they faced at the hands of ignorant people, that's when I felt twisting knots inside me. I had felt those feelings before and knew them all too well. It was anger, it was hatred.

At first, it was so uncomfortable; all I wanted to do was *get rid of it, fix it, fight it,* or do something, anything to end the dreadful feeling I felt. But something within me told me not to run.

Instead, I paused and turned toward the hurt. Then, with mindful awareness, I did something completely contrary to the dark energy within.

I offered a hand upon my heart and held the pain with love, acceptance, and understanding.

That's when waves of tears fell from my eyes. For over twenty minutes, they flowed freely, but they weren't tears of grief, but of peace—like a child being found in the dark, finally being seen, the light of my nonjudgmental awareness brought those fragmented parts back to wholeness. Because they didn't need to "be expelled," chased away, or made wrong; what they needed most was my loving, caring attention. That's when the healing happened.

For most people, the natural reaction is to push away or push through the uncomfortable feelings we feel. For example, we may hear some bad news from a friend, colleague, or even on TV, and instead of being with the discomfort, we pick up our phones and start scrolling on social media; we compulsively eat or even turn to drugs or alcohol to numb the feelings. But the problem is, as I have previously mentioned in this book, is that those unprocessed emotions don't leave; they actually get stored inside our bodies and, when conditions are right, come back with more strength than before. This has great consequences both for ourselves and, even if we may not realize it, for the world at large.

As the great thinker Martha Beck put it, "How you do one thing is how you do everything." Thus, our lives are like microcosms of the universe, and how we deal with the energies within us also tends to be how we deal with the world around us.

With this in mind, I can't help but draw parallels between that personal experience of hatred and anger within my body and the hatred many people are feeling and responding to the mass polarization found in our society today.

As I write this, the Palestinian-Israeli conflict grows by the day. The tension between Democrats and Republicans is at a record high in this century, and even after years, there continues to be an undercurrent of distrust between individuals who are vaccinated and unvaccinated.

No matter what "side" you're on, everyone feels they have been wronged by the other and that they are in the right. But rather than meeting the discomfort and listening to one another, we scream, distrust, or worse, we physically lash out at one another. But, if we stop for a moment and listen to what everyone is saying, we find that at the end of the day, we all want the same thing—peace, happiness, and safety. How beautiful is that? But how we are all going about it is all wrong.

Now, don't get me wrong. I do believe there are times for force. The atrocities of Hitler called for affirmative action. Even in the Bhagavad Gita, the timeless scripture on life, there are very strict circumstances when one is allowed to take up arms in a righteous war. However, according to the text, these are not such times. For something truly to be a righteous battle, where physical force is justified, one must do everything, and I mean *everything* in their power, to work for peace. This means conflict resolution, mediation, diplomacy, and more.

However, in the case of much of the polarization we see today, it seems we are skipping this step and instead going at each other's throats and expecting this level of thinking to bring about the peace and security we are all seeking. Einstein said the definition of insanity is "doing the same thing over and over and expecting a different result." How can we expect to heal the world's hurts by using the very same energy that created them?

When we approach challenges in this manner, we may be efficient but not effective. Sure, anger may be loud and get a rise in the media, and maybe one of the "sides" will get what they want, but since the outcome was created with the same negative level of mind, down the line, who knows when, maybe a day, a week, or even years into the future, the same negative energy will manifest, but be even stronger than before.

Think of the father who angrily hits their kid when they misbehave because the father just wants some peace and quiet. Sure, maybe it works at first. The kid shuts up. However, research shows this quick-fix approach has damaging effects down the line. For example, in a 2016 meta-analysis from the University of Michigan involving 75 studies with 161,000 children, researchers found that hitting children as a form of correction leads to a host of short and long-term negative effects, such as anxiety, anti-social behavior, lower self-esteem, impaired parent-child relationships, and greater childhood aggression—just to name a few.

Now, with this research in mind, do you think this child will bring more peace into the world or less? As such, while aggression seems like a useful way to get the "peace" we want, down the line, that same anger rears its ugly head, only to create more havoc than before.

The same is true when we push away the uncomfortable emotions we feel within our bodies. While an easy out may be to pick up our phone to get rid of the feeling, or worse, a bottle, the long-term negative effects of escaping these feelings are detrimental to our emotional, mental, and physical health. Moreover, the overwhelming research on the mind-body connection also strongly suggests that unprocessed emotions can even manifest into critical illnesses such as cancer.

What we see in the world today is a build-up of years of unprocessed emotions and hurts from both sides of this divisive story. And if we continue to approach this problem with the same negative energy that created it, we will create a toxic environment that, like cancer, will harm or, worse, even destroy us all.

So, what is the solution?

It's true we cannot just stand idly in the face of this divide. Act we must. However, how we act and the level of mind that governs our actions are fundamental. Compassion is key, which is one step ahead of empathy. Empathy takes the first step on the route to healing and puts itself in another's shoes and says, "I feel you." Compassion takes the second step and says, "I feel you," and "I am here to hold you." That is compassion in the truest sense, feeling another's pain and reaching out with care.

With this in mind, it's worth considering what might happen if we turned toward our "aggressors" with love instead.

What might happen if all of us did as Saint Francis of Assisi did when he instructed in his famous prayer, *to seek to understand, rather than be understood*?

Truthfully, I don't really know.

But I do know this idea of "seeking to understand" is echoed by the world-renowned leadership expert Stephen Covey, who studied the universal principles and habits that create success. In *The 7 Habits of Highly Effective People,* the fifth paramount habit of effective living is to "seek first to understand."

I also know that some of the greatest leaders in history grounded their movements in understanding and love. Look to Nelson Mandela, who said, "You will achieve more in this world through acts of mercy than you will through acts of retribution." Or to Abraham Lincoln, who once said, "I don't like that man; I must get to know him better," reminding us that the path to peace is paved not with resistance, but with the willingness to understand—even those we once called our enemies.

I also know the laws of this universe also follow this same thought, such as the principles of quantum physics, which have found that what we put our attention on expands. The process of germination, which time and time again shows us that the seeds we tend, grow.

Lastly, I know that when I met that anger and hatred in my body with the energy of love—healing happened.

That's what I know, and I have a hunch we might achieve the same positive results if we approached today's global challenge of division with the same love and understanding.

What do you think?

HOW TO BE AN ALCHEMIST

~

When the Dalai Lama and
the Tibetan people were exiled from their homeland,
the Dalai Lama brought the Chinese
political officials to his mind every single morning.
But rather than rolling in rage as
most people would have done,
He meditated on the image of his perpetrators
and offered them love and compassion instead.
He noted that the process was not easy.
It was hard work that he had to do every single day.
But as challenging as it was, that process liberated him.
How powerful is that?
Despite having everything stolen from him,
They could not steal his peace.
Not a slave to his anger,
he was truly free.
And in turn, his life continues to be

an example of the power of love
and compassion in action.
In a world that is so divided,
we would be wise to follow the footsteps of this
great soul and let love and compassion lead
the way.
How about you?
How can you bring more love and compassion
into our world today?
We need your light.
So go out there and shine bright!

~

DEAR SPIRIT...

~

Give me the strength to love
when everything inside me
just wants to judge,
To be kind when all I want to do
is run and turn away,
To live with an open heart when
I feel like being closed.
Teach me, Spirit, to be able
to hold the whole world like you do,
With love and care...
Thank you, thank you, thank you.

~

WISDOM FROM MY ELDERS

~

I sat perched on the edge of my chair
as a wise grandmother
spoke with words of wisdom
I still carry in my heart today.
"We need to learn to forgive those who
think differently than we do," she said.
"Forgiveness and unconditional love
are the wings that will carry our world
to the healing it so desperately needs."
I pondered her words, rolling them in my mind
like a baker does with dough.
I thought, for some eighty years,
this sacred woman has been doing her best
to live a good life.
She's seen wars, death,
and decades of cold winters.
She's watched her children grow,
from boys to men,
from girls to women.
She lived,
really lived,

a rich and long life—
walking down a road
paved by generations before.
So, I figure, she must have some idea
about what makes a good life.
And while forgiveness and unconditional love
may be difficult at times,
If I want to live a good life, too,
I'd be wise to follow.

~

36
THE FRUIT OF FORGIVENESS

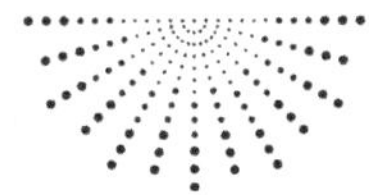

After wearing the same clothes for three days, I grinned when Antonio, my hostel owner, handed me a large black sack containing my neatly folded laundry.

"It's 45 *soles*," he said with the muted expression he wore around his white beard.

Handing him the money, I quickly dashed to my room to change. But to my dismay, when I opened the bag, my clothes smelled like moldy cheese. Honestly, they were worse than when I gave them to him. It appeared he had washed them, but left them sitting wet in the machine all night, a recipe for stink in the jungle.

I went back to the hostel office to express my concern. But Antonio's boulder frame sat like an immovable stone.

"It's not my fault. That's how they came. They were in the bag you gave me for so long that the smell stuck. I even used double the soap," he said with a cold stare.

I gritted my teeth. In all my years of doing laundry, never once had a machine been unable to wash the stench. What I felt really stank was his unwillingness to take responsibility for his mistake.

Already short on cash, I didn't want to give him the laundry again and spend another 45 soles on something I had already paid for.

With a couple of deep breaths, I pushed the mild annoyance aside, left, and placed my wardrobe on the clothesline, hoping the sun would suck out the dampness. Then, I carried on with my day, not thinking too much more about the incident.

I didn't know it at the time, but soon realized just how much this experience affected me. Later that evening, I listened to a talk on the act of forgiveness, which included an exercise to practice. The speaker mentioned that we do not need to condone the action, but when we forgive the person, we release the hold they have on us.

When the forgiveness exercise began, I was invited to bring to mind someone who I had been harboring a resentment toward. Because it was so minor, I was intrigued that Antonio was the first person who arrived in my awareness. As instructed in the exercise, I brought him to my mind's eye and forgave his actions.

What happened next shocked me.

Tears began to flow from my eyes, a heaviness lifted from my shoulders, and warm waves of love flowed up and down my body. I then remembered a prior conversation with the man. I remembered that Antonio's wife had passed and how challenging it was for him. I saw the pain, the hurt, the sadness he carried. I saw why he was so hard, and with that awareness, waves of compassion and care flowed through me.

After the experience, I was amazed at just how much weight I had been carrying from something so seemingly small. Then, I began contemplating all the pain we unconsciously inflict on ourselves when we harbor larger resentments.

The next morning, I sat in the garden with my friend, sharing my realization. Turning toward the clothes on the line, I smiled and said, "It's okay. I forgave him. At his core, he is really a beautiful man."

Then, something magical happened.

Out of nowhere, Antonio came to the garden to inspect his plants. *"Como estas?"* I called to him, flashing a grin. He looked pleased and then approached us. "Beautiful garden you have here," I went on.

His smile widened, and he started pointing out the wide variety of trees and plants. He told stories of kids in the neighborhood, the large snakes he found running through his garden, and tales of his early life.

Then, pointing to the tree in the far corner of the property, he said, "This one even has some great fruit." With those words, his large body wobbled toward it. A minute later, he was in front of us, holding two bright yellow oval-shaped fruits.

Reaching out, I accepted it and took a bite from the soft, syrupy core. Fantastic flavors of honey, sugar, and lemon danced in my mouth as little drops of juice drizzled down my chin. The taste was as sweet and warm as a tender embrace. Breathing deeply, I paused to take it all in. At that moment, I tasted the sweetness of the fruit of forgiveness.

Forgiveness is a profound spiritual practice. While it can be hard, if done regularly, it opens us to the gateways of true love. It frees us from suffering and liberates vast amounts of energy we can use to live more rich and meaningful lives.

Forgiveness does not mean forgetting. It does not mean we condone the negative behaviors of another. What it does mean is that we let them go. Truly let them go. Because when we choose to forgive, we are really freeing ourselves. The Buddha once said that holding onto resentment is like picking up a hot coal in the hope of hurling it at your perpetrator. We're the ones who get burned the most in the process. Because when we hold onto resentments, we store the pain in our bodies and unconsciously walk around, burning ourselves all day. In the end, it blocks the flow of life's energy, makes us sick, and keeps us stuck.

But when we forgive, we liberate that energy from our minds and bodies and allow the energy of love to work through our lives.

Sometimes forgiveness is as easy as dropping that hot coal. Other times it happens a little at a time, and that's okay. We need to be patient with ourselves when embarking on this journey. Because sometimes, it's just downright hard. But when we see just how much we are hurting ourselves through lack of forgiveness, it can inspire us to do the work.

The International Forgiveness Institute (yes, there is such a thing!) recommends a four-step model for forgiveness:

The Uncovering Phase

In this phase, we honestly examine our hurts and pay close attention to the negative feelings alive inside us. This can be a difficult part of the process, as it requires us to bring the uncomfortable emotions to the surface, which we may have been pushing away for a long time, maybe years, or even decades. But facing reality as it is, not as we would like it to be, is the beginning part of healing.

The Deciding Phase

Once we see the coal we are carrying, we can use it as motivation to take the next step. We might not know how we will do it, but here we make a firm resolve to find a way to forgive. We can even say to ourselves, "I don't know how I will do it, but I make a commitment to forgive." Personally, in challenging times like this, I firmly believe it is helpful to reach out to a Higher Power to ask for the support, strength, and guidance you need to help you let go.

The Work Phase

This is the phase when we do the heavy lifting to forgive those who have wronged us. We actively examine the nature of the person and the circumstances they went through that may have caused them to wrong us. With this new understanding, it's possible for the gates of compassion to open to their hurting.

From fourth to sixth grade, I was a bully to a number of kids. The pain I inflicted on the few individuals still brings tears to my eyes every time I think about how I had wronged them. The thing is, while I was troubling those kids at school, I was suffering the same struggles at home with my older brother. I simply passed on what I knew. While I am not saying this to condone what I did, I share it as a point of reflection on the nature of pain. Because in the end, when we dig deep into the lives of the people who have wronged us (and, yes, sometimes it takes lots of digging), we find that indeed, "hurt people, hurt people."

In this phase, we bring in the heart of forgiveness, which is acceptance of the pain that has been dealt us. This does not mean we accept what the person has done as just, but rather we embrace a willingness to feel the pain deeply. Once we do that, we realize just how much it actually hurts and never want to pass it on to anyone, even the ones who have wronged us.

The Outcome/Deepening Phase

This is the phase of joyful tears. We begin to feel the weight being lifted from our shoulders and gain a new sense of meaning. Like reaching a mountain summit, the journey can be difficult. But the blessing of forgiveness is well worth every effort. In this step, we grab hold of the gift gained from the challenge, and, like an alchemist, we transform the hot coal into gold.

And in the end, really, that gold is love. Think about the genuine connection shared between Antonio and me. None of that would have happened had I held onto my resentments. Because every hurt we hold becomes like a wall that keeps us from getting what our heart truly longs for.

Love is the ultimate destination, always there, waiting to embrace us. But when our resentments and past hurts weigh us down, we are kept from experiencing it. But if we can commit to the path, feel, and let go, we will gain Life's greatest treasures. And there is no greater boon than being connected to love. It is life itself and the source of all good things. Thus, if we want to live lives connected to love, we must find it in our hearts to forgive. When we do so, we will first free ourselves and, in turn, the whole world around us.

How powerful is that?

TO FLY

~

Forgiveness is a sweet nectar that sets you free.
For resentments are like mud that keep your
    wings
from opening to the great open blue.
Don't you want to fly?
Open your heart.
Wash away the crud!
And let the balm
of forgiveness
take you to the sky.

~

37
HEALING THE WORLD FROM WITHIN

I wanted to yell at the drunk man babbling to me in a daze.

Now, what made this situation awkward was that the drunk man was a friend, whom I had just sent money to hold him over while he was stranded in a hostel, 1,000 miles from home, during the COVID-19 pandemic.

Just that morning, I had been a little reluctant to wire him the funds when he asked, because I knew he had a drinking problem, which usually ended in bitter fits of depression. But without me even requesting, he assured me he would only use the money for rent and food. So with that assurance, I felt better about helping him out. Yet that very evening, he used the money I sent to get drunk. And there he was, slurring over the phone about something that made no sense.

To say I was angry would be an understatement. I was pissed. At the time, I was also strapped for cash, and here he was using my money to hurt himself. I could feel a fire in my belly as I wanted to lay it on him.

But thankfully, literally just before I hopped on that call, I had attended an online holistic workshop that presented the Hawaiian forgiveness practice called Ho'oponopono, the modern version of which was developed by the *kahuna* Morrnah Nalamaku Simeona in the 1970s and later popularized by Dr. Hew Len, who apparently used this technique to heal an entire mental ward, simply by uttering four simple mantras as he reviewed the patients' files from the comfort of his desk.

While this ancient practice has been around for thousands of years, it was new to me. Although I was pretty skeptical of the validity of the story, I figured I might as well give it a shot. So as I spoke to my friend over the phone some 5,000 miles away, I put my hand on my heart and repeated the four healing phrases:

I am sorry.

Please forgive me.

Thank you.

I love you.

Again and again, I rolled the mantra around in my mind as my inebriated friend spoke, and something very interesting happened. I began to see mental images of myself over that past week. I saw how I would turn to caffeine, work, and food in moments of discomfort. And while they weren't mind altering substances like alcohol, I began to see that the underlying energy I was acting out was exactly the same. I was acting out of longing, a feeling of incompleteness, a void.

I saw and felt that pain within me, and with the four mantras, I offered love and forgiveness to those parts within myself. Then, when I loved and forgave myself, my heart opened. And the anger I was harboring for my friend was transformed into compassionate care for his hurts.

Now, what happened next, to this day, still astounds me. My friend's loud and obnoxious tone transformed to calm and contemplative to the point where he broke down, literally in tears, over how bad he felt about getting drunk.

He then talked about his problem and how he wanted to change. He then committed to change. And while it didn't happen overnight, and he had to call me many times for support during the following months, in the end, he let go of the destructive habit that had plagued him for years.

The Power of Compassion Over Shame

Now, as I reflect on that experience, I am still utterly amazed at the power of forgiveness and the power of this technique. Because I know, had I chewed my companion out like I initially wanted to, none of that healing would have happened.

Research in neuroscience shows that when we feel ashamed, our brain's learning centers shut off. This means that change is pretty much impossible in a shameful state. So while it's common practice to shame someone to get their act together, it literally has the reverse effect of what we are trying to achieve. Because the truth was, my friend didn't need anyone else shaming him—he was already ashamed of himself! But the beauty was that once I approached him with love and compassion in my heart, he felt it, and that loving space was the perfect environment for him to open up and heal.

How This Technique Works

In traditional Hawaiian understanding, as in many other Indigenous traditions, we are all deeply interconnected. So the idea is that any disharmony we encounter in the world "out there" is also a reflection of disharmony within us. Thus, when we work on healing ourselves, we contribute to healing the collective.

With this in mind, rather than trying to change the other person, the practice of Ho'oponopono invites us to look within and work on ourselves by asking: Where do I also enact this pattern? What old wound, belief, or emotion is being triggered? Then, when we find that part of ourselves, we love it.

This practice is grounded in the principle of profound responsibility. Because when we take responsibility for our inner reactions, we stop feeding the conflict externally with our added negativity. When we do this, as you saw in my story with my friend, we are better equipped to respond positively and proactively to a conflict-heavy situation. Moreover, simply our changed internal energy has a healing effect on the environment.

The Science Behind Collective Energy

The idea that our thoughts and emotions can influence the larger environment was highlighted by Rupert Sheldrake, a British biologist and author, who proposed the concept of a morphogenic field—

an invisible field of information we are all part of. Put simply, the idea is that when we shift our thoughts and emotions, we can influence this field and affect collective change.

Now, if an invisible field of collective energy sounds too woo-woo for you, I'm sure we have all experienced how one person's mood can affect an entire group, such as an angry person bringing a storm to a party or a happy person lighting up a room. Now, the cool thing is that scientists have actually proven what we intuitively know. Our brains have mirror neurons that pick up on others' emotions. Studies on emotional contagion show that feelings like anger, stress, and calm spread rapidly through groups without anyone saying a word. The HeartMath Institute has even found our hearts emit measurable electromagnetic fields that change with our emotional state, and can literally influence other people's nervous systems. Moreover, they have even found that a calm and peaceful heart literally has the power to positively affect group dynamics.

The Practice in Action

This is where the Ho'oponopono draws its power. Through going within and finding peace in ourselves, we literally emit that peace into the world and can influence it for the better.

How cool is that?

So the next time you find yourself in conflict with someone, before you blame and shame, turn within, and start using the four mantras.

I am sorry.

Please forgive me.

Thank you.

I love you.

Then take responsibility for your part. Ask yourself, "Where is this in me?" Forgive yourself. Love yourself. Then watch how you and the world around you change for the better.

FREEDOM

~

Forgiveness is a gateway to heaven.
Our hate, anger, and grudges
are like hot coals that burn us with their fires.
Let us remember
that as humans,
Each of us is filled with faults and foibles.
For just as others have wronged us,
We, too, are filled with shortcomings.
But at the core of everyone,
basic goodness resides.
Knowing this,
let us practice the art of forgiveness
and see that those who have hurt us
are simply just hurting themselves.
Because if we hold on to resentments,
we burn ourselves.
We become slaves who have willingly
given up our freedom,
But the choice is ours.
Let us choose freedom.

Let us drop these coals
and give our troubles to the fire.
Let us free ourselves and forgive.

38
BREAKING FREE FROM THE TRAP

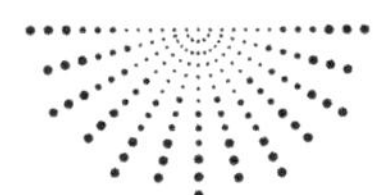

Be kind, for everyone you meet is fighting a hard battle.

— IAN MACLAREN

She scowled at us from her porch through the window as our light brown Toyota Avanza crawled through the narrow white gates to the duplex house in the desert mountains of the Mexican village of Teotihuacan.

My wife, sister, and brother-in-law hopped out of the car and started bringing the various suitcases and boxes stuffed in the back of the van to the second floor—our new home for the following year.

Climbing the rickety metal stairs, I carried a large suitcase up, then a second, and when I came down for the third, my brother-in-law, whom we call Coyote, had a solemn look on his face, one I had never seen before.

"What's wrong?" I asked. His face was in a scowl. Shaking his head, he said, "Your neighbor is so mean." Apparently, while I was putting the bags away, the old lady who lived below gave Coyote a hard time for using the driveway to get to the backyard, which was, apparently, just for her. While he tried to be kind and reason with her, the lady did not have it and sent a long string of negative comments back at him, eventually causing the scowl I saw on his face.

For the record, my brother-in-law Coyote is probably one of the happiest guys I know. Really, I have never seen someone smile so much! He's the kind of guy who waves to strangers in the streets and lights up a room just by being in it, and so seeing him with that frown on his face made me slightly concerned about what living here would be like.

In the weeks to come, we soon found out. The old lady below us was not only concerned about cars driving in her driveway but what felt like everything! Every time we would enter or leave the front gate, we would have to pass by her open front door, where she would be sitting in a little wicker chair, giving us a look of death as we went. Then she would pester us for all sorts of things, such as being too loud, our dogs running around, the way we opened the gate, or even breathing, it seemed! And at times, it even felt like she was cursing us through the concrete walls. Eventually, the nagging was so bad that even my wife didn't want to leave the house on her evening walks because she dreaded confronting the vile woman.

We were frustrated, yes, upset, of course, but deep down, we had an intuitive knowing there must be something deeper causing all this friction. Then, one evening, my wife and I discussed the old Zen story about a man who walked through the woods and was suddenly accosted by a dog. The man jumped back, just missing the dog's bite by an inch. At first, he was filled with a mix of emotions, fear, confusion, and even anger toward the creature. But after a mindful pause, he noticed the dog's foot caught in a trap. And with that understanding, the man's heart opened with compassion.

Without fully understanding, we began to pray for the woman below us. We prayed she would find peace, ease, and happiness. Then, Valentine's Day came around, and my wife and I had an idea. You should know that in Mexico, Valentine's Day is not reserved for just lovers, as it is known as *el Dia de Amor Y Amistad,* the Day of Love and Friendship. With this in mind, we went to the market and bought a bouquet of yellow-tip Mexican roses.

Then, from home, we crafted a handmade card inscribed with the words: "Happy day of love and friendship. May this day be filled with joy and kindness. With love and friendship, Your neighbors, Andréanne and Adam."

When we arrived at our gate that evening, her door was closed. With flowers in hand, I took a deep breath, prayed, and knocked three times. Vicky, the woman who helped the elderly lady with cooking and cleaning, answered. With a smile, we handed her the roses and said, "This is for the Señora. To say thank you on the day of love and friendship. Can you please give it to her?"

Smiling softly, she agreed and closed the door.

What happened next is a true testament to the power of love and friendship. The next day, after an evening walk, we found the elderly lady sitting in her customary chair, looking outside her front door. But something was different; her once sunken and sullen face was stretched wide with a smile, and she had a sparkle in her eyes.

"Thank you so much for the flowers," she said in her native tongue.

"Thank you for being our neighbor," we replied, smiling.

The glow in her eyes grew, and like that, it seemed that a metaphorical door had opened between our shared hearts—a door that led to love.

In the weeks that passed, our once confrontational interactions were transformed into warm-hearted conversations with hellos, smiles, and goodbyes. Even if she did mention something about the noise upstairs or our dogs barking, she didn't bark at us. Instead, her voice was soft, calm, and kind. In turn, we were more thoughtful about how we walked around the house or when to let the dogs out to play.

But it didn't stop there; the metaphoric door between our hearts grew even wider. One day, when I was leaving the house, I saw her sitting in her chair, staring into the distance. I climbed the two steps to her front door and started chatting. "Good morning, Señora," I beamed at her. She beamed back. "Good morning, my son," she replied.

"How are you today?" I asked.

That's when her smile faded.

"Oh, bad," she said, shaking her head. "It hurts everywhere. My body, my back, my limbs. Everywhere!" She said, nearly in tears, before she went on. "It's cancer... I can't eat, I can't sleep, I am always tired. It's so painful." She had been diagnosed over a year ago and had been undergoing chemotherapy, along with a string of other operations. And with that, I began to see where her foot was in the trap.

Then I entered her house and sat in the chair beside her, listening intently as she shared even more.

"I am so lonely," she said, shaking her head. "You know I have fourteen kids!"

"Wow, that's a lot!" I smiled.

"Yes," she smiled back for a moment, only to shake her head again. "But they're all gone. Everyone is gone! My husband, my kids, I'm all alone!" She went on with water welling in her eyes. Then she turned and looked into the distance at the seemingly cruel world that took everything from her. I placed my hand on hers, squeezed it, and sat with her in silence for a good long while.

After that, our visits with the lady grew longer. We'd even stop by just to see her. She'd offer us tea and little cookies and tell stories of her life. She'd share about the grandkids she was proud of, or simply just how hard it was for her. We'd laugh, listen, cry, and exchange the beautiful range of human emotions that come with true friends.

Then, when it came time for us to leave the apartment upstairs one year later, our experience with the old lady was much different than when we first arrived. Coming down with a bouquet of flowers, we told her we would miss her. She squeezed my hand tightly and hugged me for almost a minute. Then, looking deep into my eyes, she said:

"You take care of yourselves. Okay?"

"We will," I replied with a smile....

"Thank you for everything," we said. "It's been a gift living with you. We will be thinking of you, and we will be praying for you."

Her eyes twinkled, and her mouth curled into a smile. "Thank you," she said.

My wife and I held her hands, squeezed, turned, and gave one last wave before we turned and left. Then, hopping into our car, tears of joy welled up in my eyes as I reflected on the power of love and friendship. It was the key that opened the locked door between us, the key that opened our hearts to healing.

Given our initial treatment from that woman, my wife and I could have easily dismissed her as some crazy neighbor to avoid. But had we done so, we would have missed an amazing opportunity to serve, offer care, and, most importantly, gain a good friend.

Because, like that dog, this older woman's foot was caught in the trap. She faced tremendous physical pain and experienced deep loneliness. Her reaction to us and the whole world around her was simply a manifestation of that pain. Like that frightened dog trying to fight for freedom, everything around her became a threat. However, when my wife and I met that hurt with the power of love and friendship, healing happened.

This lesson extends to all life. While it can be easy for us to react to someone's unpleasantries with anger, if we pause for long enough, we will find our aggressor's foot is in a trap. Be it the trap of ignorance, pain, or disconnection from our Source—the biggest trap of all. But, just like us, our aggressors long to be free, to love, and to be loved.

While it's not always easy, if we can pause for long enough to see the trap, we can step outside ourselves and offer love in response to anger. It will take patience, effort, and compassion. But if we respond this way rather than react, we can help heal the hurt. We can help heal the world.

And in the end, also gain a few more good friends.

MEETING HATE

~

When the fires of hatred or fear
feel as if they will burn you,
Do not flee.
Instead,
Let the eternal flame of your open heart
embrace everything.
For the cool waters of kindness, care, and love
contain a power so vast,
They can extinguish everything.

~

39
THE POWER OF GENTLENESS

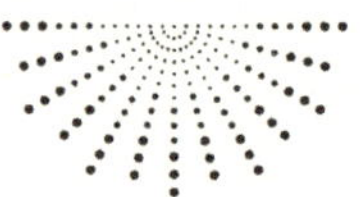

"Hey! Get back!" I screamed as I swiped my arm across the open space between me and the four growling dogs. It was seven at night in the shanty town of Teotihuacan, Mexico, and little Lobo—my one-year-old blond mutt—and I were surrounded by street dogs. We were on their turf, and by the fierce looks in their eyes and their full showcase of teeth, I could tell they wanted us out.

"Get back!" I shouted again as I braced myself for the fight. Doing my best to protect my dog, I slashed my fist from left to right to see if I could scare the pack away. But the street dogs held their ground, growling and barking even more fiercely than before.

Then, suddenly, as if the wisdom had been dropped from heaven, the words of one of the world's greatest basketball coaches, John Wooden, came to mind.

"Gentleness is more powerful than force."

Now, you may think that taking advice from a basketball coach on how to deal with a pack of wild street dogs might not be the wisest choice. Still, you should know this sage advice helped guide John Wooden through the turbulent trials of life and eventually helped support him in winning ten consecutive NCAA championships! But more importantly, this wisdom helped John lead a good life, one that went far off the court and would eventually inspire millions around the globe on how to win the game of life. This maxim was one of his guiding stars. So, if this mindset helped him win, I figured it could help me, too.

Armed with those words, my entire consciousness shifted. I gathered myself and took a few conscious breaths. I became calm. Then, with gentleness as my guide, I continued to circle back and forth with my arms still stretched out, but my tone was softer now. "Shhhhh," I said as my arm and palm pressed forward in a stop signal.

"Shhhh...It's okay, it's okay, shhh," I gently said, as if I were rocking a troubled baby to sleep.

What happened next amazed me. Their eyes suddenly softened, they stopped barking, and they started to back away slowly. Then, almost all crossed the street and left us alone—all but one, that is. Lagging behind, still on our side, was a very large yet skinny brown dog. But he wasn't growling anymore. Instead, he was wide-eyed and full of curiosity.

Then, slowly, with my free hand, I reached into my bag and grabbed a treat I had been saving for my pup, Lobo, and threw it to the hound, who looked like he could use it a lot more. When I did, the skinny mutt's eyes lit up like the stars. He bent down to eat it. Then, he wagged his tail, smiled with full teeth, and sniffed little Lobo from behind. Then, like that, we were friends.

As I reflect on this story, I am in awe of how powerful gentleness really is. It's a force so great it can tame even our greatest adversaries. Thus, it's a force we would be wise to adopt if we want to solve some of our world's conflicts. This stance not only works for basketball coaches and wild dogs but also for all the turbulence in this world.

The force of gentleness is the same energy that Desmond Tutu used in efforts to dismantle apartheid; it is the same force that guided John Lewis through the fight for civil rights. And it's the same force we can use to deal with our current challenges.

But let's not kid ourselves. It can be hard to walk with this type of integrity, and so much easier to let anger take hold when we look at the countless injustices we see. However, before we let anger win, we would be wise to remember the words of one Buddhist sage who said:

"You can solve some problems with aggression, but you can solve all problems with gentleness."

As I have mentioned before in this book, living with these principles has nothing to do with passivity or inaction. We do not need to be doormats and let others walk over us. That is weakness. These principles are far from that; they are rooted in strength and wise action. Wisdom that understands a fundamental law of nature. We reap what we sow.

So, if we want to live in a more peaceful and loving world, we'd better ensure our actions contain the seeds we want to grow.

Thus, with those thoughts in mind, may you meet this day with gentleness, kindness, and care toward all beings, knowing that, like that skinny brown mutt I met on the streets of Mexico, even your supposed foes could be friends in the making.

THE LIGHT

~

Love is the light that will lead us
through the darkness of despair.
It is the bridge
that will bring us across the divide.
It is the battering ram that will
break down the walls that segregate us.
Love is the key that will
open doors to all locked hearts.
In these times of great transformation,
reach for it
again and again, and again,
For it is our greatest weapon.

~

40

HEALING THE WAR BETWEEN CATS AND DOGS

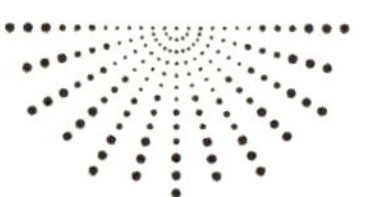

She hissed at him while she bared her fangs at his black, pointy face. He showed his teeth and growled; it was getting ugly, and fast. I pushed them both aside and stood between them. It was the first time the two had met, but conditioned by a lifetime of hurt and ancestral wounding, they were trained to be at war.

Kim, the black and white mutt, was hit by a car in his early years and was also beaten by unruly men in the past, which made him deeply distrustful of strangers. On the first day we met, I was too quick to pet him, and he snapped at me, breaking my skin.

Shasti, our little orange kitten, was taken from her mother before she was two months old and left in the gutter to fend for herself. When we found her, she was covered in mud and fleas and on the edge of life and death. Needless to say, when these two creatures came into contact, the age-old war between cats and dogs came easily to them.

It had only been a few days since we found little Shasti when my mother, who was visiting at the time, decided with my wife to "condition" the two creatures. I was mortified when I first saw it happen on the back porch. Eyeing each other down, Shasti's paw was in the air, ready to strike, while Kim tried to put his mouth around her head.

Like a father trying to protect his child, I came rushing forward, waving my hands in the air like a madman. "Get out of here!" I shouted at Kim. He jumped over our rock fence and went whimpering back home.

"Adam, don't!" my mom ordered. "We are just letting them get to know each other."

"What are you talking about? He was about to swallow her!" I replied defensively.

But my wife and mother both scolded me, "They were fine!"

They may have thought so, but what it looked like to me was a battleground. So, for the next couple of days, I was like a vigilant hawk chasing away Kim every time I saw him hounding her down. And every day, my wife and mother tried to dissuade me from doing so.

However, during one of those moments when we were arguing over how to deal with the two, my wise wife said something that changed everything. In a calm and determined voice, she said:

"We have to let them get to know each other. If we don't, they will forever be at war."

Her words went straight to my heart, and I knew she was right. Humbled, I let go and decided to trust her.

Diligently, my wise wife and mother continued to work with the two animals. Trained to hate each other, it was not easy, as many times, Shasti wanted nothing to do with Kim and would hiss and claw at him every time he got close. Kim, on the other hand, wanted everything to do with her, but not in a friendly way. I still remember one night when I opened the curtains of our house, there I found Kim staring right at Shasti through the glass with his beastly eyes, and Shasti stared right back, eyeing him down with disdain. Literally and figuratively, there was a wall between them, and for some time, I did not know if it would ever fall.

But my wife and mother didn't give up on the two creatures. Whenever they found them together, with supervision, they would let them spend time with one another. If Kim were ever too rough, my wife or mother would raise a gentle finger and say, "Hey, hey, hey, gentle, gentle, gentle…" Then, they would give him an affectionate touch. They did the same for Shasti.

Like this, little by little, as the days turned to weeks, the more time they spent together, the more tolerant they grew of each other, and eventually, they became fond of one another—actually, very fond of one another.

Truly, I was wowed to see how much they grew to appreciate each other. Every day, when the sun rose, and I opened the door to let little Shasti wander out into the world for the day, Kim came out to greet her with a big smile on his face. There was no hissing, no growling, nothing. Instead, they played a little game of chase. He darted toward her, and she quickly skipped into the bushes; this went on for some time until it was Shasti's turn. Turning around, she started for him. His eyes lit up, and his tongue broke free from his mouth; then, with a big toothy grin, he darted away from her and started running around in circles in our backyard while the little orange fireball tried to keep up. Back and forth, they ran at each other until they had nothing left in them. Then, they found a little spot in the shade and lay beside each other until it was time to play again.

I won't lie and say they were perfect; like all friends, they still had their squabbles, and they got annoyed at each other every now and then, but for the most part, they were friends, and it wasn't just me saying this; even my neighbor's daughter chuckled to me the other day as she said, "Shasti and Kim are besties!"

Now, that is real transformation, the type of transformation I feel is so needed in today's wild world. You only need to look around for a moment at the ongoing wars to see we could use some serious healing.

And while drawing parallels from this story for our global conflicts may seem silly, are we not just playing the classic tale of cat and dog?

I think so. And the good news is, like Shasti and Kim, we can heal our conditioning, too.

Just like cats and dogs, we have negative biases. We make quick, unconscious judgments about people, groups, or cultures based on our past conditioning, which is developed through personal experience, societal stories, and even ancestral memories. However, research in social psychology shows that through deliberate effort, people can change racial, social, and cultural biases for the better by spending quality and intentional time with people they may have been conditioned to be at war with.

This is exactly what was done at the Building Bridges Program, a peace organization that brought together groups of Palestinian and Israeli adolescent girls to spend quality time together.

Given the conflict between these groups, you can imagine their initial meetings were much like Kim and Shasti's, with teeth and fangs ready to fight. However, the more time these young women spent together and the more they listened to each other's stories, the more they could see the world from each other's perspective. Consequently, little by little, the walls of bias that kept them apart crumbled, and even after the program, many of these young women from both opposing sides continued to be some of the best of friends.

All of this makes me think of the wise words of Nelson Mandela, who said, "No one is born hating another person because of the color of his skin, or his background, or his religion. People must learn to hate, and if they can learn to hate, they can be taught to love, for love comes more naturally to the human heart than its opposite." This wisdom has far-reaching effects. For if we continue to "other" each other, point fingers, blame, and hate one another, we will forever be at war.

But if we pause for a moment and slowly make space to question our current conditioning and reach out, we see that, in the end, we are not really that different after all. Sure, maybe we have different beliefs, cultures, and skin tones. But at our core, every one of us bleeds red, and we just long to love and to be loved.

Right now, with a divide so big, it sometimes just seems impossible to bridge the gap. However, if a bruised cat and a broken dog can find a way to reconcile and find peace, don't you think we can, too?

I think so.

LIGHT IN THE DARKNESS

~

It takes but a single light to illuminate
A field filled with darkness.

~

41 THOUGHTS ON A DIVIDED WORLD

As I turn on the news and see the divide between people everywhere, a story keeps coming to mind of a woman whose teenage son was murdered by another adolescent. The injustice was overwhelming, the pain unbearable, and like all who have lost something they loved at the hands of ignorance, the mother was fraught with grief, despair, and even anger.

She cursed herself, life at large, and the boy who had stolen what she cared for most. However, despite her initial anger, something within her told her she was getting nowhere by playing into her emotions.

Then, in a dark night of the soul, somewhere within, she found the strength to choose love instead of the easily available emotions of anger. Despite her internal resistance, she decided to visit the murderer of her son every week while he was in prison.

Was it challenging? Of course. Did she resist? Undoubtedly.

However, as the weeks and years passed, her understanding of the situation grew, and as a result, so did her compassion. She found out her son's killer came from alcoholic parents who beat him as a kid and, through a series of unfortunate events, found himself in a gang, which brought him down the dark road where killing another became an easy option.

Did that justify his actions? Of course not. But she found that through her understanding, she could open her heart and eventually even love the young man.

The same thing happened with the young man, who at first was wary of this woman's visits. Having been wronged by others so much in his life, he distrusted nearly everyone and wondered if the woman simply wanted to curse or condemn him. However, when he was met with nothing but unconditional understanding, his heart also softened. He opened up to her, repented for his actions, spoke of his hurts, and even shared his long-held dreams before the days of the gangs.

After three years, the young man was released on parole, and guess who was the one to open the doors to him? It was that woman. Moreover, she even had him stay in the same room as her deceased son. And in a year's time, she adopted him and became the mother he never had, and he became the son she had lost.

Reflecting on this story and the transformative power of forgiveness and true love in action, I am brought to tears. It literally transforms us and the whole world around us.

It would have been so easy for her to dwell in anger and blame. Many would have even supported her and said it was justified. But if she did, that's where she would have stayed. However, through doing the hard heart work, she gained that which she had lost. This is the transformative power of love. It always brings us more.

I believe the loving wisdom found in this story is crucial for us to remember at this time of division. Filled with grief, many are pointing fingers, blaming, and even pushing back with violence. Many feel their actions are justified. But if we follow that train of thought and action, like the distraught mother at the beginning of the story, we will forever be at a loss.

However, what might happen if we approached our world's current challenges with the same understanding and mindset as that mother? What might happen if we did the hard work required to open our hearts to the so-called "other"?

Like that mother, I know that if we really lived by the principles of love, we would transform our losses into something greater. This is love's power.

But as I have said again and again throughout this book, it will not be easy. I stress this fact so we can mentally prepare ourselves for the journey ahead. Because we will need to stretch our capacities and put ourselves in another's shoes. We will need to be patient and even forgive what may seem unforgivable. However, despite the challenges we may face on the road to understanding, if we hold steadfast to the principle of love, no matter what trials come to shake us from our resolve, we will transform ourselves and the world at large.

42
A FIGHT WITH AN AMERICAN

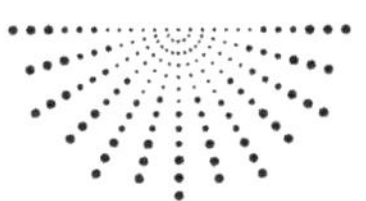

Her eyes were as round as the full moon.

"Oh my God, we got keyed!" she exclaimed as my wife relayed the story to me.

It was Wednesday, just before noon, when she'd rushed to the courier office to get the week-old package that was going to be returned that day. She had to practically fight with the agent to stop them from sending it back, eventually she convinced them to go into the warehouse, pull the package from the truck, and give it to her. While that battle was won, to her dismay, when she exited the office and approached the car, she noticed that the driver's door looked as if it had been clawed by a cougar.

"I think it's because of the Massachusetts plates..." she added when telling me about it, absolutely distraught.

We were traveling through Canada at the time, and the "American" car we were riding around in was a loaner from a friend. This made the idea that it had been damaged in our care all the more distressing. Thankfully, prior to this event, I had noticed those scratches were already there, but in my wife's frantic rush that morning, she had failed to see them.

While there was instant relief to discover that no damage had been done to the vehicle on our watch, I couldn't help but feel saddened that, given today's polarized climate between the United States and Canada, it wasn't a far stretch to think we would get keyed simply because we had American plates.

Heck, just the day before, on a visit to my uncle's, he jokingly said his neighbors slashed our tires because the car was from the US.

On top of this, I have noticed more grand negative generalizations of Americans in everyday conversations, such as: Americans are greedy. Americans are racist. Americans are selfish, and so on. Now, I know the majority of these generalizations are caused by a few politicians and their supporters. However, I feel it's seriously important for us to question whether it's safe to blanket an entire nation given a few people's actions.

A Pattern of Overgeneralization

I noticed this type of overgeneralization in 2015, when the Venezuelan dictator Maduro's corruption sent millions of Venezuelans fleeing to neighboring countries as refugees, my father among them. At first, many countries opened their arms welcomingly to these refugees. Yet, while most Venezuelans were kind, caring, considerate people, some, in desperation, had turned to crime, stealing, and taking advantage of people's good nature.

Note: to date, the number of Venezuelan refugees is approximately eight million. Now, within this vast number of desperate people, it's pretty obvious there would be less than favorable characters. The problem was that their loud and unjust behavior caused many people to overgeneralize and label all Venezuelans as bad apples.

I saw the very same type of thinking towards Russians in Bali, which since the war on Ukraine, experienced a massive influx of Russian's escaping the conflict. And just like in Venezuela, the bad ones left a bitter taste for many Balinese, making them assume that all Russians contained a certain negative characteristic. Now, having met thousands of Venezuelan refugees, Russian expats, and American tourists, I know these negative generalizations are far from the truth.

Why Does This Happen?

The reality is, what's happening is a well-known psychological and sociological phenomenon called overgeneralization. This happens when people take the behavior of a few individuals and project it onto an entire group.

Cognitive psychologists have found that we are prone to many cognitive biases (also known as "thought errors"). Such errors occur because our brains like to take mental shortcuts to make things simpler. While this is extremely helpful in many circumstances—say, seeing dark clouds and grabbing an umbrella without checking the forecast—it can also backfire when facing more complex situations, such as judging the character of an entire group.

One such cognitive bias is known as the availability heuristic. This happens when we hear/have vivid experiences, like hearing about corruption in the U.S. or meeting a rude Venezuelan refugee, the experience sticks out. And since it's vivid and emotional, it's easier to remember. Thus, it's more available for us to access, making it much more likely for us to assume it's common. This leads people to jump from "I had a bad interaction" to "they're all like this."

In-Group vs. Out-Group Dynamics

Moreover, social identity theory explains that we naturally divide people into "us" and "them." While this is far from the truth, we tend to see our in-group as diverse ("not all Canadians are the same") and tend to lump the "out-group" into one identity. So rather than looking at the behavior of a few individuals as unjust, we're more likely to say, "All Americans are greedy."

Fear

To add to this, when fear is added to the equation, over-generalizations spread faster. The tariffs put on Canada by the United States could seriously affect the Canadian economy, making many Canadians scared. Such rampant fear makes it much easier to blame "all Americans" rather than dealing with the complexity of political systems. We do this to create a sense of control—the idea is that if we label "them," we feel safer. But the truth is, this creates only a false sense of safety.

Why This Matters

So, now we know why this happens. Before we blanket entire nations, point fingers, and blame, we should really pause for just a moment to ask ourselves: "Is this really true?"

If we don't, we are destined to fail. Because let's face it. We are in trying times. Times that need the cooperation, ingenuity, and genius of all nations. As such, ideas about keying a car shouldn't even be on the periphery of our repertoire.

Instead, we should be focused on building bridges, not spreading ourselves further apart. While I think it's beautiful that many Canadians are feeling a sense of nationalistic pride and only buying local, if we get caught up in the *us versus them* mentality, which is so easily available, we won't be able to solve the crazy problems we face. We can only accomplish that together. The corrupt powers that be know this. Divide and conquer is the name of the game. So if we really want to "stick it to the man!" we have to unite, not just as a country, but as a world. Because behind every flag is a human heart, just like yours.

THE RIVER

~

Have you seen how the river flows?
She does not complain about the obstacles
that come her way,
Yet her patience and persistence efforts
are directed at where she wants to go,
Has the power to turn boulders into dust.

~

PART V
TRANSFORMING OBSTACLES INTO GIFTS

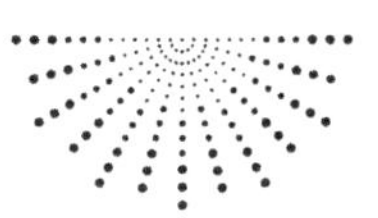

43
HIDDEN TREASURES INSIDE CHALLENGES

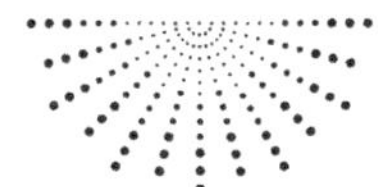

"Life is full of sh*t!" a wise medicine woman once told me with a big toothy grin. "But the thing is, we need the sh*t," she added with glowing eyes that cradled her wrinkles. "Because without the sh*t, we can't make fertilizer, and without fertilizer, you can't grow beautiful roses!"

What a simple but profound truth she had to share.

If we open to life in this way, we begin to see the hidden treasure within every obstacle. We begin to see that every challenge is actually an opportunity for us to grow. We begin to realize that even the very things we disdain the most could actually be gifts in disguise.

Think about it. Maya Angelou transformed her traumatic childhood into timeless poetry. Helen Keller turned her blindness and deafness into a brilliance that inspired millions. Steve Jobs transformed being fired from his own company into the wisdom that made Apple revolutionary. Truth be told, there is always a hidden gift found within every challenge. But if we are honest, tending to the garden of our lives is not always easy. As the story suggests, sometimes, it's just downright sh*tty. But life's beautiful fruits and flowers are always worth the work.

44
LOVE IN DARK PLACES

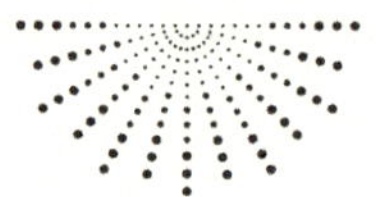

Now, as crazy as it may sound coming from a guy who wrote a book on love, I used to hate myself. Even as a kid, I secretly harbored thoughts that I was somehow "bad." And by the time I hit my teens and early twenties, the tormenting voices of negativity grew exponentially.

Where did these wild thoughts come from in a child so young? Well, I am not entirely sure, but what I do know, as I have expressed before in this book, is that the first seven years of our lives, we are sponges, taking on the beliefs, ideas, and ways of looking at this world through our environment, culture, and social upbringing. This means that even one negative experience in this formative stage can leave an imprint that will follow a child for the rest of their lives.

Yet, I had no idea about that when I was in the thick of it. All I knew was that it felt like there was an ongoing war inside me. And in all honesty, I probably hated those overcritical voices that were in my head more than they hated me! Really, I just wanted them to be gone. So for years, I tried what I thought were heroic healing efforts to expel the hatred inside me "once and for all!" and like a madman with a sword, I swung at my shadow.

However, after many failed attempts, it became evident just how fundamentally flawed my approach was. Carl Jung, the famous psychiatrist, spoke extensively about the shadow, which is those parts of ourselves that we don't fully accept. You know, those less-than-admirable qualities we tend to wish weren't there. Now, in Jung's perspective, if we don't fully accept and integrate these parts of ourselves, they tend to grow in the dark.

But what was I doing? I was trying to get rid of these parts within me, attacking them with the same level of energy that created them: violence and aggression.

But what happens when we do that? What happens when we approach the darkness of this world with this mentality?

We can find the answer to this query by reflecting on how our society treats garbage. We have a quick-fix approach, which sends it away to far-off places where we don't have to think about it anymore, or we may even burn it, assuming we have actually eliminated it for good. But is that really true? Even if it is burned away, are there not chemicals floating in the ether still polluting our oxygen?

This quick-fix approach doesn't stop there; we follow this same method with the challenges of homelessness, treating the people in this condition as if they were garbage themselves. We push them to the cold corners of our city streets and do our best to stay away from those parts.

Now, while we may not see the "problem" anymore, it's still there, growing and hurting in the shadows. But this quick-fix mentality avoids the hard and patient work required to bring about real, lasting change, and, honestly, robs us of a great gift.

What is that gift? The gift of the shadow is our full self. You see, when we fail to fully acknowledge and respect those shadowy parts of life, we lose the wisdom they have to share. Because these parts, if acknowledged and integrated, can become our greatest teachers.

Have you ever reflected on the wisdom of a butterfly? Its journey of transformation is worth contemplating. When the butterfly begins its pilgrimage, at first, it only thinks of food and the fancies of its flesh. But the truth is, that can never satisfy its soul's deeper longing: transformation. So, the butterfly willingly faces its own death. It prepares a coffin and sinks deep into the darkness, resting with its shadows. Unafraid, the creature uses the time of darkness as fuel for its radical change, and in the end, is reborn and becomes one of life's most beautiful creatures and symbols of our hidden potential.

Now, it was only through the darkness that this marvelous being got its wings. Similarly, our hardships, our pains, and our shadows, if used, can become our greatest allies. Personally, I know this to be true, for within me there's a wellspring of love that many have said was even unnatural. While I do believe that love is our nature, I will be the first to say that it did not naturally come to me. I had to work for it. To do that, I had to move away from fighting the darkness within to loving it.

Now, the gift was that with so much negativity within me, I had ample time to practice with the opposing force of love! This helped me grow exponentially.

Think about it, you don't go to the gym to lift nothing. You go there to meet resistance, and through that resistance, you grow in strength. So while other people had to wait for a negative person to practice being loving, I had the opportunity to practice loving the so-called "unlovable me" for twenty-four hours a day with the wild antics of my mind. This is the gift of the shadow.

And what a blessing that was, because in time, it not only helped me develop more love within myself, but it also helped me deal with others I might not initially find so agreeable. For if I could sit with the darkness within myself, I could do it with others, too. I could cast aside my initial judgments that may have viewed another person as "bad" and instead open my heart and see past their shadows. Because, in the end, those shadowy parts are not who we fundamentally are. They are just shadows. That's all. At our core, we are light. Everyone is. Everyone.

Now, I will not lie and say it was an easy task, far from it. Through my personal healing journey, there were so many times when I was impatient and just wanted it to be over and done with. But I know if that had happened, I would have failed to reap the treasure this great teacher, my shadow, had to share.

Now, this topic is a useful one for us to contemplate as a people, especially when we look at the global challenges we face. All we need to do is turn to the news for a minute to see the shadows of fear and hatred running rampant through our society. When we see it, it can be easy to want to treat these larger problems like garbage, hide them away, and just get rid of them once and for all!

But if we long to really change what we see, both in ourselves and in the world at large, we cannot attack these problems with the same level of violence and aggression that created them. If we long to create more light, we need to be that light. We need to be willing to be with the darkness long enough to allow its wisdom to help us grow. For it is only from this place of awareness that we will find the right actions needed to transform the challenges we face in the world today.

So, wherever you are, and whatever shadows you are dancing with at this moment, be they within yourself or in the world at large, I want to remind you that those shadows are not you, and they are not those people you are contending with either. With this awareness, I want to urge you to meet that darkness with love in your heart and let it be fuel for your consciousness.

If we all do this, together, like the caterpillar, our world will transform and grow beautiful wings that will carry us through our collective trials.

HIDDEN GIFTS

~

There is a strange paradox in life,
where it seems that in order to grow
first, we must descend into the darkness.
The seed sinks into the earth before it
sprouts into existence.
The caterpillar crawls
into the blackness of the cocoon
before it is transformed
into the beauty of a butterfly.
The baby grows in the night of the womb.
It is the darkness that is the fuel for
all these great revolutions.
And for us, it can be the very catalyst
for our exponential growth.
So why then do we
fear the darkness in this life?
If we just change our perspective,
we will see that all these trials and
challenges that come our way,
If used,
could be our greatest gifts…

WILL WE ANSWER LIFE'S CALL?

~

If you have tuned into anything going on
in the world these last few years,
You know it's been a hard go:
A global pandemic
Climate catastrophes
Shaky economies
Wars
This is "Big Stuff!"
And at times like these, it can be
overwhelming or even scary to think about.
But we need not shy away from the struggle,
For it is in the face of our greatest hardships
that the best within us is called forth.
Just look at athletes.
They put themselves
in rigorous training regimens
that put their bodies, minds, and emotions
in the face of enormous resistance.
And they do this willingly.
Why?
So they can reach gold-level standards.

And right now,
we are in Life's training ground,
And with these global challenges before us,
she is calling out the best
within each and every one of us.
Now the question is:
Will we answer her call and use
our current crises
to bring out the gold within us?
Or
Will we be passive spectators and
watch the world we love burn?
We should think carefully about our response.
Because the future of our world
depends on how we answer this question.
We may think we are too small
to make a dent in the grand scheme of things.
And alone, maybe we are.
But we are not alone; we are in this together.
All great things were created one act at a time.
Thus, we must remember that every action
we take is meaningful.
Even those small,
seemingly insignificant acts matter.
Such as choosing to offer
love and understanding
in the face of opposition,
Or
Holding your tongue
when you want to lash out
Being mindful of your consumption
Reaching out and being kind to your neighbor
Every action we take casts a vote
for the world we want to live in.
So, what world do you want to live in?
Are your small daily choices
voting for that world?
If yes, then keep doing them.
If not, then today's the perfect day
to make a different choice.

Today is the perfect day to use
these global trials to bring out our very best.
Whatever that looks like, the world needs it.
It needs you.
We need you.
Not tomorrow.
But today.

45
THE GIFT OF CHAOS

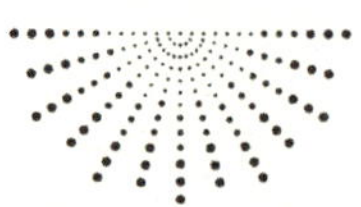

I wandered through the permaculture garden while long waves of grass grew high into the sky. It had been nearly a month since I had visited, yet everything was so different.

A new entrance welcomed me into what seemed like an entirely new garden. Where there was once a large shed, piles of planks lay scattered. Patches of earth sat messily around while garden beds overflowed with weeds. I continued until I made my way to a garden plot where I sat down to pot some seedlings. And I was shocked, because I couldn't even find a shovel to do my work. Put frankly, the garden was in chaos.

Note: Usually, this place was pristine, with perfect lines of crops neatly kept, with organized tools, and guided by perfect permaculture principles.

Yet, the place was in chaos!

Why?

My hands were immersed in the earth as I potted some baby eggplants, then I looked over my shoulder and smiled at what I saw.

There, in the not-so-far-off distance, two beautiful cabins were being built on the property, and along with this, there was a complete overhaul of the land. Pathways were being ripped out so new ones could be laid, garden plots were filled so they could be moved to more ideal locations, and entire buildings had been broken down so something new and better could be built.

Smiling as I looked at the transformation before my eyes, I couldn't help but draw parallels to the times we as a society are currently facing.

Here we are, with political, economic, social, and environmental systems in what feels like utter chaos! Yet, the truth is, like the garden, this is all part of the building process. It's worth noting that a primary principle in chaos theory suggests that things often need to get messy before things can get back to order.

Just like in the garden, things need to be moved, shifted, and even broken down so something new can be created.

You've probably experienced this firsthand every year when you do your spring cleaning—pulling up boxes from hidden corners, piling clothes here and there while dust builds in the air.

It gets messy. But that's all part of bringing things back to order.

The same is true for the chaos we are experiencing in the world right now.

For thousands of years, ancient cultures spoke about this time we'd be entering.

The Vedic traditions called it the end of the Kali Yuga—the end of a time of great ignorance. But in the end, a golden age of wisdom would be born.

Now, while a golden age of wisdom may be hard to believe when we turn on the news and watch the crazy drama of world events unfolding, the truth is that for the golden age to be created, things need to be reorganized, and this means things may get pretty chaotic.

But chaos is often misunderstood.

Most of us associate it with disorder, confusion, or even destruction. But across many spiritual traditions, mythologies, and even systems thinking, chaos is seen as a necessary force for change and creation.

In Greek mythology, Chaos was not bad—it was the raw state of existence before the cosmos (order) was formed. Out of Chaos came the earth, the sky, and everything else in existence. Thought leader Michael Beckwith uses the term "Chaordic" (Chaos + Order), suggesting what looks like chaos in our lives is often a Divine reordering.

Now, I won't lie and say this reordering does not come with a price. Heck, when we look at the current state of the world, we can see the cost is *huge*. So many people are hurting because a few people use their power for their own selfish means. With all this, it can feel overwhelming to look at the current state of the world.

But we can take heart, knowing that within this chaos lies our golden opportunity for change.

For it is in this chaos that the old systems and unhealthy paradigms of greed, selfishness, and ignorance that have been running our world for so long are finally being brought to the light. With that, they can be broken down and reorganized in a way that supports us all.

Just look at what's already transpired since much of this darkness has risen to the surface:

With more people realizing that change starts from the ground up, local politics and community organizing are thriving

People are choosing to buy locally, thereby strengthening their economies and supporting the environment as a whole

With all the environmental stress on the planet, there is a rise of regenerative agriculture over industrial farming, and a desire for alternative energies

Moreover, after being so disillusioned with the world, many people are asking themselves bigger questions like "Who am I?" and "Why am I really here?"

Thus, while the chaos of this world can seem overwhelming, if we use it, it can be the very catalyst for great transformation.

Note:

I said "if we use it." So while this change is inevitable, I believe it's essential that we are all active participants in the change we wish to see.

For if we want to grow a beautiful garden, we have to put our hands in the earth and get dirty. What this looks like for you will be different from your neighbor's, but each of us is responsible for doing our little part to create the change and order we wish to see in the world.

The work required to create that change is both personal and collective.

On a Personal Level

We need to do some spring cleaning with our inner worlds and clear away habits, mindsets, and unhealthy beliefs and patterns that have been negatively impacting our lives.

Like the state of the world, this might look a little chaotic at first; to meet this, we may need to do shadow work, double down our efforts in our spiritual practice, or go to therapy to help us move from chaos to peace and order.

On a Collective Level

We need to continue to tune in to where we are called and offer service there.

Look to your community.

Is there an initiative or cause that speaks to your heart? Ask yourself how you can use your gifts to make a difference, and then go out there and serve.

Because when each of us meets the chaos of life, both within and without, bit by bit, we create positive ripples that reach out into the world and transform it for the better.

So yes, we live in some pretty chaotic times.

But hey! Such times are ripe for positive change. And the gift is that the power to make that change is within each of our reach. Because it begins with you and me, each doing our part.

Now the question is, what's your part in these times of great change?

Questions for Reflection

- What can I do in my personal life to bring more peace and order there?
- Are there any boxes in my metaphorical basement that need clearing? Habits, mindsets, unresolved trauma?
- How will I work to clear these?
- Are there any causes that speak to my heart?
- Where do I feel called to offer support in the world?
- How can I make a difference in my community today?

THE CALL

What can I say about
what's going on in the world today...
Left and right, as I talk to people,
I see an overwhelming energy of fear.
Nuclear threats have turned
the Doomsday Clock
to 89 seconds to midnight—
the closest it's ever been in recorded history.
The economy is shaky,
leaving many of us feeling
like we are walking on unstable ground.
Threats of World War III
murmur in the background.
Put frankly, we are in some wild times.
And while many of us don't want to look,
we cannot escape it.
The house is on fire, and
smoke has entered the living room.
Now the question is,
what are we going to do about it?
What can we do?
Is there even anything?
This question is a very personal one,

posed to each of us by Life itself.
It's a question we will all answer differently.
For some, their conscience may
call them to the streets with picket signs,
While others will be called to focus their efforts
on raising their children
to the best of their abilities.
For others, it will take them to the mat to pray,
Or a combination of all.
Each person's call will be unique
to their makeup.
But we cannot deny these calls any longer.
For we are *ALL* being called.
And answer we must.
What that looks like for you,
only the wisdom of your conscience knows.
Activated in the stillness,
your assignment waits.
Listen to the wisdom of your soul,
and take your sacred stand.

SAY "YES"

~

When we surrender to Life,
we are free.
This is not a passive state
Or some act of resignation.
No, far from it.
The act of surrender I am talking about
does not mean we give up our will
Or not try to change the things
that can be changed.
But what it means
is you stop arguing with the moment
that's in front of you
and using your will
to wish it was something different.
It means you don't complain
that it's cold, rainy,
or that the driver in front of you
is driving too slowly.
It means you stop trying to push away
those uncomfortable feelings you feel inside.
It means you look at all the moments

that life presents you with an inner "Yes"
and you relax and soften into them.
And when you do that,
You will find you develop a poise that is
unshakable despite external conditions.
No longer will you need things to go your way
to wear a smile on your face;
It will always be there.
Because for you,
every moment will become a gift.
Circumstances, good and bad alike,
shall all be used as fuel
to set your consciousness aflame.
Every moment will be a great teacher,
another opportunity to grow.
All this is possible when we
stop fighting what is
and instead say
"Yes" to Life.

46
I DON'T LIKE THAT CAT: A PATH TO SUFFERING

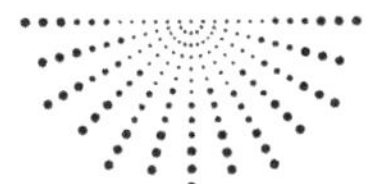

The torrential rain poured upon us just before we walked.

"Did you hear that?" my wife exclaimed with ghost eyes. "Oh my God," she said as she reached into a stream of water and pulled out a screaming kitten no bigger than the size of my palm. Abandoned or washed away by the storm, my wife held the creature's frigid body close to her. Cold, hungry, and desperately wanting her mommy, the little kitten nipped and clawed at us as we carried her back.

The days that followed were just as chaotic as the storm we found her in. There were late-night runs to the city for kitten formula, waking up every 2 hours to feed her failing little body, two emergency vet visits, and cleaning up bloody stools from puddles around the house. To add to the existing chaos, all this was happening in the midst of tending to our newborn son, who was only a little over four weeks old at the time.

And as cute as the little creature was, I will admit there were times when my little self resented her. Fatigued from lack of sleep, in the morning, all I wanted to do was meditate. Yet, when I would go to sit, her little claws would dig into my skin as she looked for a nipple to feed. I'd get up to warm some formula to nurse her, yet after only a few moments, she would howl in pain from the cool air; I'd make a warm water bottle to keep her cozy, and then my wife would come out with my four-week-old asking for a hand. It seemed that because of that cat, there was always something pulling at me. Yet, despite the chaos of the storm, one thought kept me grounded and even helped me welcome the challenge before me with a smile.

"I am being purified."

Like the rain that fell and brought that cat to us, water has a purifying quality. On the most basic level, we use water to wash the dirt away. Perhaps that's why many ancient traditions use it for a deeper and more spiritual purpose. For example, some Native American traditions will use sweat lodge ceremonies to help expel the bad water from a person's body. Hindu priests, in purification ceremonies, will infuse water with healing mantras before they bathe you with it, and in the Christian traditions, they will baptize someone in water to wash away all the negative energy of one's past life. And this cat, whom we nicknamed "Storm," was washing away all that I no longer needed. Just as the water of a rushing river eventually chips away at the stone, life's challenging experiences have the power to chip away at all that no longer serves us.

Let me explain:

Do you recall the story of the Golden Buddha from Part I of this book? Let me give you a quick refresher. In the 1500s, in a small village in Thailand, a huge Buddha statue was covered in mud to hide its value from an invading army. The army took the village by storm and, for many years, ruled there. But because of the layers of mud, the statue's worth was hidden for centuries. Until one day, a monk noticed a crack in the statue where he saw a luminous light. He chipped away at the mud and discovered the Buddha's golden core.

Similarly, there is gold within us—Divine potential waiting to shine and express its unconditional joy and happiness. This luminous part of us can be at peace in every situation, for peace is our very nature. But like the Buddha's golden nature was hidden by the mud, we cover our Divine nature with our self-created limitations, negative thinking, beliefs, and preferences.

Now, there are plenty of problems out in the world that need our attention, but whether or not we allow them to take our equilibrium is up to us. In my case with the kitten, it was not the cat and all her needs and demands that were the problem; the problem was the way I was looking at the situation.

How was I looking at it? Through the lens of my preferences.

Through the lens of my likes and dislikes. I wanted things to be a certain way. I wanted more sleep, and I didn't want to be clawed at and interrupted during my morning meditation, my little self, that is. In other words, because of my preferences (my likes and dislikes), I wanted reality to be other than it was. Now, this is a recipe for a losing battle. Because, as Byron Katie has said, "When you argue with reality, you lose." And then adds very cheekily, "But only 100 percent of the time."

You see, our preference for how we think reality "should be" (our likes) is like the layers of mud we put on, conditioning ourselves to a limited nature. If we have a strong preference for a food cooked a certain way, and it's not, we may get irritated. If we have a strong preference for a person to treat us in a particular manner, say kindness, yet they treat us cruelly, we become distraught or even angry. If we wish for the sun, yet all it does is rain on our parade, we get upset.

But here is the thing: rain is part of life, and all our preferences limit us to a small self that needs reality to be a certain way for us to be happy. But because the very nature of reality is filled with fluctuations, our likes and dislikes will eventually lead us to the road of dissatisfaction. Because reality will never conform to all our wants and wishes.

Now, don't think I am saying we need to put up with abuse or challenging situations. What I am saying is we don't let external situations steal our peace. If we need to act, we must act to make things right. But we should do so from a place rooted in our golden core, rooted in our Divine nature. Why argue with reality and get upset if it's raining, both literally and metaphorically? Just bring an umbrella or even sing and dance in it!

And guess what? When you act from this calm and wise place, you'll come up with better solutions. The well-known Broaden and Build Theory from the field of psychology has found that positive emotions lead to better thinking and creative problem-solving.

Consequently, when we don't let life's inevitable storms steal our peace, we are better equipped to face the conflicts in front of us.

Thus, when we view the challenges that come our way as the rain that's here to melt the layers of mud so we can get to our golden core, then every challenge has a purifying quality. With this perspective, everything, and I mean EVERYTHING, that comes into our life becomes a teacher and, thus, has a lesson, a message, and a gift to share with us. Then we begin to see whatever is in front of us, be it good or bad, as an opportunity to connect more with our unlimited nature, which, by its nature, does not need any external condition to make us smile with inborn peace. This is true freedom.

It's the same freedom Stephen Hawking generated in his mind as his frail body failed him. It's the same freedom Maya Angelou had as she wrote her poetic prose that would help a "Caged Bird Sing." It's the same freedom Admiral James Stockdale cultivated while he was thrown into Vietnam's prison for nearly eight years, using the experience to chisel his character and bring out the best in him. This is true freedom.

Because true freedom is chipping away all that is not us—all our limitations. This makes me think of Michelangelo, the famous sculptor who, when asked how he created the great work of the statue of David, said, "I saw the angel in the marble and carved it until I set him free."

Similarly, each of us has this Divine and angelic nature within us. Yet, like Michelangelo needed to chip away at the stone to set him free, we must chip away all those limitations that hold us back from expressing who we truly are. Our likes and dislikes for how we expect reality to be are a big part of this liberating process. But don't get me wrong, there is nothing wrong with enjoying a sunset, feeling the joy that comes from completing a project, and feeling the warmth of a loved one in your arms. Yet, needing these things to make us happy traps us in stone. But if we are to be angels and fly through life, bringing our gifts in the greatest service to the world, we must relinquish these little wants and wishes and learn to be happy with whatever life gives us. Because let's face it, there will always be storms that come our way. But, like the water, Life's storms can purify us to be our best selves.

With this in mind, as we face inevitable storms, let's remember that whatever challenges come our way are not necessarily "bad." They are simply opportunities for us to smile in the face of life's crashing waves.

They are our opportunities for us to spread our angelic wings and fly.

47
LIFE LESSONS FROM AN EIGHT-YEAR-OLD SAGE

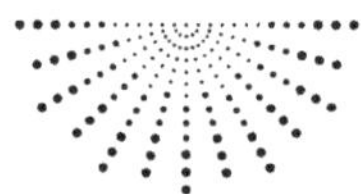

"What are you proud of?" I asked as I peered into Katlin's deep blue eyes on the final day of a camp I had helped organize. The blonde eight-year-old girl looked up from her paper, clenched the red crayon in her hand, and then tilted her head to the left as if in deep thought.

"I'm not sure…" she said shyly.

"Well, try to think about this week at camp. Was there any moment when you were afraid but were able to overcome it?"

At this question, she lit up like a spark in a fire. "Oh yes! I was pretty afraid of making new friends, but I faced that fear, and now I have lots of friends!" she replied, glowing.

I smiled at her enthusiasm and asked, "And how did you overcome your fear?"

She looked down, no doubt thinking deeply about this question. It took time, but eventually, she spoke.

"I was kind to people!" she said with a big smile and a sparkle in her eyes.

I smiled right there with her, appreciating her achievement. "How do you think you can take what you learned here at camp and apply it to other areas of your life?"

She looked up and shared with all her enthusiasm, "Well, I guess I could be kind to everyone! And then everyone would be my friend!"

I continued to grin joyfully as I listened to the wisdom of this little 8-year-old sage who inadvertently picked up on a universal truth to overcome all fear: love and kindness.

Her simple answer reminded me of a 2,500-year-old story that came from the Buddha when he instructed his senior monks to go into a dark forest to do a three-month silent retreat.

Unfortunately for them, there were demonic spirits that dwelled in the forest and did not like those monks being there one bit and did everything they could to scare the monks off. And they succeeded. Not long into the monks' retreat, they all fled the forest, riddled with fear.

When the Buddha heard of their troubles, he prescribed a very simple antidote: Love and Kindness Meditation.

In this practice, the monks would bring the image of that which they feared to their minds, and rather than running from it or fighting it, they would offer thoughts of goodwill towards it.

The meditation mantra went something like this:

"May you be filled with loving kindness, held in loving kindness. May you be happy."

And so on…

They would practice this again and again, until they could viscerally feel a genuine care for the spirits of the forest.

Amazingly, this simple practice of visualization and sending goodwill and wishes toward their fears not only helped the monks overcome that which they feared but also created a field of positive energy around them that was so irresistible that in the end, the forest demons that once attacked the monks came to them and offered them gifts!

Now, this is the power of love and kindness, and it is the same power that young Kaitlin used to overcome her own fears, and it is the same power we can draw from to overcome the ongoing fears we personally and collectively face today.

Because let's face it, in today's world, it can often feel like we are walking through a dark forest filled with demonic spirits. Consequently, without the proper practices, it can be easy to feel overwhelmed and want to run away just like those monks did.

Let us remember that each of us holds powerful keys within us to face these fears and overcome all the challenges that come our way.

Those keys are *love and kindness*.

But in order to reap their rewards, like those monks and Kaitlin, we have to practice and put in daily effort.

With this in mind, let's commit ourselves to doing the work required to create a kinder and more loving world.

So, as you go about your day and face your fears, rather than running, see how you can practice love and kindness instead.

Then watch how love's illuminating rays light up your day, and all who come your way.

PART VI
THE POWER OF VISION

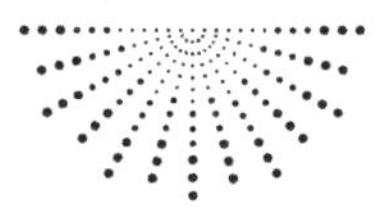

48
BEYOND OUR EYES

Where there is no vision, the people perish.

— *PROVERBS 29:18*

Love does not perish—it thrives. Thus, to live with love is to live with vision. Vision is the power to transform, to create, to evolve, to move past our old and outdated scripts, and to stretch ourselves from the earth to the stars.

Because, in the end, all great personal, social, and spiritual change begins with vision—it all starts there! Just as an architect draws out a plan before they build, if we want to build a better world with the foundation of love, we must envision it!

However, this is much easier said than done. Because in order to do so, we must see past our current circumstances, suspend our beliefs, and live in the realm of hidden potential.

Vision is seeing the oak in the acorn, the community center in the rundown building, the book in the blank pages, and peace on the planet despite our current crazy circumstances.

It's seeing beyond what our eyes can see and living in the field of possibility.

The power of vision is one of the greatest powers known to mankind.

For it is through living in that possibility that we turn our long-cherished ideas into reality.

With this in mind, let us remember that regardless of the challenges we currently see on the planet, if we hold the vision of love and peace alive in our hearts as we take constructive actions to bring that vision to life, positive planetary change is inevitable.

49
CRAZY DREAMS FOR A BRIGHTER WORLD

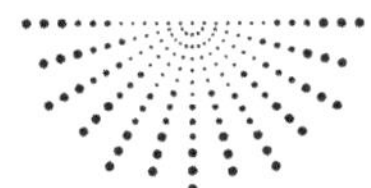

One fateful day in the 1920s, the renowned scientist Albert Einstein said, "Imagination is everything, it is the preview of life's coming attractions."

Perhaps that's why Martin Luther King Jr.'s most famous speech didn't start with a five-step plan but instead invited us into a dream.

Because when we look at our world's current crisis—the post-pandemic problems, a rapidly changing climate, and mass-scale corruption and injustice around the globe—it can be easy to imagine a bleak and scary future. There is no denying it: We are in dark times. But I feel in times like these, it is important to remember the wise leaders throughout history who triumphed through turbulent times and remind us to hold to our visions, despite the seeming negativity.

Leaders like Harriet Tubman, who, in the face of segregation, courageously led hundreds to freedom through the Underground Railroad. Or Eleanor Roosevelt, who, in the face of the Great Depression, rising fascism in World War II, and the Cold War, still championed justice, morality, and the Universal Declaration of Human Rights with undying optimism. Or Thich Nhat Hanh, who held steadfast to a vision of peace and compassion even as bombs fell around him during the Vietnam War.

With leaders like these as our guides, we can borrow their wisdom and see with their eyes. Eyes that were able to see beyond the current circumstances and even within the clutches of darkness hold onto a vision that illuminated the world.

Just as they did, we need to see beyond our current challenges, dream, and walk forward to create those visions with courage and faith.

With this in mind, let us envision a world beyond division, where kindness, generosity, and equality are the norm. Where our global challenges are replaced by global flourishing, and the world on which we walk is no longer seen as separate but sacred. Let us envision a world where everyone's needs are met, and poverty is but a thing of the past. Let's dream of a world of peace, where wars are things we only read about in history. Yes! Let us see a world where corporate greed is replaced with community generosity, and the culture of individualism is exchanged for an awareness of our interdependence within all things.

Yes, let us dream what some may say is a crazy dream!

Because history and all its lessons have shown us that some of the greatest feats ever achieved were all once thought to be crazy. Think about it. It was crazy to think that humans could fly, until we did. And even crazier to go to the moon, until we did that, too! It was crazy to think that the slave trade could end and that blacks would have equal rights to vote, until that vision became a reality. All these great revolutions were thought to be crazy at some point, but because of the commitment and tenacity of many willing to hold on to empowering visions and act accordingly, despite external circumstances, these once crazy dreams became the world as we now know it.

Similarly, if we seek to create the positive world we want to live in, each and every one of us is responsible for holding steadfast to those powerful and positive visions at this time. Be it in our families with our children, amongst our circle of friends, with our colleagues at work, or whatever communities we find ourselves in, right now, life is asking us to see beyond what our eyes can see, and like the great leaders before us have done, hold onto visions that will illuminate our world.

50
SEEING CLEARLY

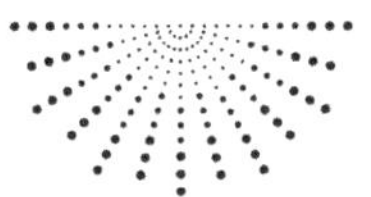

I was a sh*t disturber as a teen. Forgive me for being crass, but it's true.

At fifteen, I was kicked out of school and was on a first-name basis with the law because I was found excessively drunk, running around town, and causing a ruckus.

After I got caught breaking into a liquor store one summer evening, it got really ugly. However, by grace, shortly after that incident, I came into contact with an Indigenous medicine woman who transformed my life for the better.

And while we did many external things like sitting in sharing circles with other young people, going to ceremonies, and so on, I know one of the greatest gifts that woman had given me was the gift of simply seeing me.

She saw past the drunk, unaware, and foolish kid who just wanted to party and get high and peered into the depths of my soul and saw me for who I really was. And in doing so, she helped me remember the light that lived within me.

Because the truth is, all of us, and I mean all of us, at our core, are basically good.

When we act out and do wrong, these actions are not coming from our true nature but simply conditioned responses caused by trauma, pain, and past or present suffering.

As a great saying goes: "Never judge another man until you have walked a mile in his moccasins."

It can be easy to look down upon others from the high horse of righteousness. But before we judge, it's essential to consider that these individuals doing "wrong" are simply playing out an old script inherited from the culture in which they were raised, their parents, and the generations before them. They have been conditioned by the pain and trauma they have experienced.

However, at their core, they are not those actions.

They are souls who have simply been jaded and hurt by a cruel world.

As such, I feel it is so important for us to remember the wisdom that medicine woman gifted me all those years back—to see people. To see that at their core, there is a beautiful, bright, and glorious light that lives within them.

Because it is through this practice of "seeing" we will be able to melt away the darkness that lives in this world.

It won't happen overnight, and maybe not even in this life, but despite that, we must go on looking toward the light. And I can testify with my life, as well as having practiced this for years:

This stuff works! But we have to work it.

So, the next time you find yourself confronting a challenging individual where your judgments flare up, remember who you are really talking to, beyond the personality, the hurt, the pain, the aggression, and animosity—or whatever else you see.

Remember, you are talking to a spark of the Divine. They may have forgotten this, but if you remind them through how you see them, you just might watch them transform before your eyes.

I see you.

51

HOW TO AVOID A CAR CRASH

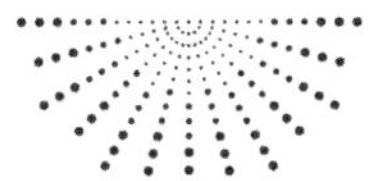

One winter night, a young man was driving down a lone country highway when he hit a patch of ice. The car spun into a wild skid. The driver held his breath as his heart pounded like a gong, and his 3,000-pound machine headed right for a lone telephone pole.

Racing right towards it, the driver eyed the pole in terror.

However, just before a collision, the driver remembered some sage advice his father once gave him:

If you ever hit a skid, look and steer to where you want to go.

With this in mind, he redirected his focus and turned his eyes toward the road. And while the momentum of the past kept the car moving toward the pole, he did not look at it. Instead, he kept his focus on where he wanted to go.

He kept his focus on the road. With that, he was able to steer the car away from the pole. But still riding on speed from the past, the car was still in a skid—but now headed towards the ditch on the other side of the road. But just like before, the driver turned to the road and kept his focus on where he wanted to go. Like this, he made small adjustments, left and right, until he regained control of the car and was eventually safe to continue on his journey.

As we consider the global challenges we face as a society, it's helpful to contemplate the sage advice given to that young man by his father. Because ultimately, we are the drivers in this collective story. And how we respond to the crises we currently face will either bring us to a crash or lead us to safety. We can look at the hardships we currently face (the telephone poles) and be filled with fear of what might happen in the future. We can complain, blame, and focus massive amounts of attention on all the problems we see in this world—and just focus on what we don't want.

But if we do that, we will be just like the driver at the beginning of the story and steer our world directly to the places we want to avoid.

Now, don't get me wrong in thinking I am suggesting we stick our heads in the sand and sing Kumbaya. Because we must acknowledge the truth of the matter. As a species, we are heading for metaphorical telephone poles. More than one, in fact, which I have mentioned again and again.

We have threats of environmental collapse, global wars, and economic turmoil, just to name a few. Yes, there are "big" problems out there, and if we don't do something about them soon, our skid will lead us into a crash. But by solely focusing on the problems we see in the world and by excessively complaining and blaming, we are doing no one any good and are simply driving ourselves toward destruction. Hence, just like the driver in our story, we must redirect our focus to where we want to go.

If we want a more just world,
we must put our attention there.
If we want more peace,
we must put our attention there.
If we want more love,
we must put our attention there.

Again, and again, and again.

We must redirect our focus to where we want to go.

We must keep a vision of a better world firmly rooted in our minds and hearts.

Then, we must take constructive action to create that vision.

While it will take time to see results due to the momentum of our past, if we continue to focus on the world we want to see, we will eventually get to where we need to go.

52

DROPS OF HOPE IN A BURNING WORLD

Take care of the kids, and the future will take care of itself.

"So, how do you feel about the future?" I asked the teenager through his white mask.

He was a counselor at a summer camp I helped organize. The younger kids were running freely in the open air on the hot summer day. Yet, despite social distancing and quarantine orders having been lifted for nearly a year, we still sat quietly six feet apart on top of a concrete skate ramp as he hid behind his mask.

"To be honest…" he said while he shook his head, "it looks pretty hopeless to me."

He then began to ramble about all the challenges we face as a society: the pandemic, the unstable economy, and the wars around the world.

His voice cracked into a sad hum, and my heart slowly broke while he spoke. For a moment, I was at a loss for words.

What could I say to help bring this young man hope in what looked to him like a hopeless world?

I reached within and remembered the words of wisdom from many ancient traditions that had helped me through these challenging times.

I reached for prophecies.

The Prophecies

You see, these times were predicted by spiritual traditions all around the world.

For example, in many Indigenous traditions in North America, as well as in the global South, the ancient prophecies predicted the very trials we saw during the pandemic and continue to see today. They spoke about the sickness, the darkness, and even about artificial intelligence! Abrahamic traditions also shared similar predictions about "the end of times." Even the ancient Mayan civilization, with its advanced astronomical technology, predicted the end to occur in 2012. Many feared that date was the literal end of the world.

However, what many failed to see was the truth that these forecasts were actually pointing to a beginning, not just an ending. Eastern traditions called this period of humanity the end of the Kali Yuga, signifying the end of the darkest times we have known for thousands of years. The Baha'i teachings also echo this wisdom and suggest we as a society are actually entering into a glorious process of transformation, where unity and peace are inevitable.

Now, if the idea of spiritual prophecies seems like some far-fetched idea, drop the idea, and simply look to science, which actually shows we are less violent, more educated, happier, and healthier than we have ever been before. It's true.

In a cross-sectional study of 143 nations in the years 2000-2008, we found that people live longer and are happier in today's modern societies. Extreme poverty has dropped from over 90 percent to 10 percent, and child mortality rates have diminished significantly. Equality for women and racial minorities has transformed remarkably for the better. To think that less than 200 years ago, it was okay to have people as slaves! And yes, we have so much room to grow in the area of equality, but we are growing. The upward trend in global health suggests we are actually entering a brighter age.

Now, as 'kumbaya' as this may all sound, I'll admit it's still pretty ugly out there. We see youth mental health diminishing at pandemic rates, wars popping up like tumors around the globe, economies standing on glass, and the threat of environmental collapse. Many wonder if we will even make it as a species. With all this, we may think: Moving to a better age? I don't think so!

To this, I point back to the prophecies, which suggest these global challenges are all part of our collective healing. It looks like chaos on the surface, but as I have mentioned before in "The Gift of Chaos," if you have ever organized your house for a spring cleaning, you know that sometimes you need to shake things up to get things in order. And while it may be messy at first, the chaos from reorganizing and sorting through what's needed and what's not is exactly how to bring things back in order. Similarly, the challenges we face as a globe are shaking us up to clean out all that is no longer needed in the new, beautiful world that is emerging.

And sometimes that looks messy. Really messy.

But we can take heart because the wisdom from ancient traditions, and now, also modern science, indicates we are in a positive state of transformation. As such, we need not fear; we can move forward with confidence.

"For me, as I hear stories like those in the prophecies, I am hopeful," I said to the young man.

And as I did, I could see drops of hope fall into the fire of his eyes. I could tell they were not enough to extinguish the flames that had grown through the two challenging years of the pandemic, but I knew if he continued to hear thoughts like these enough times, he would regain his faith in humanity again.

After my encounter with that young man, I wondered how many others felt just like he did. How many young people looked off into our world with thoughts of *What's the point?*

With that, I feel that we as a globe have a responsibility to be beacons of light to future generations. We need to let them know it will be "okay." We need to remind them this is a process, and we will make it through and thrive in the end.

I don't expect the future to be easy. Adversity is inevitable, but such trails are the fuel for our transformation. We can either kick and scream and fight it, or we can use the challenges we currently face as the fertilizer for our growth. As adults, the latter is what we need to model for young people.

For as we do, we become beacons of light in this sometimes dark world. Such a light is like a ray of sun that shines through stormy seas. It brings hope, something youth desperately need in today's changing and challenging world.

With this in mind, let us accept that responsibility. And let every interaction with a young person be like drops of hope for a world on fire. When we do, that hope will create a cascade of rain that will extinguish all these flames.

An assignment, should you choose to accept it: Find a young person this week and inspire hope in them through a mindful conversation.

53
THE LIGHT IN DARK TIMES

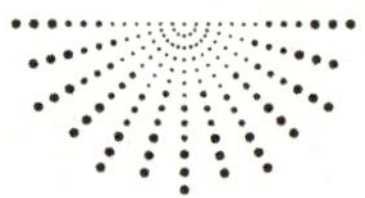

The goodness of one soul may effectively neutralize the mass karma of millions.

— PARAMAHANSA YOGANANDA

I'll be honest. It's getting pretty dark out there in the world...Even here in Bali, a tiny island no more than a hundred miles long, tucked away in the South Pacific, we can feel it. And each day, as world events continue to play out the daily dark drama, many of us feel powerless as we look to the forecast of a seemingly bleak future.

Yet despite this, I've been finding lots of solace, strength, and security as I contemplate the wisdom of saints and sages from traditions around the world, who continue to remind me that, despite the darkness, there is a power greater than any shadow that covers this world.

That power is love.

Paramahansa Yogananda, the great saint whom I've mentioned before in this book, once said, "Only Love can redeem us...The Power of Love is the greatest of all powers. No power of authority is greater than that. Love can conquer all."

He goes on to say: "Love destroys evil."

This wisdom echoes what Martin Luther King taught us about love being the only force that can overcome darkness.So while it seems like everything in this world is trying to divide us, there is a greater power operating in the background, working to unite us.

Our job as warriors of light is to tune into that Force and let it lead us.Because while it may seem like we have no power to make a difference in the crazy show our world is witnessing, we have so much more power than we think.

Listen to the words of a student of Yogananda, who said, "Your daily attitudes, actions, and prayers have a deeper influence than you may realize." This wisdom aligns with her guru's teachings, that: "Individual effort can be even more important than mass karma. One who in every way tries to uplift himself, harmonizing body, mind, and soul with the Divine, creates positive karma not only in his own life but in his family, neighborhood, country, and world...The goodness of one soul may effectively neutralize the mass karma of millions."

That statement is so powerful, it's worth pausing to contemplate once more. "The goodness of one soul may effectively neutralize the mass karma of millions."

How empowering is that?

It means you and I, despite our distance, have a powerful impact on this world simply through our individual attitudes, prayers, and actions.

For we are connected to a greater power than all the negativity we see in this world.

That power is Spirit.

That power is Love.

It is always there, it is always with us.

We simply need to connect to it.

With that in mind, let us connect to this love, and let it lead us to the light.

PART VII
THE SACRED

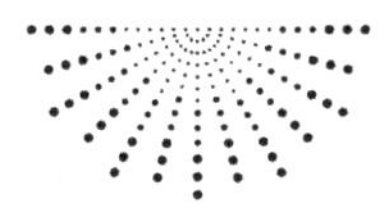

54
THE GREATEST LOVE

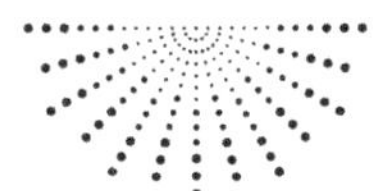

It is through our relationship with Spirit that we gain everything we seek in this world.

There are times when war is necessary.

The Mahabharata, the book of Sanskrit wisdom, tells the tale of a great battle between two families, the Pandavas and the Kauravas. Yet this is no ordinary feud; it is a battle between light and darkness.

In the epic tale, the noble Pandavas fought to reclaim their kingdom against the wicked Kauravas. As mentioned before in this book, in the Vedic scriptures, there are very few cases where war is seen as "just." Prior to going into combat, great acts of diplomacy, negotiation, and mediation efforts must be made before any act of war is declared.

That being said, despite heroic diplomatic efforts to keep the peace, a battle was imminent.

Thus, Arjuna, the leader of the noble Pandavas, and his enemy Duryodhana began to prepare their armies for war. To do so, they traveled to the neighboring kingdoms to gather allies.

Duryodhana, the cruel Kaurava king, went to Krishna's castle to seek his support. If you're unaware, you should know that in Hindu mythology, Krishna, a strong and wise king, was also depicted as the embodiment of the Divine, or in other words, God in human form. But clouded by arrogance and ignorance, Duryodhana failed to see him as such. For him, Krishna was but a king with a powerful army that could aid him in his fight. Thus, strategically, like a chess move, Duryodhana went to try to convince the Holy King to join his side.

When Duryodhana arrived in Krishna's quarters, he was sleeping on the couch. While there were cushions on the floor by Krishna's feet, which his disciples often sat on, Duryodhana, lacking humility, sat on a chair by Krishna's side while he waited for him to wake.

Shortly after this, just like Duryodhana, Arjuna, the prince of the noble Pandavas, came to the palace seeking the Holy King's support in the war. He entered Krishna's room, but unlike Duryodhana, Arjuna recognized the Divinity within Krishna. So rather than sitting on a chair, he stood humbly at the king's feet with his hands folded in prayer and patiently waited for the Lord of the Universe to wake.

When Krishna finally arose, he saw Arjuna standing before him in prostration.

"What have you come here for, dear friend?" Krishna asked warmly, but just as he did, Duryodhana protested, "I was here first!" he demanded. "I should get the right to start!"

Being the Lord of the Universe, Krishna knew why they had both come, but insisted that since he saw Arjuna first, he should begin with his query.

In the end, both of them made their pleas to the king. After listening intently, Krishna replied with the wisdom of the ages, "I will aid you both. To one, I will offer you my army of 10,000 strong soldiers... To the other, you will have me. But I will not pick up any arms, and I will not fight. But I will offer you my guidance through every step of the battle."

Then he looked to the Pandava prince Arjuna to make his choice.

Without a second thought, Arjuna chose the counsel of the Divine over his epic army.

From his rival's choice, Duryodhana felt as if he had won the lottery. He was the second to decide, yet still he walked away with an army ten times the size of the Pandavas. He thought Arjuna was the biggest fool in the universe and left the room, thinking he had already won the war.

But history would tell a different story, one useful for us to contemplate as we wage our own wars in the struggles of life. After he made his decision, Arjuna humbly asked Krishna to be his charioteer and guide him in the battle. The Divine being did, and through his wise counsel, the noble Pandavas prevailed in the battle of light over darkness, despite being heavily outnumbered.

When asked why he chose Krishna over his army, Arjuna replied, "Where there is Krishna, there is victory!" Or, in other words, where the Divine is, there is victory.

Arjuna had the wisdom to know this great truth—to know that when given a choice between the material and the spiritual world, the spiritual forces that make up this universe will always win in the end.

Thus, this allegorical tale symbolizes how the wisdom of the Divine in our lives is strong enough to overcome any battle we face. Just as Krishna guided Arjuna's chariot, if we let the Divine guide and lead our lives, no matter how trying the trials, we shall overcome them.

Where there is Spirit, there is victory. This is a great truth and a helpful story for us to contemplate as we face the inevitable battles in our lives. Because, like Arjuna, we are all warriors in the battle between light and darkness. While wars may not always necessarily be outside us, the truth is, there is an inner war between our higher and lower selves at every moment of the day.

There is the part that wants to lash out when we are "wronged" and the other part that tells us to be calm and understanding. There is the part of us that is greedy and wants to take more than we need, and the part of us that is happy with enough. This war is being waged every day, every minute, and every moment. But how can we win against the ever-insistent battles we face? Where do we find the wisdom and strength to overcome the enemy within us?

Like Arjuna, we must humble ourselves and draw that wisdom and strength from Spirit.

It's worth noting that in this classic tale, Arjuna symbolizes the soul, or in other words, the part of us that is connected to something bigger than ourselves. Duryodhana, on the other hand, is symbolic of the ego—the part of us that sees ourselves as separate from the spiritual plane and looks to the material world for its salvation. But as you can see in this story, if we follow King Ego's path, we realize that nothing in this material universe can lead us to true victory. On the other hand, if we have enough humility and wisdom to be like Arjuna and seek counsel from Higher Wisdom, we will win the war.

The best-selling author and highly effective psychiatrist Phil Stutz, well known from the Netflix documentary *Stutz*, echoes this wisdom. In his work with clients, he invites them to connect to what he calls "higher forces," because he has found that through that connection, his clients draw unseen power to overcome their struggles. This might look like a client visualizing beings of light surrounding them while they resist a bad habit. Thus, just like Krishna and Arjuna, to overcome our lower nature, there is a partnership with this spiritual power. However, just like Arjuna had to reach out to Krishna for support, Stutz suggests, "If we don't recognize the power of Higher Forces, they can't help us."

Moreover, Viktor Frankl, one of the world's most renowned psychotherapists, whom I reference frequently in this book, had quite a similar theory. In his research-based modality, logotherapy, which has touched millions worldwide, he suggested there is more to humanity than just our bodies and our minds; there is a deeper nature, which he called *the noetic dimension*, or in other words, the spiritual dimension.

For Frankl, the spiritual dimension is where we draw our unique human powers that give us the capacity to overcome the starkest of circumstances. It is the source of our free will. It helps us find meaning in challenges, gives us strength, and, ultimately, provides us the capacity to love.

Armed with this theory, Frankl was able to treat schizophrenics, the clinically depressed, and those with severe anxiety with outstanding results, where other mental health professionals fell short. Why? Because the other practitioners simply treated the minds and bodies of their patients. But Frankl saw past his patients' current mental and physical impairments and connected to their noetic/spiritual nature.

For example, instead looking at a schizophrenic as someone with a neurological disorder, he looked deeper. He saw that while they had certain mental and physical conditions, at a soul level, they had a desire for meaning, just like everyone else. This resulted in different interventions that supported these individuals much more successfully than other practitioners' attempts.

Thus, it was through connecting to that higher spiritual power that healing could happen.

This is the power of connecting to these, as Stutz's would say, "higher forces." Just as a lightbulb draws its brightness from the invisible force of energy so it may shine, so too can we draw power from this Source. Like a current of energy, when we connect to these Higher Forces, we draw the power we need to overcome all obstacles that come our way. And when we draw the power of Spirit, we are drawing from the power of love. Perhaps that's why the Christians say "God is love."

Love is the ultimate force that moves, creates, and shapes the universe. But how often do we forget this in our hyper-secular world? How often are we rushing around like Duryodhana, only looking to this material world for assistance? But the truth is, if we really want to win the battle of life, we need something more. And to do that, we need to develop a relationship with this loving power.

As you've heard in many previous chapters, I've spoken a lot about the importance of relationships, whether with ourselves, our family, our neighbors, the natural world, and even our enemies. Now, while these are all crucial relationships to maintain if we are to live rich and meaningful lives, I truly believe the most important relationship for us to develop is our relationship with a higher power. The Source.

Because at the end of the day, it is through that relationship that we gain everything we seek in this world. Think about that for a moment. Which begs the question, what are we all seeking anyway?

While philosophers and religious traditions have wrestled with the semantics of this question for eons, we can roughly agree that, at the end of the day, we are all searching for the same thing: *Happiness*.

The Stoics called it *eudaimonia;* the Buddhists called it *Nirvana,* and modern psychologists call it *flourishing*. Whatever you want to call it, essentially, we want to feel good. It's the driving motivating force for all human action.

Think about this for a moment. A businessman works many hours to put a new product on the market. You ask him why? He tells you he is doing it to make more money. When asked why again, he responds that he's doing it to support his family. You keep asking why, and this time he says it's so he can achieve financial freedom and be comfortable. Again, you ask, to which he eventually replies, "So I can be happy."

If you observe your own life, your goals, your daily actions, and your habits—even the bad ones—you will find they all stem from the desire to make you or the people around you feel better. You do them to make you feel happy. Because at the end of the day, it's really what we're all looking for.

But here's the thing. Where does our modern world, which spends trillions of dollars on advertisements, make us look for happiness? Again, like Duryodhana, we are told to look to the material world for our salvation. We are made to believe that external achievements, fame, a promotion, a romantic relationship, money, and so on will bring us the peace we seek. While nothing is inherently wrong with these pursuits, the problem comes when we think these things will grant us the fulfillment our souls desperately long for.

But here's the truth: When we look to the things of this world for our peace, we are like chasing a mirage to quench our thirst. It simply can't suffice. Because at the end of the day, the external things of this world are all but counterfeits of true happiness.

So now the question is, where can we find the source of happiness? In Sanskrit, there are three names for the expression of the Divine: *Sat* (Pure Truth), *Chit* (Pure Consciousness), and *Ananda* (Pure Bliss).

Ananda is a happiness beyond measure, the source of ultimate happiness. Thus, while we have been made to believe we can find fulfillment in external things, this ancient wisdom suggests that connecting to the spiritual nature of life is the source of all joy.

In turn, this Force is what we've been looking for all along. It's the ultimate purpose of life. It is our ultimate *ikigai,* as the Japanese put it—our reason for being.

Perhaps that's why the Christians say, "Seek ye first the Kingdom of God, and then all things shall be given." They understood that once you connect to the spiritual plane of existence, you get what you have been tirelessly searching for in this material world. You actually get the world and more.

In the next section of this book, as we continue our exploration with love and relationships, if it's available to you, I encourage you to look at this higher power not as some distant, far-off energy but as something very close. I encourage you to see it as a presence that cares for, cherishes, and loves you, not as some far off being in sky. That's a relationship. It's personal. Then, like Arjuna was with Krishna, we can call upon this Force like a great friend to help us in times of need.

With that in mind, let's continue our adventure as we explore another facet of love, the source of love itself.

WARRIOR OF LOVE

~

The battlefield of this world lives
within you and me.
Every time we choose love over fear,
Moderation over excess,
Understanding over judgment,
We create a ripple
that vibrates into this universe.
With this in mind, body, heart, and soul,
Let us be strong as we face those daily battles
and know that it is not just for us
But in service to the planet at large.
And let us remember that we
are not alone in the struggle.
In times of need,
We can always call upon
this Great Universal Force
And like a good friend,
it will come running to help us.

~

55
A LOVE STORY

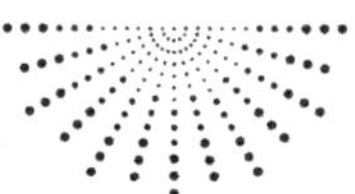

A cool dawn breeze blows against a light blue sky cradled in Bali's beautiful clouds, and on this new morning, I am contemplative about the new life ahead of me. Because any day now, my wife and I will welcome a little boy into this world.

Even as a writer, putting into words the overwhelming love I feel within my heart for my partner and my unborn child seems like a herculean task so big I could not do it justice, so I won't even try. I will simply be frank and say, "It's a lot of love!" And I feel so blessed to be given the privilege of being the husband to a woman I cherish so dearly and a soon-to-be father to this little miracle.

But the craziest thing of all is that if fear had won, none of these gifts would ever have happened.

Let me explain.

I first met my wife, Andréanne, in the spring of 2021 in a little retreat center in the quiet village of Carp, Ontario. With a desire to escape the world, I moved to that little oasis shortly after the COVID-19 pandemic took the world by storm.

Many months after I had arrived, Andréanne came to the retreat center for some well-deserved rest, following heavy demands at work and a year spent caring for her ailing mother, who had just passed.

When we met, the chemistry was palpable. Yet, at the time, celibate for years, I was more likely to become a monk than pursue a partnership. Thus, when it came to romantic relationships, I had made a habit of closing my heart off to others.

However, despite both trying to avoid each other—which she told me later was the same experience for her—we were like magnets that kept finding ourselves drawn to one another in nooks all over the center. We found ourselves doing ceremonies by the rocks together. We stumbled upon each other on our evening walks in the woods. She boosted my car. We went for a drive. We even had a dance party. Again and again, we bumped into one another and shared intimate, heartfelt connections.

And even if my futile attempts to get away from her worked somewhat during her stay, I still could not get her out of my head. It was maddening, to say the least.

But still, despite the very real energy between us, I had placed a wall between us and had no intention of breaking it down. On the contrary, I wanted to build it even higher. I wanted to build a castle with a great big moat between us! Whatever I could do to keep her away. So, on her last day, before she returned to her life in the city, I made a point to address what was there, hoping we could both acknowledge it, let go, and then happily move on with our lives.

Before our meeting, to gather myself, I meditated and prayed deeply for the highest outcome, then went to find her.

"I think we need to talk about the elephant in the room," I said very seriously as I cornered her in the living room, sitting on the couch.

She looked up from the book she was reading and squinted as if looking at the sun.

"What's that?" she replied.

"This... This energy between us..." I said as I fumbled my hands in front of my chest.

"Oh. Okay," she said with a sigh of relief as she closed her book and looked intently at me.

But at the same time, I could also tell by the look in her eyes that she was a little shocked that I had spoken about the forbidden elephant we had both been feeling all week.

"But we can't do anything about it..." I said, my mind already made up. "It just won't work," I added, shaking my head left and right.

During that week, when Andréanne was running through my mind, I had already imagined our future, the dates, the losses, and how I would end up breaking her heart. Ultimately, I saw that, in the end, this relationship was doomed to fail, so why even try? But really, even if I didn't know it at the time, I was just afraid. I was afraid of opening my heart and letting her in.

Thankfully, she's a lawyer, and she countered my argument. "What if we are just present with what's here? It could be anything we want it to be," she said. "What if we enter this relationship to heal?"

And, of course, when I wasn't zooming thirty years into the future, imagining all the possible things that could go wrong, and was just present with the moment, I was open to the possibility.

We shook hands and went into the woods to pray and perform a ceremony to welcome our healing relationship into the world. Then, after so many years of guarding the gates to my heart, I finally opened the door a crack and let her in.

Her love was like a healing balm, and with her sweetness and care, she smoothed the rough edges I could not touch on my own and helped heal the hurt parts I had hidden away.

Perhaps it was just hormones and chemicals running through my body, but regardless, the first couple of months were really like magic; we did ceremonies by rivers, went on hikes in the woods, and rode our bicycles through the Gatineau hills, leaving offerings of flowers and tobacco everywhere we went.

But still, despite all the beauty we shared, that same scared part of me that kept me from entering the relationship in the first place was trying to sabotage it. It conjured up negative thoughts about how flawed a person she was. The judgmental voices told me she wasn't spiritual enough, adventurous enough, good enough, and so on. But of course, we all know those voices were but projections of my own judgments and insecurities.

Thankfully, these voices all came around the same time I was scheduled for my yearly four-day wilderness retreat, where I would go solo into the woods, fast, and unplug so I could reconnect with my Higher Self and get the direction I needed for my year ahead.

There, in the silence, surrounded by trees, my busy mind stilled, and I could hear the voice of my soul calling to me.

"Just love her, Adam..."

Again.

"Just love her..."

It was like a commandment from a higher power. But not simply an order for an order's sake. But an order in the truest and purest form. An order for the sake of bringing things to order. It was as if, through following this wisdom, I would bring my life and its fragmented parts into order.

Thus, with this commandment summoned unto me, I stopped giving that whiny voice so much free space to run wildly in my mind. Instead, I just loved, regardless of what it would say. And of course, without giving it so much attention, it eventually quieted down. This resulted in our relationship growing even greater in love and care, and those sharp edges around my heart were smoothed even more.

But, when Andréanne started to get visions of the children we would have only four months into our relationship, my walls went up again, and for the third time, I searched for the back door.

"I think you're talking about some other guy," I replied as I imagined the future failures that seemed so certain. At 34, I knew she wanted them soon. But I still wanted my freedom. There were things I needed to do. Projects to create and work to bring to the world, all of which I assumed would be hindered if I had a little one to take care of. And after these conversations, we both considered the very real possibility this beautiful treasure we briefly shared would soon leave us.

But again, prayer and connection to something greater came to save the day. In a ceremony, about a month after these initial conversations, the children we would have came to me in a vision. And just like the summons I had in the wilderness a few months back, they commanded me.

"It's not about you," they told me. "It's about the next seven generations. The future needs good kids."

Again, it was like a Divine Order, an order that commanded my immature ego to give up its illusion of freedom to submit to the strength and power that comes with responsibility.

Of course, there was still a choice. But deep within me, I knew that listening to this Divine Order, like before, would bring true order to my life and the world at large.

With this wisdom, the very next day, I asked Andréanne to marry me. And the rest is, as they say, history, a beautiful history, a beautiful story, one I could not even have imagined.

Since I listened to the commandment of love, my life has truly transformed. I went full-time into the career of my dreams, moved to Bali, and now have the pleasure of waking up with joy next to a woman who loves me unconditionally and encourages me to be a better man every day. My connection to my Creator is deeper than it has ever been. Long-held boyish tendencies have been cast aside and replaced with a new sense of responsibility and commitment. The shift is more than 180 degrees. It's 900 times ten. Truly, in all honesty, I know if I had let fear win, my life would not even be 10 percent as rich as it is now. Which really makes me contemplate: How can we ensure that fear does not win?

Upon reflection on our love story, only a small part of which I've shared, the power to overcome the small self governed by fear came from connecting with the big Self. It came from connecting with Spirit.

The small me clouded my vision from seeing reality as it was. With it as my guide, I was walking through the world with mud-covered glasses, where everything I looked at was distorted, messy, and ugly.

But when I plugged into the Universal Source through meditation, prayer, connection to nature, and ceremony, these practices became like healing water that washed away all that was not true.

The truth was, there was something so beautiful in front of me, yet my mind, ideas, and judgments had distorted reality. But when I connected to that Universal Power, I saw what was true.

I saw love.

56
WHERE TO FIND STRENGTH

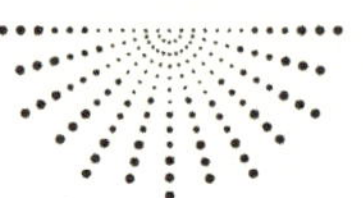

Grant me the serenity to accept the things I cannot change, the courage to change the things I can, and the wisdom to know the difference.

— THE SERENITY PRAYER

"I don't know what to do," he said to me as he shook his head. Plagued with PTSD, anxiety, depression, and the physical distress that comes from a body on constant high alert, he came to me desperate for an answer. I looked into his eyes, weathered by sleepless nights. They reminded me of a look I had seen all too often before—one in my very own mirror many years ago.

Staring into his darkened daze, I told him a story.

One about me in my early twenties, where, due to some major events, like him, I sank into a depression. My life felt like chaos—like everything was out of control. Desperate to bring some order back to my world, I tried to control something. Anything I thought would bring me what my heart was desperately seeking: Love. Yet, sadly, I looked in the wrong place. I looked outside and saw a culture that placed so much value on image. And as a result, I began to place so much emphasis on how I looked.

It started with a little bit of food monitoring, followed by a little bit of exercise. After a while, I got some positive feedback from the world, like: "You look great!" The approval felt good, especially after coming from such a vulnerable place. Then, before I knew it, it became a full-blown obsession. Until the next thing I knew, I had unknowingly developed anorexia.

If you aren't familiar with the illness, it's pretty wicked. It's a severe eating disorder characterized by an intense fear of gaining weight, a distorted body image, and extreme dietary restrictions. Due to a lack of caloric intake, a person with anorexia's body is in constant starvation mode, which means their nervous system is in a constant state of high arousal, where fight, flight, and freeze are the norm. This is met with a host of mental and emotional problems, such as anxiety, social isolation, unrealistic standards, and harsh self-criticism.

Thus, with my judgmental mind leading the show during this period of my life, it was like I was roommates with the meanest person on earth.

"So, how did you make it through?" my friend asked, eagerly awaiting the end of the story. Because, despite our struggles being quite different on the surface, at the core, our problems were the same—both of us felt trapped in a negative cycle of suffering.

Giving a single answer to his question was difficult. On my healing journey, there wasn't just one thing. On the contrary, I felt as if I had tried everything! From traditional therapy to neurolinguistic programming, I drank ayahuasca, underwent hypnosis, and completed a ten-month program with Gabor Maté.

I practiced Kundalini yoga to rewire my mind and participated in an eight-week mindfulness-based stress reduction course. I worked with compassion therapy, did affirmations, used Louise Hay's mirror work, and engaged in various cognitive-behavioral approaches. Heck, even years later, I saw a specialized nutritionist to help me regain weight.

Each approach was unique, and each one gave me the tools I needed for where I was on my healing journey. And while the modalities were all seemingly different, there was a golden thread of truth woven through every one of them.

What was that golden thread?

It was Spirit, the Sacred, God. Whatever you want to call it. This Divine energy was the golden thread woven through the tapestry of my healing journey. And like a drowning man in the sea, connecting to it was the lifeline that kept me afloat and, ultimately, carried me home. For it was this act of connecting to "something bigger" that guided me to the different therapeutic approaches I needed to pursue at the time. In my many moments of despair, I would pray for help. And while it was not a quick fix, without fail, the right person or opportunity would present itself to me and give me the tools I needed to carry on with my journey.

Like this, bit by bit by bit, day by day, I chipped away at the negative neuro-pathways in my brain. And in time, those darkened voices that plagued me for all those years faded like a distant dream. It was a powerful process of transformation, where, instead of looking for love outside, I connected to that Great Love that lived within me. I connected to my Source. This is how I healed. This, ultimately, is how we all heal.

57
UNTYING THE IMPOSSIBLE

Have you heard the tale of the Gordian Knot? It was a complex, intricate knot named after Gordias, the father of Midas, who tied the knot. According to prophecy, whoever could untie it would become the ruler of Asia. Thus, thousands tried to unbind it and claim their kingdom. Yet, the knot was so complex, so challenging, and so seemingly impossible that for hundreds of years, everyone who tried to untie it failed. That is, until the year 333, when Alexander the Great came along. But rather than taking the traditional approach and trying to free the knot with his hands, he took his sword and slashed it clean.

While I don't condone many of Alexander the Great's deeds, this story highlights the importance of reaching for something beyond ourselves to overcome those obstacles that at times feel impossible. Thus, like Alexander, we need a sword to cut through our greatest struggles.

What is that sword? It is Source.

Yet, how do we normally approach our big challenges?

More often than not, particularly in Western culture—which champions the maxim of being the master of one's destiny—we are taught to grit our teeth and push through challenges with sheer determination. While willpower is undeniably a crucial factor in achieving success, it alone cannot carry you through every trial. Indeed, if we are to overcome our greatest hardships, our will must be guided by wisdom.

To illustrate this point, I invite you to imagine you are lost at sea, desperately trying to get home. No matter how much rowing you do, if you're going in the wrong direction, you'll still be lost. Similarly, if you're struggling with a major life challenge, more important than will is the wisdom to guide your will.

Abraham Lincoln understood this as he faced his version of the Gordian Knot—abolishing slavery in America. To which he famously said, "I have been driven many times upon my knees by the overwhelming conviction that I had nowhere else to go." This is true wisdom because it begins with the humility to know we do not know everything, and regardless of all our intelligence and ingenuity, in times of great struggle, we need to reach for higher ground, and there is no higher ground than connecting with Spirit.

Perhaps that's why the first principle of Alcoholics Anonymous (AA) is submitting to a higher power. Like Lincoln, they understood that when we are so tangled in life's knots, we can't do it alone and need something more to give us a greater perspective. We need a connection to a higher force. We need a connection to the spiritual world beyond what our eyes can see. We need a sword to slice through these seemingly impossible problems before us. This sword is always available to us. Yet, like Lincoln, we must humble ourselves and reach for it. When we do, it will help us rise above life's toughest tests.

Now, back to you.

Are you trying to do it alone?

What is one 'knot' in your life right now you can place in the hands of Spirit today?

OUR GUIDE

~

While the seas of life may
be stormy and
the clouds thick,
still, I must trust in
This Great Universal Force.
She is my compass
and will always lead me north.
And even if I cannot see
the next step before me,
I must trust
and let her lead the way.

~

58
GOD IN THE GARDEN

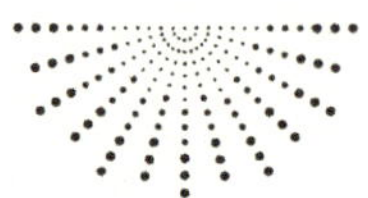

The Saturday sun beat down upon me as I wandered through the garden pathway. Kadek, the Balinese permaculture expert, buzzed around like a bee with a spade in his hand. Then, standing in front of a baby banana tree, his shovel pressed into the soil and unearthed it with a few precise swings. Yanking the tree from the ground, he dragged it twenty paces over to a plot surrounded by more banana trees.

"It's better if they're all together," he said. Then, with the spade, he made a perfect hole to transplant the tree. He placed it in and buried it with earth.

Still a novice gardener, I noted how effortless and natural the whole process was for him. It was the work of someone who had truly mastered their craft.

"For sure, now they're around friends," I said jokingly to him, then patted him on his shirtless shoulder and said, "So what are we doing today, boss?"

Kadek laughed as he wiped the sweat from his brow.

"Come," he said, waving his hand as he turned and walked me over to the side of a garden path.

"We're going to put flowers here," he said as he pointed to a plot of green, "but we need to get rid of the grass and weeds so we can plant there."

"Sounds good to me," I said, rubbing my hands together.

Then, Kadek handed me a shovel, and we got down on our knees and started working. Knowing how skilled he was with his work, I first thought about watching his technique. But I figured, it's just digging up dirt. How hard can it be?

But I soon realized it can be pretty hard, and I mean that quite literally. While there were no rocks below us, the high temperature and lack of recent rain made burrowing into the earth feel like chipping away at stone.

Kadek saw my form and quickly corrected me. "Like this," he said as he angled his shovel horizontally.

Then, attentively, I watched how the master did it. In and out, his hand plowed through the soil like butter.

Then, after following his expert guidance, the job was much easier, allowing me to cover much more ground than before. Still, in my rapid movements, I was suddenly met with an unexpected surprise. Pulling out a piece of dirt with my blade, I watched as a swarm of ants erupted from the earth. Then, placing the soil into the mound beside me, I apologized.

"I am sorry, ants," I said sympathetically. "Sorry I took your home."

Kadek looked at me and chuckled; like a stone, he was unmoved. "It's okay. They will find a new home," he said nonchalantly.

Perhaps because he intimately understood this was simply how nature, growth, and life worked. And there really wasn't anything to fuss about.

I nodded and continued to clear the way for the flowers to be planted. Then, suddenly, I realized this simple experience with the permaculture expert spoke to a universal principle we all experience.

Let me explain. Through years of training, Kadek achieved a level of mastery that allowed him to see the bigger picture. While a novice gardener might see nothing but green, the master sees the whole. He sees above the earth, below it, what once was and what could be, and thus, knows the big and small actions to take to help the garden thrive.

Similarly, there is a Divine Intelligence that knows exactly what's needed most to help grow the beautiful gardens of our lives. As said before in this book, that intelligence goes by many names. Some call it the Great Spirit, while others call it the Universe, God, our Higher Selves, or some just call it Love. Whatever name you want to call it does not really matter. But it's helpful to remember there is a wise gardener in our lives, shifting things around to help us grow. It wants to plant flowers where there were once weeds and move banana trees to be closer to their family. Yet to do that, it's got to shake things around, uproot things, and sometimes, the process is quite dirty, and maybe even uncomfortable.

Think about your own life for a moment and the challenges you have overcome. Maybe there have been times when it felt like the ground below you was collapsing, yet if you have found the gift within those hardships, you will probably say something along the lines of:

"I would never wish this on anyone, but that challenge was the best thing that ever happened to me."

This is not always an easy stance, especially if we feel like we are the banana tree being ripped from the earth. But if we take a step back and stop looking at the weeds, we begin to realize there is something so much bigger and so much wiser guiding the show.

How beautiful is that? It means we are not in this alone.

With that, we can have the faith we need to face the sometimes earth-shaking challenges that come our way.

Note that when I talk about a Divine Intelligence guiding the show, this does not mean we are passive observers simply subject to the whims of Fate. Like in the story, the shovel is in our hands. The question is, will we let our egos guide the show, or will we listen to the wisdom of the Intelligent Gardener? The first choice is a hard one to bear, and the latter helps us grow beautiful roses.

But ultimately, the choice is ours.

What will you choose?

59
BUILDING ON THE ROCK

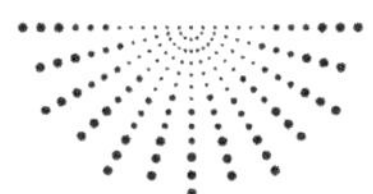

Nearly everything was taken from him. Thousands upon thousands of dollars were stripped away in days, leaving him with little choice but to hop on a plane to some Asian country to teach English to pay his bills.

With the turmoil before him, it was hard to imagine that a week before, he was living comfortably on investments with the means to do nearly anything he wanted. Yet, with the chaos of the world, there was chaos in the market, and the seemingly solid ground of security he had depended on for so long broke beneath him.

"But you know what, man," he said to me calmly and with sweetness in his voice. "I've been feeling called to pray, and for some reason, I've felt happier and freer than I have in a long, long time."

I smiled deeply as I listened to my past client and friend's deep realization. Because he touched upon a universal truth that many of us search our whole lives to discover.

That truth is this: We can't find our security in the material world.

Why not?

Because the very nature of this material universe is impermanent.

The Buddha discovered this 2,500 years ago and noted that everything in this universe shall come to pass and is essentially empty.

Since then, scientists have come to the same conclusion, illustrating that despite the solid-looking nature of this universe, only 0.0000000000000000000042 percent, to be exact, contains any matter; the rest is just empty space.

Yet, despite the impermanent and fleeting nature of this material world, how many of us still run to it for our salvation?

How many of us seek security in our finances, our professions, or whatever it is in this material world we look to in order to make us feel safe?

While there is nothing inherently wrong with these things, the problem arises when we look to them for our source of security. Because, eventually, these things will be stripped away. This could happen in one weekend, as it did to my client, or at the moment of our death. But regardless of when it happens, whether we like to admit it or not, everything will come to pass sooner or later.

Now the question is: if we can't take refuge in this impermanent universe, then where can we find it?

You may have heard the Christian parable that speaks of the fool who builds his house on the sand. When storms come, there is no foundation to hold him, and he loses everything. On the contrary, the wise one digs deep and builds his house on the rock, so when the storms come, he is grounded in a foundation so strong that nothing can shake him.

What is that foundation on which the wise build their lives?

The Spiritual Dimensions

We can see this truth profoundly expressed through my client, who, despite having everything taken from him, still found refuge in prayer—which is another way of saying he found refuge in the spiritual nature of life.

Or with Nick Vujicic, who, despite being born without limbs and battling severe depression in his youth, found through reading scripture (spiritual wisdom) deep purpose and meaning in his suffering, which gave him the strength, stamina, and inspiration he needed to become a beacon of hope for millions worldwide.

Or with Immaculée Ilibagiza, who survived the Rwandan genocide by hiding in a tiny bathroom with seven other women for ninety-one days while her country was on fire. Despite witnessing the horror and injustice, rather than being swallowed by hatred for her aggressors, she found peace and strength through the practice of prayer and forgiveness.

And that same power that gave them strength in those times of great need is available to all of us. Both science and spirituality point to the same humbling truth: The material world we see is not the whole story. While science shows us a universe that's mostly empty space, governed by invisible forces, spiritual traditions go one step further and teach us there is an intelligence to those forces—call it consciousness, universal truth, or a Divine presence, whatever—this force can give us the strength we need to weather any storm.

Now, as the global storms grow by the day and everything we thought stable is being stripped away, that ancient parable of the two builders raises an important question for us to consider. It invites us to ask ourselves where we are laying our foundation.

Note, building our house on the rock is much more than a philosophical idea; it can and should be applied in a very practical way. Just like my client, Nick Vujicic, and Immaculée Ilibagiza all took constructive action, we need to "practice" to bring this spiritual wisdom and energy into our daily lives.

What that practice looks like for you will be unique, but there are some common ways found in traditions from all around the globe, such as:

- Meditation
- Prayer
- Spiritual study
- Connection with a spiritual community

Just to name a few. The trick is to find out what works for you and then to take refuge in that practice again and again. And if you already have a practice, double, triple, or even quadruple down on your efforts. As I have mentioned before in this book about how athletes deliberately put themselves up against resistance, we need to do the same. Because we are up against a challenge greater than many of us have seen in our entire lives. As such, we need to train our spiritual muscles so we can be those beacons of light in a very dark night.

With that, let us remember that despite the chaos we see in the world today, we are connected to a power greater than any trial we see. Heck, we are connected to the power that created the entire universe.

That power is always with us; it's here to help us; we simply need to turn to it—again, and again, and again.

Questions for Reflection:

- Have you been seeking your sense of security in the material world? What might it be like if you anchored more of your attention on the spiritual nature of reality?
- What practices can you do to keep yourself spiritually plugged in?
- Do you need to double, triple, or quadruple down? If so, what does that look like?
- When will you start?

60
ON FAITH

I write this three weeks after the world declared a state of emergency due to the COVID-19 virus. And like many people, I have been wrestling with the paralyzing voice of fear. Can you blame me? It's hard to escape the barking concerns of today's frightened world. Many are threatened with thoughts of our loved ones being lost, an economy that might collapse, and unknown turmoil that might happen after all this chaos is over. Let's face it: we are entering new territory that none of us has ever seen. Without a clear picture of where our world is going, many of us turn to the default images, running through reels of apocalyptic movies in our minds, further letting the virus of fear sink in.

But within all this madness, one wonders where we can find the strength to carry on when it feels like we are standing on glass. Where can we find hope when it seems like our northern star has fallen? How will we rise when it feels like fear is pulling us down?

What are we to do?

I got the answer sitting at my writing desk the other day as I stared through my amber wooden-framed window. There, a frantic fly was flying for freedom. I watched as it persistently slammed its body against the glass with all its might. And even though it was just a fly, I felt a sense of admiration for its tenacity and determination.

But I knew that no matter how hard it tried, on its own, what it was attempting to accomplish was unattainable. Now, while it might sound strange, as I watched the little guy and his futile attempts, I couldn't help but be filled with compassion. Thus, with love in my heart, I swooped my hand in to help it on its journey home. At first, when it saw me, it dashed from my palm and banged its body into the glass once more. I tried again, and this time, it was curious and crawled along the edges of my fingers. But just before it entered the safety of my cupped hands, its old patterns of fear kicked in, and it resorted to what it had always done. Terrified, it slammed its head against the wall.

While I tried a few more times to help, I saw it had already decided. So, I shrugged and thanked the critter for the wise universal teaching.

How often are we playing the part of the fly in today's modern world? Since the age of the Enlightenment, our Western culture has become a product of individualism, a people that prides itself on independence and self-reliance. The common belief is that with enough willpower and effort, we can accomplish anything!

Don't get me wrong, self-effort is a valuable trait and something to be fostered. But the problem comes when we believe we are the sole rulers of this universe. When we do so, we cut ourselves off from the natural laws of life. We think we own the world and, thus, can dominate it. We build farms in deserts, inject our food with chemicals, and change its genetic makeup to make it grow. We think we're winning at first, but we have to look at our world's climate crisis to see where this type of thinking gets us.

The truth is that no matter how much we "accomplish" as a species, there comes a time when we face obstacles so big that the task becomes just like that impenetrable glass. In such times, we would be wise to follow what great leaders, many of whom I mention in this book, have done in the past when facing similar odds.

We can look to Dorothy Day, Sojourner Truth, the Dalai Lama, and Martin Luther King Jr., and see how they faced their giants. In the face of the impossible, all these great exemplars did the same thing: they reached for a higher power. Today, we are facing even bigger challenges than them, challenges so grand I believe the only way to meet them is to humble ourselves and turn to something larger.

Now, I am not religious. But I do believe in God. And I know that can sometimes be a loaded word in today's world. I understand why. The dogmas of many spiritual traditions have done atrocious things, slaughtered millions, and robbed cultures, all in the name of *GOD*. Now, we don't need to be religious scholars to see these wicked acts were nothing more than small-minded, arrogant men seeking to control.

So, if the word "God" gets in the way, replace it with another, call it the Universe, the Great Spirit, Love, Creator, or even what modern physicists call the "quantum field." Whatever name you call it does not matter. What does matter is we know that force is here. It is here for us, and just like the story of me and that fly, it is trying to help us. When we truly know this, we are confident because even if we are standing on unstable ground, we know something is holding us, guiding us, and taking care of us when all seems like it is breaking. It is this certainty we can reach for when everything else is uncertain. With this knowing, we can relax and trust that something greater is unfolding.

And if we are honest, we need this. So many of us are hurting in our shaking world. Our cultural rates of anxiety, depression, and loneliness are the highest recorded in history. And it's no wonder. Our world can look pretty grim when we look at life as purely matter-based. Think about it. It is hard to connect to greater meaning and purpose when society's general narrative is that we live in a random and purposeless universe. It's hard to feel like we belong when our primary cultural story is that we are separate.

But when we add the element of Spirit, I believe we add the antidote for much of our world's shared pain. Spirit is the piece of the puzzle of life that shows us we are not merely isolated beings making our way through a matter-dense planet, but instead, part of an interconnected universe that is all purposeful, all loving, all good, and all beautiful. In this space, we find true belonging because we know we belong to something so much greater.

It has only been a short time since science and spirit have been at war. The hostilities started in the 1600s when Galileo made his famous discovery of the sun-centered universe. This contradicted the church's doctrine at the time, and thus, the battle began. Over the next few hundred years, Materialism was born. Descartes founded Dualism, further dividing matter and spirit. Darwin brought forth natural selection. Science held firm to the world that could be seen, while religion held to the unseen.

I find it a shame that, because of a few fundamentalist religious folks, so much wisdom from spiritual traditions has been forgotten. Guilty by association, many have associated ideas of spirituality with being far-fetched and unscientific. However, if one studies modern science and spiritual principles, one finds that much of what ancient sages have said about the nature of our universe is in direct correlation with theories from today's leading physicists and neuroscientists, such as the idea of universal consciousness, which is currently being accepted by many in the scientific community.

Based on the cultural conditioning of a matter-only universe, I know it can feel strange for some to reach for this universal consciousness. For so long, we have been taught to do it on our own. We have been told it's just us out here, alone against the world. But I hope we can dig deeper and see the connections between science and spirit. Because when we are humble enough to reach for that force, we are cured of the virus of fear. Because we know we are holding hands with something so much larger, we know we are not doing it alone, and what a grace it is to know that we don't have to.

But don't take my word for it. Try it yourself, like a scientist, test it. Come with the same curiosity and intensity to know, with openness to possibility, miracles, and the unknown. Find that truth within yourself. Take a day to sit in silence. Read from the wisdom literature, look into quantum physics, connect with people who have had that direct connection, pray, and reach for that force, and see what you discover.

We are in trying times, this is for sure, but when we are connected to this great universal force, we can rest assured that we do not need to face these challenges alone.

61
THROUGH THE EYES OF A SAINT

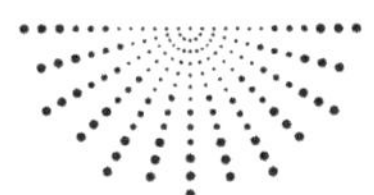

Nobody can do anything to me, no condition can come into my life that God has not permitted.

— SRI DAYA MATA

In today's challenging world, many of us are feeling uncertain, anxious, and even afraid about what might transpire in the coming months.

And when we look at the world through a three-dimensional lens, it's easy to understand why.

But what if we look at our current dilemma through the eyes of a saint?

Here is what the saint Sri Daya Mata had to say about facing life's challenges:

"If you really believe that there is a Power in this world, then you must really believe that that Power has control over your lives. Which means that this power is allowing this to be here. Nobody's doing anything to me that God does not permit them

> to do. Nobody can do anything to me, no condition can come into my life that God has not first permitted to come into my life. There has to be that belief that God is the One who is controlling my life."

You see, when we look at our current circumstances through this wise lens, faith is the natural byproduct, because we see that despite the many woes we face, there is a Divine, supportive, and loving intelligence working in the background, allowing these challenges to be here.

Why?

Adversity brings out the best in us.

I have spoken before about how athletes deliberately put themselves up against resistance, fully knowing it is in the struggle that they break through their limitations.

Similarly, what we are all experiencing as a collective is a mass opportunity to transform and bring our greatest gifts.

Now, the question is: Will we turn away and run from the challenge, or will we use it to bring out the best within us?

The choice is ours.

HELP IS HERE

~

Life is filled with challenges.
Wild waves with ups and downs,
that can sometimes feel just unbearable.
But in those times when we feel as
if the world is pressing upon shoulders,
we must take heart
and remember, we need not do it alone,
For Life's big open hands are here
just waiting for us to reach for them.
We simply need to open ourselves,
and ask...

~

62

HOW TO BECOME FEARLESS

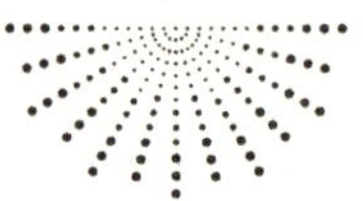

It was early Tuesday afternoon when I felt an itch in my throat, a telltale sign I was getting a cold. Unfortunately, that same day, I noticed my eight-month-old son had started coughing along with me, letting me know he had caught it, too.

Upon realizing this, I got seriously worried—not for me or him but for my nearly ninety-one-year-old grandmother, who for the past few days had been holding, hugging, and kissing him as much as she could.

Deeply concerned for her health, I cautioned her about getting too close to my boy. But without flinching, and with a face as calm and cool as a quiet winter morning, she said, "I am not afraid of germs."

Then, joyfully, she continued to hold and love her coughing great-grandson.

Now, in a time when one of society's biggest fears is germs, and at an age when most people are typically the most cautious about them, I found my grandmother's fearless response both admirable and inspiring.

Knowing my Nana, I had a hunch about what made her so fearless but still decided to ask her outright.

When she responded to my query, she did so again with that same calm and cool tone, anchored in ninety-one years of wisdom: "Well, I've just come to realize that the Universe has an intelligent plan, and if I go, I go. If I don't, I don't, and in the end, there's no real use worrying about it."

Interestingly enough, that same perspective my grandmother used to stand in the face of what so many fear was the very same approach Rosa Parks used as she sat defiantly in the face of racial segregation. It's the same principle Joan of Arc leaned on as she courageously ran into battle. And it's the very same practice we can apply when facing our own fears.

What is the practice?

Faith in something greater.

You see, when we turn our attention away from our little, frail, and limited selves, and instead lean on the universal force that grows the plants, gives birth to stars, and made the entire cosmos—when we take shelter in a force so great, what is there to fear?

Nothing.

Really. There's nothing.

And with that fearless spirit, like Rosa Parks, Joan of Arc, and my grandmother, we can lovingly turn to the sacred tasks before us, to the best of our abilities, without worries or concerns.

Now, I find this lesson especially valuable in the chaotic times we collectively face, where so many of us wrestle with fears for our future, for our world, and for ourselves. And of course, we still should be cautious and do our due diligence. But rather than letting excessive thoughts of fear overwhelm us in times as challenging as these, let us learn from the wisdom of my ninety-one-year-old grandmother and take shelter in something so much bigger.

Because when we do that, we become fearless.

63 LEADING WITH THE SACRED

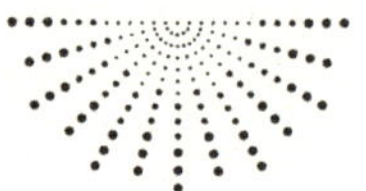

Our scientific power has outrun our spiritual power. We have guided missiles and misguided men.

— MARTIN LUTHER KING JR.

"Focus on crime! Focus on crime! Focus on crime!"

The mob of pro-gun protesters roared at us in the anti-gun rally. We were head-to-head as pellets of rain fell upon the demonstration outside the city hall. With the dark clouds looming above us, the two groups were ready for battle.

The screams of the pro-gun protesters were so loud I could barely hear Councillor Campbell giving his speech through the microphone on the damaging effects of handguns on Ottawa's community.

Then I looked into the gray sky and watched as the large drops of rain fell upon us. Then wondered: Could we have stopped this?

I think we could have.

But before I continue, let me backtrack a bit to give you more context.

This was all taking place outside the city hall building at a demonstration I'd organized to ban single-use plastics in Ottawa's municipal buildings. Important bills were being passed by our politicians that morning, and our hope was to encourage them to support our cause. At the same time, with violent crimes on the rise in the city, there was another demonstration on the other side of the building, encouraging politicians to ban handguns.

"Hey, would you mind if we shared your space?" asked Joe, Councillor Campbell's advisor. "There's a mob of pro-gun protesters where we're supposed to speak. It could get pretty ugly if we go there."

"Sure," I said, "We're all allies here. The more the merrier."

While it was great to have the extra people at the demonstration, it was already 9:15, and the demonstration was supposed to start at 9:00 and end at 9:30. With that, as an organizer, I felt the weight of trying to squeeze two demonstrations into one thirty-minute slot.

Prior to this unexpected turn of events, that morning, in meditation and prayer, I received guidance that as the MC of the event, I was to open the morning by singing a traditional Indigenous Water Song to show respect to the Algonquin Nation whose land we were inhabiting, to give thanks to water, the earth, and most importantly, to bring in the energy of Spirit into the event.

But with the time crunch pressing upon me, the many new faces there, I lost my balance, and my mind began to race like a frantic hamster on its wheel. *What was I to do?*

The action began.

"Welcome, folks," I said to the thirty-plus faces. "It is a gift and an honor to have all of you here showing your support to make this world a better place. Before we begin, I think it's important to acknowledge that we are on unceded, unsurrendered Algonquin territory. I believe when we engage in any type of change work, it's of the utmost importance that we share this, for we cannot move forward in a good way without first acknowledging the hurts that have happened in the past and that continue to go on to this day..."

Nods of agreement swept over the thirty-plus people in the crowd.

"Now, I have learned many things from working with the Algonquin Nation. One of these was the importance of paying respect to the water. For water is the very thing that gives each and every one of us life! And because of this, it's so important to pause and give time to respect it."

This was the moment I had planned to sing. It was the moment I planned to pray.

"So, let's take a moment of silence to give respect to the water."

Then, with fear of not having enough time, I waited two short seconds, giving the water, life, and Spirit nothing more than a head nod before I went on to introduce our first speaker.

Around that time, the pro-gun protesters discovered that the anti-gun demonstration had moved to where we were. Ready for a fight, the twenty-five or so of them came pressing around us armed with picket signs. They left our environmental rally to continue with our three brief speeches, but when we handed the stage over to Campbell and our friends in the anti-handgun demonstration, that's when the angry pro-gun screams soared through the sky. Campbell tried to speak, but between the yelling and pouring rain, you could barely make out what he was saying.

That's when I looked into the sky and wondered if everything would have unfolded differently had we taken a moment to pause, pray, and respect the water. Some scientific research suggests that water holds memory; like a sponge, it takes in the energy of its environment. For example, in a double-blind study published in *Explore*, researchers found that when water was treated with positive "intention"—say, the feeling of love or joy—the water produced ice crystals that were rated as more beautiful. Moreover, other research led by Lynne McTaggart found that positive intentions from large groups of people effectively increased the pH of polluted water sources, making them more suitable for drinking.

Just think, we humans are about 60-70 percent water. As such, it's possible that intentions, positive or negative, could affect our mental and emotional states. Perhaps that's why, during the full moon, ER workers report an increase in panic alerts. Because just as the moon governs the tides, it could also raise the waters within us, thereby affecting our emotional states.

So, as I gazed up at the gray sky, I couldn't help but think that if I had followed the guidance I received that morning, led with love, and sang that sacred water song, the rains above would have been charged with that love and perhaps softened the hearts of the angry protesters.

But why didn't I speak up? Why didn't I follow the guidance I received that morning? Why? Time was a factor for sure, but honestly, I choked. The thing that held me back most was fear. In the age of science, the sacred can be seen as silly, so in turn, I withheld it from the equation. But in doing so, I believe I did a great disservice to myself, my community, and the world at large.

Now, some may say that singing a song wouldn't have changed anything during that demonstration. Angry people are angry people, and they would have still yelled and screamed either way. I agree that no-one can say how the events of the day might have changed had we first started in sacred reverence. But what I do know is that when I've organized other events with the intention of Spirit leading the way, the most beautiful things have occurred.

People came to me afterward with tears in their eyes; political councillors held hands and sang. Others told me their lives had changed in revolutionary ways and that these events were different from any they had experienced before—they were deeper, richer, and filled with something more. That "something more" was Spirit.

Now, this experience of the transformative power of the sacred goes much further than me and my little demonstration efforts. Satyagraha, the non-violent resistance movement that liberated India from British rule, was founded on Vedic spiritual principles. This further went on to inspire and empower civil rights movements around the globe, like the fight against racial segregation in the United States, which was guided by non-violent resistance (*Satyagraha*) and the principles of *Agape* (brotherly love and love for God). Spirituality was not just part of these movements; it was the very foundation on which they were built, and therein was the source of their strength and success.

In today's modern world, where science is king, it can be challenging to speak about things like spirituality openly without fear of backlash. Some call it "woo-woo," and others who want to be politically correct encourage us not to mix politics and religion. Of course,

I understand why. As I have mentioned before, there have been so many atrocities brought to this world in the name of *God*. However, I would argue that these "atrocities" have nothing to do with spirituality and are merely delusional men wielding it for power.

But despite all the controversy, personally, I believe that forgetting our Source would be foolish. Because we are in dire times that require relentless strength. And I truly believe that organizing our lives around spiritual principles is where we can find such strength. Look to Nelson Mandela, who, for twenty-seven long years, endured unjust imprisonment. Yet armed with the spiritual principle of forgiveness, he was able to transform his anger into something that brought peace and harmony to people in South Africa. Viktor Frankl, the Jewish psychotherapist, drew the strength of Spirit to shine a light that inspired millions even in the face of one of the world's darkest places, the concentration camps. It is this strength of Spirit that gave David the power to fight Goliath, and it is the very strength we need to face the giant challenges before us.

So, with these thoughts in our hearts, minds, and souls, may we move forward today, tomorrow, and in the years to come, remembering to connect with this Universal Source. For it is the power that will empower us to overcome anything that comes our way.

DEAR SPIRIT...

~

Teach me to surrender my fears
and allow me to be embraced
by your loving arms.
Let every thought of worry
be transmuted into trust
and any sense of lack
be replaced by a
free-flowing current of enoughness.
May I always remember that
all I ever really need
is right here.
Teach me to be here…
Thank you, thank you, thank you

~

64
PRAYER

Prayer is the process of turning our minds and hearts to Love itself. Just as a light draws its power from electricity to shine bright, through prayer, we connect our small selves with a spiritual power that gives us the energy we need to shine bright in this world.

Moreover, prayer provides guidance in moments when we feel we are lost. It gives us strength when every part of us wants to quit. And ultimately, it can give us the power we need to overcome every trial we face.

But perhaps even more importantly, it can also bring us joy.

Because prayer is not just about asking for things; it's also about connecting and communing. It's about friendship, which involves sharing our hopes, our dreams, our gratitude, and our deep appreciation.

Put simply, prayer is about a relationship.

Perhaps that's why D. A. Carson said, "Effective prayer is the fruit of a relationship… not a technique for acquiring blessings."

Because through prayer, we deepen that relationship with our Source, the universal Love within all things, and through this bond, we are changed, and the world is changed as a result.

Great leaders, thinkers, and reformers knew this. That's why people like Dorothy Day, Helen Keller, Malala Yousafzai, and so many unsung names would go deep within, to pray, and connect with that Great Love. Because they knew it was through this intimate connection that they were able to help shape the world around them for the better.

Like them, we can draw on this great power.

Like them, we can deepen our relationship with our Source.

Like them, we can change the world for the better.

65

ONE PRAYER CAN CHANGE THE WORLD

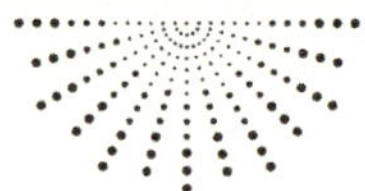

I sit alone at the kitchen table in the Southern Plains of Alberta, visiting my Elder and adopted spiritual father, Leonard Day Rider, before I leave on my next adventure to Mexico. It's 5:30 a.m., and the house is quiet, with everyone fast asleep. The sun has yet to shine and sing to the fields. And there in the canopy of darkness, I can hear the howling of the chinook wind barreling in from the west. Its presence is so strong I can feel it shake the entire house. It's breathtaking, really. It is like a song calling me to the moment; it sings. Then, in this little house on a farm in the sacred plains of North America, I pray.

Pray that everyone who comes to meet this day is filled with love and light.

I pray those in the small community I am staying in are happy, that their connection to the Source is strong, and that they can meet this day's challenges with grace and ease.

I pray that the words on this page are charged with love, peace, and wisdom and that they may touch all those who read them....

Soaked in this presence of prayer, I give thanks to my Elder, Leonard Day Rider, the wise medicine man, for being one of my greatest inspirations.

Just the other day, as we were talking in the low light of his bedroom, he looked at me and spoke with great humility.

"I wasn't really given the gift for healing people like some..." he said, chuckling. "I mean, I can sit and talk to people, share stories, and give guidance, but I can't really 'heal' people per se. I'm not really that kind of medicine man..."

Then he paused and looked off into the distance.

"But the most important thing I can do for them is to keep them in my heart, pray for them, and trust that the Creator will take care of them. Of course, I have to do my best and do everything I can to support those in need, but there are many things I have no control over.

"Take what's happening in Ukraine right now... There's really not much I can do at the moment, but I can pray for them. And some may not think it's much, but I feel that if my prayer can reach across the world and help just one person, it's worth it."

The depth of his words and deep humility struck a chord in my heart. I remembered the story about a woman who was on the verge of death in a car wreck on a highway in Los Angeles.

Floating above the crash, she could see her own body and hear the anxious thoughts of everyone on the road. She heard the paramedics worried about what to do, the police officers thinking about how to best patrol the perimeter, and, it being midday in L.A., she could hear the many impatient people.

She heard thoughts like, "Geez, what the heck is taking so long up there!" and "Oh, man! I'm gonna be late!"

Just before she left this world completely, she came upon a red station wagon and heard a woman's voice, not thinking about herself, but of others. Her voice was crystal clear: "Dear Creator, please be with whoever is over there. Let them feel embraced by your love. Be with them. Hold them. Help them." And at that moment, the woman felt herself being drawn back into her body from where she'd been floating in the air, and she was revived.

Now, the crazy thing is that before she returned to her body, the woman managed to remember the license plate of the red station wagon. When she recovered, she looked up the driver to say thank you for her compassion and care. When she found her, the two women embraced as they celebrated the miracle together. And the rest, as they say, is history. Now, I share this story to remind us just how powerful each of our individual prayers and intentions can be. They can literally reach out across the world and touch those in need. This is the power of prayer.

I wonder how the world might look with all its challenges if everyone took the attitude my Elder Leonard Day Rider does and humbly stepped beyond ourselves, stopped complaining, and started praying. I can confidently say that we would live in a kinder, more loving, and more beautiful world. Now, as I have said many times before, we will still have to do our part to create the changes we wish to see in the world, but why should we do it alone when we can partner with the Creative Power within all things?

With these thoughts in mind, let us always remember to pray—with everything.

Give thanks for this day, your home, this breath,

Things big and small—Pray. Pray. Pray.

In times of joy and in times of deep struggle.

Pray for wisdom.

Pray for strength.

Pray for courage.

Pray for all your needs.

Pray for all those in need.

Because every prayer counts and every prayer is heard, even if we don't see it.

And this is sometimes the hardest part of prayer. Because things might not look like we want them to at first. Heck, sometimes it may even appear like things have gotten worse. But we have to have trust and realize that sometimes our prayers take their due time. This could mean years or even lifetimes. Thus, we must be patient, and we must have faith.

When gardeners plant their seeds, they don't pull them up the next day to see if they have grown. They let go and patiently water them every day, even if, on the surface, they have nothing to show for their efforts. But they trust that if they keep showing up, the law of life will support them. So, too, we must be with our prayers. We must offer them up. Let go, and then continue to water them with our attention, our faith, and trust.

So, as we look to our world and the many events and challenges beyond our control, let us remember the wisdom of Leonard Day Rider, reach out, and pray.

Thoughts to Ponder / Actions to Embody

- Is there anyone who could use your prayers today?
- Offer your thanks and gratitude for the big and small things in your life today.
- Bring someone in need to your mind, and with your full concentration, see them in wellness, see them happy, and see them healed in body, mind, and spirit.
- Pray, pray, pray—all day, every day.

66
THE SCIENCE OF PEACE

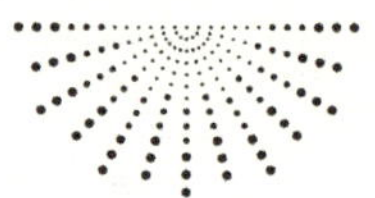

It was a hot summer's day in 1993 in Washington, D.C., when four thousand transcendental meditators set out to do what so many thought was impossible—prove that meditation could change the world...

Well, more specifically, in eight weeks, they wanted to prove that meditation could reduce violent crime by 20 percent. Put simply, their hypothesis was that by "being peace," we can positively influence our external world. This idea was first brought to the public in 1974 by the Indian sage Maharishi, who claimed the quality of life of society would noticeably improve if at least 1 percent of the population practiced the Transcendental Meditation technique. Note, the Dalai Lama has shared similar thoughts, suggesting that if all children started to meditate at age eight, all violence in this world would end in one generation. While these sound like wonderful, warm, and fuzzy claims, this group of meditators wanted to prove it.

At the time, violent crimes were actually on the rise, and the Washington chief of police didn't buy it. It's worth noting that he actually said their chance of those meditators reducing violent crime by 20 percent was as likely as it snowing in summer. But despite his little faith, after eight weeks of the rigorous scientific study, violent crimes reduced by a whopping 23.6 percent! Now, before you suggest that it was some stroke of luck, it's worth noting the statistical probability of this happening by chance alone was less than 2 in 1 billion ($p < .000000002$).

Now, this may seem crazy, but since that first experiment, scientific studies on the power of group meditation and its positive influence on our world have been repeated with similar jaw-dropping results, so much so now there is even a scientific community committed to researching the power of group coherence in influencing global events.

Now, as I have said before, I am not suggesting we should simply pray, meditate, sing Kumbaya, and then think everything is going to be alright. I am practical and know we have to do our part in this world to bring about the changes we seek. But think about those earth-shaking experimental results for a moment. Through the simple act of being "Peace," those 4000 meditators were able to make a transformative change in their external environment, nearly 25 percent! That's 25 percent less abuse, violence, and unnecessary suffering, all because a group of meditators took the time to cultivate their inner environment. Imagine the far-reaching benefits when coupled with positive, constructive action.

Personally, I find this research quite heartening because it gives us a lot of power back, especially as we look at our current global challenges. It shows us that despite external conditions and the powers that be, we have a greater power, and it lives within. Together, we can use it and co-create a more peaceful and loving world. Those 4000 meditators did it; others have, and so can we. And so will we...

So, if you feel like you want to make some changes in the world and don't know where to start, try sitting down on your meditation mat. Then filled with peace, you can get out there and use it to create a more beautiful world.

67
ACHIEVING THE IMPOSSIBLE

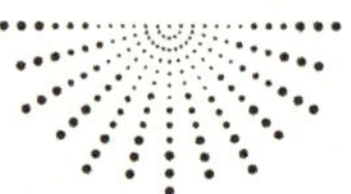

Effective prayer is the fruit of a relationship... not a technique for acquiring blessings.

— D. A. CARSON

"I am sorry, but it's impossible," the doctor said as he shook his head.

"Come on, there's got to be some chance it will heal on its own," I replied.

How I ended up on that hospital bed is a long story, but the short version of the tale is that a tree fell on me, cracking my left ankle's bone open like a hungry Pac-Man.

While he said I would be able to walk again, he would have to drill two metal screws into me to seal my bones together, leaving behind a trail of pain that would follow me for the rest of my life.

"No!" he said firmly. "I already said... It's impossible."

Then he turned and marched out of the room to tend to the other patients at the orthopedic unit at Ottawa's Civic Hospital.

I watched his white coat trail behind him as he went, then defiantly shook my head.

"Just you see," I mentally affirmed. "It will heal..."

I can't blame the doc for believing what he did. He'd only been trained in eight years of medical school, saw hundreds, if not thousands of broken bones, and none of his textbooks in Western medicine could have prepared him for the knowledge and support I had available to me—the limitless power of Spirit.

With only four weeks to the scheduled surgery, I embarked on an intensive healing routine. Inspired by the work of Dr. Joe Dispenza, for two hours a day, I would visualize my broken bone in perfect alignment, seeing and feeling as if it were already healed. I took Bach flower remedies, energy workers visited me, and probably one of my greatest areas of support was a community of souls praying for me.

Sure enough, when the operation day came and the team of specialized surgeons cut me open, they were astonished to see the impossible. The split bone they were there to screw back into place had "somehow" fused back into perfect shape on its own accord.

How's that for impossible?

I smile as I reflect on this story because it reminds me of the gift of these spiritual tools, the blessings that can be found in a sacred community, and the unbreakable power of Spirit.

Don't get me wrong. Modern medicine is amazing. Because of it, the average life span has doubled; we can transplant hearts, give people new knees, and do what was impossible no more than a hundred years ago.

However, despite the many advancements in medical technology, you and I have access to an ancient technology far too many of us forget in our modern world. That is the power of will, the power of prayer and faith, and ultimately, the power of Spirit.

This power is available to each and every one of us. It is limitless, and if we can tune in with it, the impossible becomes just another day in the park.

So yes, get your medical exams, exercise, eat well, and take care of the things on the material front. But ultimately, know you are connected to a power so much greater than anything in this material universe. As a spark of the Divine, the Universe is at your side, waiting for you to tune into it.

And with it, we can and will overcome every personal, familial, and societal challenge that comes our way.

With that power by our side, we will make the "impossible"—possible.

68
A LESSON FROM THE MAHABHARATA

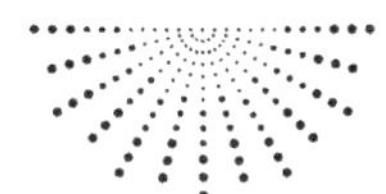

Anxiety filled me, along with millions of others, as I contemplated the mess we found ourselves in. *Oh no, it's the end of the world!* I thought as I spoke with a friend over the phone.

It was mid-April 2020, a mere few weeks after the world had found itself in the clutches of one of the largest crises our century has ever seen: The Global Pandemic. At the time, I was in a third-world country with next to no money and isolated in a little hostel, quarantined, along with the rest of the world. With that, the conversation with my friend on the other side of the world felt very much like the times we found ourselves in, dark and far from hope. So, when I hung up the phone, I couldn't help but feel the weight of what was to come. I wanted to run, to fight, to do something! But I felt paralyzed, lost, and filled with fear and doubt about what I should do.

Thankfully, I remembered the wisdom from an ancient story that brought my heart to peace.

In the classic Indian tale of the War of the Mahabharata, the Pandava army was attacked by an evil opposing force armed with weapons of mass destruction. They had never seen such powerful arms before, and even though the Pandavas were some of the greatest warriors ever seen, they had nothing strong enough to counter the opposing evil force. As such, in the fire of battle, it looked like the end of the noble Pandavas.

However, just before that happened, the leader of the Pandavas turned to his men and asked them to cast their weapons aside and, instead, to be still. Then, with hands folded in prayer, they surrendered all thoughts of violence and war and only began to think good thoughts. What happened next is nothing short of miraculous. The opposing army, unable to gain power from the Pandavas' negative thinking, became very calm. Then, with each passing minute, the Pandava army grew in power and, eventually, was so strong they were able to overcome their warring opponents.

So that's what I did. A few hours after the call, I joined 25,000 other warriors from around the world in the online arena, and armed with prayer, we sent love and healing intentions for the planet.

If you have been with me this far, you know I am a firm believer in the power of prayer. Like the Pandavas from this ancient story, I feel that one of the greatest things we can do in our current global crisis is to follow their wisdom, cast our negative thoughts aside, and fold our hands and pray. Then, filled with positive energy, we can act against the injustices we see.

Because where we focus our energy is where we will go. Just imagine you wanted to drive to Boston but were looking at a map of Chicago. In the end, despite what you wanted, where do you think we would end up? Similarly, the thoughts and pictures we send into the universe are the maps that will guide us to where we end up. There are two roads we can take at this moment: Love or Fear. Now the question is: Where do we want to go? Are we putting our attention there? If not, we'd better start now.

Because even more dangerous than the coronavirus is the virus of fear. The sickness has infected nearly the whole planet and has dished out symptoms of separation, us vs. them mentality, greed, and mass-scale panic. While it's important to be cautious against the coronavirus, we must stand even more heavily guarded against the pandemic of fear and wash our minds and emotions as much as we are washing our hands. We must practice these spiritual principles, meditate, connect in community (even if it's online), fill our minds with good thoughts, and pray with a focus on the world we want to create.

The scientific laws of quantum physics have illustrated that our thoughts are things, small micro units of energy, and any thought, if consistently focused on, with the water of our attention, will manifest in material form. This law is as true as the laws of gravity, and it works regardless of whether you believe it or not. It is the law of intention; it is the law of prayer. So, if we want to help co-create a healed world, we need to keep our minds calm and focused on a healed world.

A side note for any who struggle with automatic fear thoughts: You need not worry. Because positive thoughts are thousands of times more powerful than negative ones, just as oil rises above water, the frequencies of love rise above the lower, denser thoughts of fear. So even if those thoughts of fear come intruding in, just keep coming back to the thought of love.

Because one of the greatest antidotes to fear is remembering we are connected to something so much bigger. Some call it the Great Spirit, others call it God, and modern scientists call it the "Quantum Field." Whatever you want to call it does not matter; it is the invisible force that governs the universe. It is there to help; we simply have to still our minds and connect with it. When we do, what is there to fear? We are standing on the shoulders of a giant.

Let's face it: these are challenging times, and we need all the help we can get. But so many of us are trying to face this battle alone. But would you be so stubborn as to move your house alone? Would you drag your couch down the stairs and lift every one of those heavy boxes? Would you tussle, toil, and eventually collapse on the ground thinking, *WTF!*

Now, you could have saved yourself a lot of trouble had you reached out to a good friend and asked for help. Similarly, that good friend you can call right now is this Universal Force. It's there, standing by and happy, waiting to help. We simply have to call on it.

So, as we look to the future and face the battles before us, let us remember the honorable Pandava army, who cast their negative thinking aside and remembered they did not need to do it alone.

Let us remember we are connected to a force so grand, so strong, and so loving. And with it by our side, we can overcome whatever challenges we may face.

That loving force is here; we simply need to pause and connect with it.

69
FIGHTING FIRE WITH PRAYER

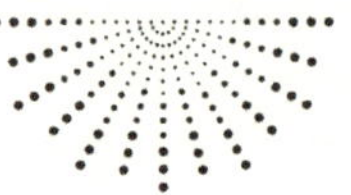

When we pray with pure heart, the whole universe prays with us.

— THICH NHAT HANH

"Fire! Fire! The forest is on fire!"

Heavy drops of sweat dribbled down my eight-year-old nephew's face. Our legs were heavy as we pushed forward through the forest, thick smoke chasing us. We doubled our speed to race against time and escape the flames.

Don't worry; we made it out. After all, it was just in our imagination.

Well, so I thought…

Let me explain: It was a little after 8:00 p.m. when I told this bedtime story to my nephew Raven as we lay in the darkness of his room with snow falling silently outside, glinting in the moonlight.

In the tale I told, the hero of the story, a young boy my nephew's age, went on a quest to save a blazing forest. His travels brought him to a mighty lake where he bowed his head, offered a purple flower to the water, and sang a sacred song to request the lake's help. The Spirit of the Water saw the offering, heard the song, then sprang into the sky and became a magnificent rainstorm that pelted down and extinguished the flames.

By the time I finished the story, my nephew was asleep. While I thoroughly enjoyed both imagining and telling the story, it didn't end at his bedside.

Later, while helping my sister tidy up the kitchen, she asked, "Did he get to sleep okay?"

"Just fine," I said with a smile. "I told him a story about a great forest fire and a little boy who stopped it when he sang to a magical lake."

She chuckled. "Thanks, Uncle Adam." Then she added, "Forest fire, huh? We could sure use some of that magic in Australia right now."

It was January 2020, and tens of thousands of miles away, in the land 'down under,' Australia had been ablaze for months. The destruction was so big the flames were felt halfway across the world. Everyone was talking about it in the news, talk shows, and daily conversations, and all were concerned. Like many, I hoped that somehow, something would happen to help extinguish the flames.

As my sister said that, I realized there was a hidden message for me in the story I had just told. And in that eureka moment, I literally grabbed my sister by the shoulder. "We need to sing the water song! We need to pray for the rains!"

Interestingly enough, I realized I had already been doing that. Over the previous weeks, I found myself unconsciously singing an Algonquin water song again, and again, all throughout the day—almost as if it was calling me to do so.

Now what happened next was nothing short of astounding. The following afternoon, I sat by a warm fireside sipping cedar tea with a woman who had worked with The Thirteen Grandmothers, the council of Indigenous Elders from around the globe who promote peace, ecological sustainability, and a unified world.

"Did you hear what just happened in Australia?" she asked with glowing eyes.

I shook my head and leaned in for her answer.

"You didn't hear about the storms? The buckets of rain? Hail the size of your fist? It came out of nowhere and dumped down on the flames. The firefighters can't believe it. They're calling it a miracle."

My eyes widened in disbelief. She smiled knowingly.

"For weeks now, the Thirteen Grandmothers have been calling everyone from near and far to sing the water song. The rains are a result of the power of our prayers."

Dumbfounded, I realized I had picked up on those people praying for the wellness and healing of the Australian bush, even though I'd not heard the request directly from the Thirteen Grandmothers. Somehow, I had tuned into the collective consciousness and added my own prayer drops to the cause.

Interestingly enough, when I recounted this story to a friend weeks later, he told me a similar story of a large church congregation that had been fasting and, like the Thirteen Grandmothers, prayed for the rains in Australia. He said that the day they broke their fast, the rains came. As I reflected on the synchronicities of these stories, I am positive there were many more groups out there who saw the need and offered their own heartfelt prayers—and through that, helped co-create the powerful change we all saw.

This is the power of us coming together in prayer. It creates a magnetic field that draws others in, and with our united mind, we can directly affect the world around us. Our collective thoughts hold power. And they hold even more power when we connect them to the Universal Force found in prayer. When we do, just like in Australia, miracles manifest. This powerful force is always with us, wanting to aid and support us. We have access to it all the time. All we need to do is plug into it. And when we do, we can unite and direct our intentions to create a more peaceful and loving world.

Alone, we are but a single drop, but together, we are the ocean.

70
AMPLIFYING YOUR PRAYERS

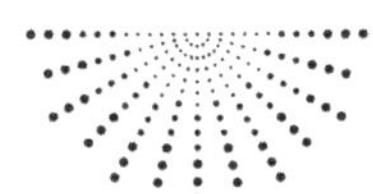

Prayer is a universal practice found in every spiritual tradition around the globe. While there are thousands of ways to pray, certain principles gleaned from ancient wisdom and metaphysical sciences suggest there are some effective commonalities that work to enhance the practice. Below, I have referenced some of these key points.

Pray in the affirmative

Affirmative prayer involves connecting with the Great Spirit within and holding a positive focus on the desired outcome. Within every one of us exists the power of the Creator, where all things are possible.

Jesus said, "The Kingdom of God is within you." Krishna declared that the Divine is situated in the heart of all living beings. Lao Tzu said that the Tao "is always present within you."

Many more wisdom traditions echo this universal truth: The Divine lives within.

Thus, when we realize that within us is the very power that created the entire universe, there is no need to doubt. Rather than wishing for an outcome, affirmative prayer sees it as already having been achieved. It sees that all is already healed and simply gives thanks for it.

Focus

Concentration is the key to amplifying your practice. It's hard to do anything well when we are not fully present. Try to imagine creating a great work of art if your mind is fixed on your plans for the weekend. Similarly, when we pray, we are creating something beautiful; thus, we need to be fully present to accomplish this.

Using a song or a chant to slow you down and rouse your devotion is a great way to gather your attention. Then, try some form of meditation, such as focused breathing, to concentrate the mind. Once the mind has slowed down sufficiently, like a magnifying glass that gathers the sun's rays into a single point to create a fire, you can use the gathered energy created from your focusing practices to direct your mind to your prayers.

Begin with devotion

When approaching prayer, it is helpful to bring the energy of love and devotion to the task at hand. As the previous point noted, focus is key to effective prayer. Love helps with this. If you have ever been engrossed in a conversation with an old friend or taken by a piece of music, you know it's easy to pay attention to what you love. Moreover, love is the ultimate amplifying force. When we are in love, we bring and create more love around us, and become like magnets, drawing events and experiences of a similar energy. With this in mind, like a joyful child embraces their father and mother with open arms, come to the practice of prayer. Bring your heart and soul to the entire process and let the fire of your love fill you as you pray.

Be grateful

The wise mystic and theologian Meister Eckhart said, "If the only prayer you ever say in your entire life is thank you, it will be enough."

This beautiful wisdom regarding the power of gratitude can be found in every major religion around the globe and is even praised in the fields of psychology and neuroscience, suggesting that an attitude of gratitude makes us feel more positive, improves our health, promotes resilience, and helps us overcome challenges. Note: Some studies even found that simply writing down five things you are grateful for once a week could increase your happiness by 25 percent.

One of the reasons gratitude is so important in effective prayer is that, like love, it creates an orbit of positive energy around you. Looking at the scientific discipline of quantum physics, we see that our thoughts and emotions produce a measurable electromagnetic field that radiates from our bodies. This field is like a magnet that draws back to us experiences that vibrate at the same frequency. Thus, when we set our intentions during our prayers, when our thoughts and emotions are connected with the energy of gratitude, we magnetically draw back experiences that make us grateful. Answered prayers are always something to be grateful for.

Have a clear vision

Just like it's critical to have a clear blueprint when building a house, when we pray, it's important to have a clear vision to build the world we want to see. In your mind's eye, see the world as you would like it to be. See it in its perfection, and let it be so.

Let go, trust, and be patient

As mentioned, when good gardeners plant seeds, they do not go the next day and dig them up to see if anything has grown. Instead, they show up daily and water them with their loving care, trusting that through their efforts, roots will shoot and sprouts will grow. Similarly, when tending to our prayers, we need to let them go and trust the process.

Remember, trust is not that hard when we realize we are dealing with the very energy that created the entire universe. It is an all-loving force that longs for our well-being. With this in mind, we can trust that all is being taken care of.

Follow the guidance

For our seedlings to grow, we need to water them daily. We do this with our consistent prayers and by following the intuitive guidance that is shown to us. This guidance may happen in moments of silence just after prayer, or it can also manifest as a feeling that encourages us to take a specific action. Whatever shows up in those moments, trust it and follow through.

If you are unclear whether something is of higher guidance, you can check in with your energy after moments of silence. If the insight radiates a field of peace in your heart, that action will create that.

However, even though peace is emitted from your body when the guidance comes, you might not like taking action at the moment it is required.

For example, we may have been praying for a form of healing in our bodies, then after periods of meditation, we get the insight we need to follow a new food regimen of more fruits and vegetables. But when the time comes to buy food at the grocery store, our habits and fears of change may create contractions in our chests. In moments like these, it's important to act on the guidance that came to you in those moments of silence.

We can use the gardener analogy again to illustrate this point. We can imagine that after a long day of work, we may not want to water the garden. But as good gardeners, we know that if we want those seeds to grow, it's important to take action and water those seeds, even if we may not feel like it.

There you have it, a few helpful points to consider when approaching prayer. While they are simple, they have been practiced for thousands of years by ancient traditions that understood these powerful principles. I pray they serve you well in life's sometimes wild journey. I also hope that in the thick of life's challenges, you will always remember that you are not alone—forever connected to a Great Loving Force who wants to help you. Like an open hand waiting for us to touch it, the support is there. We simply need to reach for it.

71
PREPARE THE FIELDS

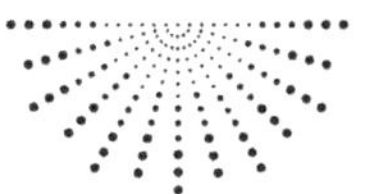

Two dedicated farmers lived in a remote village surrounded by rolling hills.

While their land was usually abundant and fertile, a terrible drought fell upon it one year.

For weeks, the rain evaded them, and every day that passed, the earth below them grew drier.

With their livelihoods on the line, as well as their families' well-being, both farmers grew terribly desperate.

Thus, when night fell upon them, in the privacy of their homes, both farmers prayed fervently to their Creator that they be granted the gift of rain.

Several weeks had passed like this, and then something miraculous happened.

Their Creator did send the rain.

But only to one of them.

Can you guess which farmer received it?

STORM

~

When a storm is brewing and
The ship starts to sink,
Everyone gets down on their knees to pray
But why should we wait for a tragedy
To connect with this beautiful
and comforting Source
That is always here with its love,
warmth, and care?
Why should we wait for a storm
to give thanks for the sun?

~

PART VIII
RESOLUTION

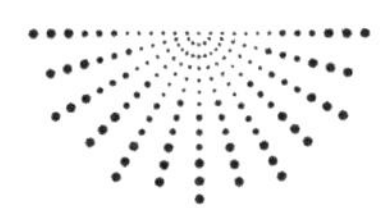

72
SOLVING THE BIG ME: PART 1

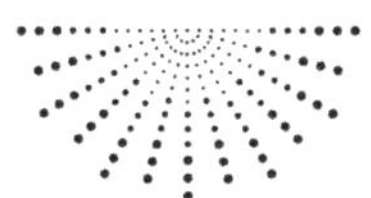

"Oh, there he is!" I exclaimed as I looked across the crowd of people huddled together in the concert hall.

There, in a red shirt, twenty feet from the left of the stage, he stood smiling and chatting as he had his photo snapped with his many fans. From a distance, I watched for nearly ten minutes before the crowd died down.

Then he was alone and I saw my opening. But it was already five minutes past eight, and the show was already supposed to have started. *It's too late,* I thought, and the cold hands of fear almost held me down. But deep down, I knew that on the other side of that uncomfortable feeling was my growth. With that knowing, I willed myself forward.

"Let's go!" I told my friend.

I rose to my feet and started shuffling through the crowd toward him. I came to a small set of stairs that led to the upper stage, and when I emerged at the top, there he was: Krishna Das, the world-renowned Kirtan musician and one of my favorite musical artists.

Staring face to face with him, I was at a loss for words. What was I to say to someone whose music had touched me so much? Eventually, what fumbled out was "Can I take a photo with you?" I exclaimed like an excited groupie.

He chuckled and made a little joke. "Well, maybe," he said with a sly grin.

"Honestly, I love your music so much, man. I listen to you every day!"

He seemed surprised.

I went on. "Yeah. I am a writer, and every day, just before I start my creative sessions, I take a moment, put your songs on repeat in the background, and let the mantras fill me while I write."

He looked appreciative, smiled, and said, "Okay. But let's make it quick. I should already be up there..."

Like lightning, I snapped a few quick photos, turned, and wobbled back to my seat, so excited by meeting someone who has supported my creative work so much. I took my seat, and in a minute, Krishna Das was front and center stage singing beautiful *bhajans*, Sanskrit love songs to the Divine.

Then I realized my mistake...

Let me explain.

Here in Bali, where I live, we have lots of waterfalls. So many that it's easy for me to hop on my motorbike and drive to these stunning sights twenty minutes in every direction.

But, while I love going to see these falls, I sometimes struggle to stop myself from judging how people act around them. Because 95 percent of the folks that come seem more concerned about themselves than appreciating the moment and taking in the waterfall's beauty. It's just one big photoshoot, with rows and rows of people snapping selfies to post on social media.

And I gotta say, it kind of breaks my heart a little bit every time I go. I mean, really, here are these magnificent works of creation, and all people can do is think about themselves and how they look in front of them?

I can almost feel the sadness of the land, the ancestors, and the spirits of the place at people's failure to acknowledge them.

And while I may have judged others for taking self-portraits at the waterfalls, here I was doing exactly that at the concert with Krishna Das. I was only thinking about myself.

Despite receiving so much from this musician, I took more from him rather than gave back. I even failed to say those two magical words that make all the difference in this life:

"Thank you."

It still hurts as I reflect on that experience.

Now, while I have my own work to do around this, I do believe this is more than a mere personal shortcoming and part of a larger social condition that, as a whole, we humans need to address.

Because I believe it's this cultural condition that has led to so much anxiety, depression, and excess.

The Bigger Problem: The Big Me

David Brooks, an op-ed columnist and New York Times best-selling author, talks about this problem in his exceptional book *The Road to Character*. He coined this cultural condition "The Big Me," which essentially is this societal obsessive focus on the self.

The Big Me is largely concerned with external forms of success, such as position, fame, and appearance. Hence, in order to keep up with its grandiosity, excess is part of the package, be it in material things or even in doings, and it loves to be busy. So concerned with the self, The Big Me loves the infamous selfie, and social media exaggerates this cultural condition.

Every "like" gives The Big Me the false sense that it is valued and loved. And when those likes fail to come, feelings of 'not enough' and unworthiness plague it. So, desperately, it tries to find ways to fill the insatiable void.

The Cost of The Big Me

But what happens when we follow this Big Me cultural trend?

Well, there is a large body of research that links self-centeredness to addiction, anxiety, and depression. Other studies have correlated social media use with similar negative outcomes.

This is not surprising, as much of social media is primarily focused on self-interest. Other research has found that when people chase after external measures of success, such as material wealth, they are less psychologically stable and more prone to psychological distress.

Moreover, The Big ME culture does not just affect us negatively, but the consequences of this hyper self-focus also harm our planet as a whole.

Think about it. In order to keep up with this "Big" culture, we need to take and take and take at rates impossible to replenish. More forests need to be chopped down, more oil drilled, and more products sold in order to keep up with an insane fascination with Bigness. And the earth feels it.

It's worth noting that gross domestic product (GDP) is the standard for how "well" a country is doing. Many believe that a high GDP means a country is growing and thus doing good. But the reality is, this measure of "wellness" does not take into account the fact that in order to grow at the insane rates we do, we need to "take" at rates that sacrifice many other, more telling measures of wellness, such as sustainability and ethical work practices.

Even more interesting is that cancer, the terrible disease that plagues the globe, acts in this very same way. Cancer cells are only concerned with their self-interest. They grow at alarming rates that eventually not only kill the host, but themselves.

As we reflect on our current climate crisis, does it not sound like a similar parallel?

The Solution to Big ME Culture

We don't have to go far to find the answer. We simply need to look outside our window and pay attention to nature to find our solution. As the mystic poet Hafiz observed:

Even after all this time, the sun never says to the earth, *You owe me.* Look what happens with a love like that. It lights the whole sky.

This idea of giving, as opposed to taking, has been prescribed as the path to a good life in ancient wisdom traditions around the globe. The Bhagavad Gita, the timeless text on how to live, instructs us toward a path of right activity that is not focused on self-satisfaction but instead on serving the whole.

"Strive constantly to serve the welfare of the world; by devotion to selfless work, one attains the supreme goal of life."

Again, the Bible suggests we should "Do nothing out of selfish ambition or vain conceit. Rather, in humility value others above yourselves…not looking to your own interests but each of you to the interests of the others."

In Taoism, the sage Lao Tzu instructs, "A man can achieve his own happiness only by pursuing the happiness of others because it is only by forgetting about his own happiness that he can become truly happy."

Even modern science highlights this wisdom. With research in fMRI (functional magnetic resonance imaging for the brain) studies, we have found that pleasure centers of the brain are more activated when serving others, as opposed to achieving personal pleasure.

The Shift

So, there it is, the solution to The Big Me Culture. A simple shift in mindset from 'me' to 'we' makes all the difference.

But I will not lie. That shift may be simple, but it is far from easy to achieve. Like all skills, it must be practiced. Even as I wrote this very paragraph, my visiting mother walked into my office and asked to borrow my only set of headphones. I was using them (listening to Krishna Das!). At the time, I could see my ego wanting to cling to "my" things. It was only for a moment, but I had a visceral sense of the feeling. I brushed it off and offered my headphones with a smile. But, upon reflection, I wonder if I may have stayed irritated had I not been writing an article on the very subject of giving!

That said, these principles must be practiced again and again and again. And we must constantly remind ourselves by reading the wisdom literature, being in the right company, and filling our minds with these ideals.

Because the truth is, we are conditioned daily to think about the self. And we must recondition ourselves to take the attention away from The Big Me, and bring it back to something beyond, be that another human being, a cause, and most importantly, to God.

Put simply, this mindset requires sacrifice. Sometimes, that may be small things like a set of headphones, or it could be our time. Or it could be to a cause bigger than ourselves. But most of the time, we can be doing the very same thing we always do, but with the consciousness of service, as opposed to self-interest.

You can use social media, pursue a client, practice positive self-care, or do your laundry, all with this simple shift in mindset from selfishness to service.

It's worth noting that the root of the word *sacrifice* means *to make sacred.* Thus, when we take our attention off *me* and our little wants, we become like the sun the mystic Hafiz spoke about, not asking for reciprocity. By adjusting our focus away from *me,* we both make this world a brighter place, and our entire life becomes a sacred act.

How's that for living a meaningful life?

SURRENDER

~

I hang the white flag and bow my head,
submitting to this Great Love.
For lifetimes, I have been at war,
fighting for "my" never-ending wants,
and every time I died, I always wanted more.
Now, all I want to do
is to come home to You!
But this "Me" of mine
has gotten me into so much trouble!
His insatiable appetite for
things of this world keeps
pulling me from what is real.
I will do my best to train him,
if that is even possible.
To exchange all his worldly wishes
for the one that will satisfy them all:
To know Truth.
So, I bow my head and surrender.
Help me, Mother!
Help me, Father!
Help me, Friend!

Help me!
I want to know "You."
That's all I want.
That's all I need.
Please.
Help me...

~

73
SOLVING THE BIG ME: PART 2

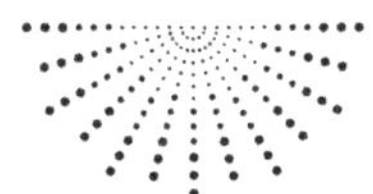

Before I close our reflections on love, I want to leave you with one final thought. It's a thought so potent that if you only remember one thing from this entire book, it's this. Because if you truly contemplate this idea, act upon it, and live it, you will find your entire life has changed for the better. Living from your authentic self will come naturally. Your relationships will become sweeter, richer, and filled with more depth. Moments once thought of as dull will be filled with new meaning. Truly, this idea really holds that power.

So what is it?

As I mentioned earlier, Krishna Das sings *bhajans,* also known as Kirtan, which are love songs to the Divine. This practice is found in the system of yoga known as Bhakti—the yoga of devotion. Now, before I go on, you should know that yoga is much more than a bunch of people on mats doing headstands. The term 'yoga' actually means "to yoke" or "to unite." Thus, real yoga is a system that helps the individual practicing it unite their small egoic self with the big capital "S" Self. And I am not talking about The Big ME Self! I am talking about the wave meeting the ocean. I am talking about uniting our consciousness with the Universal consciousness.

Thus, Bhakti Yoga—the yoga of devotion or the yoga of love—is the act of doing whatever we do, be it eating, working, or serving, with love in our hearts for the Divine. In the yoga of love, everything we do becomes an offering to our Beloved. Everything becomes an act of love.

So, when Krishna Das climbed on stage after I snapped a few selfies with him and started singing, that's when I cried. Because the minute he began chanting those love songs to the Beloved, I remembered why I was there; but in my self-absorption, I had forgotten the whole purpose of life—to unite myself with the Divine energies Krishna Das was devotionally singing about. And in that moment, just like a lover feels the pangs of being far away from their beloved, I could feel the pain of forgetting my Source. And I realized that this forgetting, this missing of what truly matters, is what many sacred traditions have long pointed to.

The Christians have a word called "sin," which can bring up many negative connotations due to religious institutional shaming. But if we break down the word in its most literal sense, "to sin" means to miss the mark. So, there I was, an archer, failing to hit my ultimate target.

It's worth noting that in the final days of Jesus's life, he offered the world two great commandments to live by. These two commandments are found in the wisdom traditions all around the globe and are sacred pathways for living a good life. In this book, I have spoken a lot about the second commandment, also known as the Golden Rule: Love thy neighbor as thyself.

But more than me just speaking about it, the Golden Rule (loving others) has received world recognition and inspired many to look beyond themselves and to reach out with love and care for others. Personally, I think this is simply beautiful. However, I have found that the first commandment for living a good life, found in traditions around the globe is often neglected.

What was the commandment?

"To love the Lord with all the heart, with all thy mind, and all thy strength."

Now, despite this being the first commandment, it's worth questioning why this rule is often forgotten. I think it's probably due to our hyper-secular culture, which tends to have a distaste for anything associated with religion. And the word Lord can often scare people. Yet, the problem is that when we forget this rule, it's much easier to miss the ultimate mark and move through life without a clear understanding of our true purpose.

What is that?

Like the process of yoga instructs, we are here to unite our small selves with our Big Selves.

The Buddhists call this Enlightenment, the yogis call it Self-Realization, the Christians call it Theosis, and scientists like Abraham Maslow have called it Self-Actualization. Whatever you call it does not matter; realizing these states is the primary purpose of us being on the planet—to Know Thyself, as Socrates would say. Thus, since this is the ultimate goal, knowing the best way to reach our destination is a helpful aid on the journey.

Now, it's true that, in the end, each of us can arrive at that ultimate realization by simply following the second rule alone. Living a life of virtue will lead you to there. But "Love for the Lord" is said to have a special place in our soul's evolution. That's why it's the first of the commandments given. But we can look past the Bible and see this wisdom echoed elsewhere, such as in the Bhagavad Gita, the Sanskrit book of wisdom.

"The Blessed Lord said: Those who, fixing their minds on Me, worship Me with ever steadfast faith and devotion, I consider them to be the best yogis."

Here, we have the Divine directly highlighting the power of love for the Beloved. It's worth mentioning that when it says, "the best of yogis," it means the best of seekers of the Ultimate Truth. That means that if you and I are on the path to becoming our most authentic selves, we are yogis as well—no headstands needed. It's also worth noting that the Bhagavad Gita acknowledges there are other pathways to reach that ultimate goal. Yet, in this verse, just like in the Bible, we see that Bhakti (love for the Supreme) has a special place on the path of our soul's unfoldment. Through Bhakti, we become the best.

I must admit that writing these words has been challenging. I actually waited until the very end of the book to share them explicitly. Because honestly, I don't want to preach. Yet, I feel there is such a great opportunity for us to know this truth and thereby benefit from it. But I also know many of us are put off by words like God, Lord, and even Creator. I get it. Like I have said before, I know the institution of religion has done atrocious things in the name of this beautiful Force. Yet would Love itself do such horrible things? I know it wouldn't. But that Great Love is right here. And like a father or mother wants the love of their child, so too does this Great Mystery.

If I am honest, more than my relationship with my wife, son, and dearest friends, I have encountered no greater love than the one I have experienced between me and my Creator. For the love I have found in that relationship truly is perfect. And I don't use the word "perfect" lightly, which can be defined as "without flaws or defects" and "complete in every way." Because in the truest sense, in that relationship, I have found perfect love. For it is a Love beyond any human limitation or condition.

And I know that's why I want to share this so much with you. When you have a gift, you want to give it. And that gift is available to each of us. We simply have to turn our hearts, minds, and souls to this Great Loving Force that is already shining its love upon us. And like a dear friend, love it back. For when we develop this intimate relationship with our Creator, we march swiftly toward life's ultimate goal. And share the greatest love our souls could ever know.

What a gift…

COMING HOME

~

When I sit still in the
silent chambers of my heart,
I remember "Who I Am."
Those little wants for
worldly favor, fame, and fancies,
seem such foolish goals
in comparison to this great bliss
that lives within.
When I search for those little wants,
it feels as if I am trading in
a million magnificent sunsets
for a tiny piece of coal.
I have been running through a desert,
playing the games in this world,
and it has made me so very tired.
For years, I've been chasing mirages,
trying to quench my thirst.
But again and again,
I find myself parched after I reach each bend,
and again and again,
I turn my eyes upward

and search the horizon
for something to free me from
this longing that follows me wherever I go.
But all this time, there has been
a river of salvation
that has been singing sweetly within my Soul.
All this time,
it has been calling me Home.
I know if I walk away from these desert sands
and turn back to the seat of my Soul,
I will find the water
that I have always been searching for.
Then why do I not turn away from that which
has brought me nothing but pain?
Habit and Fear
are the words that come to mind.
But I am tired of making choices based
on my past conditioning,
tired of letting fear guide my life,
tired of being a fool...
Tired.
I have decided to leave the desert
and turn toward the overflowing streams
that sing freely within my Soul.
If you're tired too,
I hope you join me.

~

74
FINAL THOUGHTS

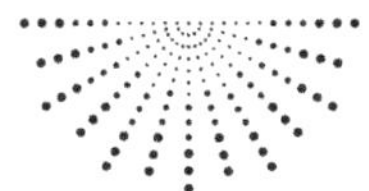

So, there you have it. A few lessons on love that I hope have helped us all gain a greater understanding of this beautiful virtue. More importantly, perhaps some of these stories will help each of us act upon this profound quality more readily in our lives.

We have covered quite a bit of ground in the pages behind us as we explored some of the many expressions of love. We've spoken about the importance of bringing love to our relationships, starting with ourselves. We discussed acceptance, self-care, and small daily practices to keep us plugged in and operating at our best. We extended that love to our family, our friends, the strangers on the street, our work, and even directed it to the earth itself! We spoke about obstacles, prayer, and the greatest relationship we can have.

We have loved.

My prayer is that during this time of our exploration of love, you have expressed and experienced and remembered some of the many faces of love in your own life. And my hope is that you'll keep up with the practice. Because life is better when we live with love—we are healthier, happier, and more engaged in everything we do. Our relationships are richer, more passionate, and filled with greater depth and understanding. We bring more presence, purpose, and enthusiasm to our work. Simply put, everything we do benefits as we bring more love into it.

Moreover, as we work to generate more love personally, professionally, and communally, the world around us literally transforms for the better. And given the crazy state of the world right now, we certainly could use a healthy dose of positive transformation.

But sticking with the path won't be easy. But hey, most worthwhile things never are. Thus, we are bound to slip and fall as we attempt to integrate this sacred quality deeper into our lives. That's okay. We don't need to beat ourselves up. We simply need to get back up and keep on trying.

To help with the process, I encourage you to pick up this book every now and then and review some of the stories. This will help prime your mind to be on the lookout for loving opportunities. Even as I write this, my cat, Storm, who I mentioned in a previous story, is clawing at my fingers as I type. Seriously, I am not joking. Now, while part of me wants to toss her little body back to the floor, which I have done in my less enlightened moments, just yesterday, I came across the story I'd written about the power of gentleness, where I reflected on John Wooden's father, who said, "Gentleness is more powerful than force." Thus, with these words of love primed in my mind, I am much more inclined to act with kindness, patience, and understanding.

That's the power of praying. And that's the power of stories. They help instruct our thinking and inspire us to make better decisions. And while this book is over, the stories don't end here. They live on with you and me. Because every day, we write new ones. Now the question is, what stories do we want to tell? Do we want to accept the norm of the doom and gloom reports we are constantly fed by the news? Or do we want a fresh narrative? One where the new normal is to love and accept ourselves just the way we are. One where each of us has the capacity to love friends and foes just the same. One where love and kindness reign supreme.

What a world that would be.

That world is within our reach through the gift of love. And it starts with you and me telling one more beautiful story today.

So, with that, as we work together toward making this world a better and more beautiful place, one loving act at a time, I thank you.

Because, honestly, this beautiful world I am speaking of is only going to be possible because of you and the loving stories you tell with the way you live your life.

Let's tell some great stories today.

With Great Love,

Adam

ACKNOWLEDGMENTS

It took nearly two years to put this book together, but since it's a collection of nine years of stories, there are *a lot* of people to thank. I cannot possibly do justice in this short section to all who made this book possible. But I will do my best.

To start, I'd like to give thanks to the Great Spirit within all things, without which, none of this would be possible. Thank you for using me as an instrument to tell this great Love story. It has been an honor and a privilege. I give thanks to the manifestations of this universal force found in the Masters of Self-Realization Fellowship lineage. Bless you, Bhagavan Krishna, Jesus Christ, Mahavatar Babaji, Lahiri Mahasaya, Swami Sri Yukteswar, and my Guru, Paramahansa Yogananda. Thank you for your endless guidance, love, and support.

Moreover, I want to pay deepest respects to many of the Indigenous nations, both North and South of Turtle Island. You took a mixed-blood kid in and, through your wisdom and traditions, helped him walk in a better way. Blessings to the Algonquin, the Blackfoot, Lakota, Cree, Shipibo, Quechua, Náhuatl, and Wixárika Nations. I am also grateful for the wisdom of the the Kānaka 'Ōiwi, Aztec, Mayan, and Hopi Nations.

Additionally, I want to offer a special tribute to all the Ancestors—your efforts and sacrifices have made this journey a little bit easier and more filled with love. Thank you. Moreover, I want to offer my love to the natural world and give thanks to the land and the spirits of place that helped bring these stories about. Thank you Mama Bali, Canada, Mexico, Peru, the Philippines, South Africa, Venezuela. And of course, to the beautiful Mother Earth that holds them all.

On top of this, I want to offer a special thank you to my blood family, particularly the women in it.

They say that behind every great man is a woman, and while I don't claim to be a great man, I believe the messages in this book have the power to create great change. And none of these lessons could have been possible without the women in my life.

At the top of that list is my mother, whose tireless support helped bring this book to the world. From helping me edit my short stories in fifth grade to university term papers and the many chapters of this book, it's thanks to your service and loving sacrifice that these pages have come about. I couldn't have done it without you, Mama. Moreover, your motherly love and model of service have been a source of inspiration. With all my heart, I say "Thank you."

Next on that list of great women is my grandmother, Mai, AKA my greatest fan. Even if no one ever read a story I wrote, I could rest assured that you would. Your love, enthusiasm, and encouragement for this work have been foundational on the path. You are a special soul who truly embodies these teachings of love. God bless you, Nana. You are a perfect example of the beautifully inclusive Baha'i Faith, which echoes the principles of unity and peace expressed in this book.

To add to this list of powerhouse women are my two sacred sisters, Athena and Zoë. I love you guys. You have been with me through thick and thin. At times, you've been my guides, challenging me to better myself and reminding me of who I was, even when I forgot. But most importantly, you've been my friends and allies in this sacred journey of life. Truly, it's been an honor to walk with you. Bless you. Also heartfelt thanks to my Auntie Alison for all your loving support to our family over the years. I love you.

Carrie, my beloved sister, how lucky I am to have you in my life. You have been a rock in times of challenge, my best woman for my wedding, and you really are a true friend.

Last, and of course not least among the women in my life, I want to offer a special homage to my beloved wife, Andréanne, mother of my children, who taught me to truly love. Having you hold and embrace those parts of me I thought "unlovable" helped bring new levels of self-acceptance and appreciation. And I am forever grateful for that. To add to this, you've been my partner, my lover, and my best friend in this epic spiritual journey of ours. What a blessing it is to have you in my life.

I also want to pay special thanks to my adopted Blackfoot father and Elder, Owl Talks, who was with me at the start of my writing journey, and whose life has served as a model for embodying these sacred teachings. Blessings also to you, Roy, for your leadership, sacrifice, and guidance on the journey. Thank you to my spiritual family at both the Farm Four and Unity Sun Dance communities. I am a better man because of you all. I love you guys.

A special shout out to Landon Rochatboeser for creating the beautiful cover art that truly helps capture the essence of this book. Bless you, too, Kyle Skinner, and your design genius for helping package it in a way that makes the cover truly shine. Jonas and Nicole, bless you both. You are living examples of many of these principles of these principles of love and service in action.

I am grateful to the characters in these stories, both living and who have passed, and even to those fictional and historical characters who gave me food for thought and the desire to share. I am also deeply grateful to the thought leaders I've quoted or recommended in these pages. I want to give a special shout out to Brian Johnson and the team at Heroic for introducing me to many of these amazing books. Your tireless efforts to bring virtue to the world are truly a gift.

As I said at the beginning of these acknowledgments, to name all those who have touched my path would require a book in itself. But I do want to offer a special thank you to all my dear friends, teachers, and supporters along the way—you know who you are. Truly, I could not have done it without you.

Finally, I give thanks to you, dear reader, for taking the time to read these pages. It's a busy world, with so many things to do. You could have spent your time doing a million other things, but you decided to focus your attention on love. That is beautiful. It's actions like yours that will help us change the world for the better.

The movement is yours now.

Let's create a more loving world together, one act at a time.

~

Mitakuye Oyasin

For All My Relations

~

LOOKING FOR MORE SUPPORT?

~

Don't let the journey end here...

If these stories have touched you in some way, and you're feeling called to dive deeper into this sacred work of love and authentic living, remember, you don't have to walk the path alone.

Whether you're navigating rough relationships, healing old wounds, or seeking deeper spiritual connection, and want extra support in applying these principles to your own life, I offer one-on-one sessions and group programs for those who feel called to this deeper work.

My approach integrates the same spiritual wisdom you've encountered in these pages, blended with science, and practical, evidence-based methods that create real lasting change.

To learn how we can work together, visit Dharma Warriors dharmawarriors.org

The world needs you.

With love,

Adam

EXTRA RESOURCES

In approximate order of mention:

- *Start with Why, by* Simon Sinek
- *A Promised Land,* by Barack Obama
- *The Road Less Traveled,* by M. Scott Peck
- *Autobiography of a Yogi,* by Paramahansa Yogananda
- *The Untethered Soul,* by Michael Singer
- *True Refuge,* by Tara Brach
- *The Power of Now,* by Eckhart Tolle
- *Loving What Is,* by Byron Katie
- *The China Study: The Most Comprehensive Study of Nutrition Ever Conducted and the Startling Implications for Diet, Weight Loss and Long-term Health,* by T. Colin Campbell and Thomas M. Campbell II.
- *Eat, Move, Sleep,* by Tom Rath
- *Food Fix,* by Mark Hyman M.D.
- *The Case Against Sugar,* by Gary Taubes
- *The How of Happiness: A Scientific Approach to Getting the Life You Want,* by Sonja Lyubomirsky
- *Happier: Learn the Secrets to Daily Joy and Lasting Fulfillment,* by Tal Ben-Shahar
- *Peace is every Step,* by Thich Nhat Hanh (or anything by this author)
- *Daring Greatly,* by Brené Brown
- *Man's Search for Meaning,* by Viktor Frankl
- *The Bhagavad Gita,* Hindu Scripture
- *Breaking the Habit of Being Yourself,* by Joe Dispenza
- *The Story of My Experiments with Truth,* by Mahatma Ghandi
- *Love 2.0,* by Barbara Fredrickson
- *Bringing Out the Best in Our Relationships with Others,* by Brother Premamoy
- *The Tao Te Ching,* by Lao Tzu
- *The Prophet,* by Khalil Gibran
- *The 7 Habits of Highly Effective People,* by Stephen Covey
- *The Dhammapada,* the Central Text of Buddhism
- *Psychology and Alchemy,* by Carl Jung
- *The Answer is You,* by Michael Beckwith
- *Courage Under Fire,* by Admiral James Stockdale
- *The Realm of the Hungry Ghosts,* by Gabor Maté
- *You Can Heal Your Life,* by Louise Hay
- *Left to Tell: Discovering God Amidst the Rwandan Holocaust,* by Immaculée Ilibagiza,
- *Finding the Joy Within You,* by Sri Daya Mata
- *The Road to Character,* by David Brooks

ABOUT THE AUTHOR

Adam Guzman-Poole is a writer, teacher, and holistic counselor and coach who helps people live with purpose and create thriving relationships. Drawing on psychology and sacred traditions from around the globe, he guides others to live with authenticity, balance, and deeper connection with themselves, their families, and the world at large.

NOTES

Made in the USA
Las Vegas, NV
23 October 2025